OTHERWISE
OCCUPIED

OTHERWISE OCCUPIED

LETTERS HOME FROM THE RUINS OF NAZI GERMANY

MICHAEL HOWARD

First published in the United Kingdom in 2010 by:
Old Street Publishing Ltd,
Yowlestone House, Puddington,
Tiverton, Devon EX16 8LN
www.oldstreetpublishing.co.uk

ISBN-13: 978-1-906964-41-2

To Robert (Bob) Wigg,
to whom my debt of gratitude
was never fully repaid.

Contents

Introduction

In the early months of 1946, a young soldier of nineteen years was sent out to Germany and, by a series of chances, very soon found himself appointed Intelligence Officer of a secret unit plying its trade among the ruins of the Ruhr. I was that young officer, and my story is told through the letters I wrote home to my parents, letters which my mother carefully preserved for the rest of her life. The secret unit was known as T-Force, but what they did and how they went about it I was to learn only gradually, as the letters reveal. The commentary I have added is intended to enlarge upon the contents of those letters, and to give a more complete picture of those unusual times. This is a personal memoir; it does not pretend to be a history. For that the reader must look elsewhere.

The blanket of strict secrecy draped over the activities of T-Force by officialdom included an embargo on the release of documents, of astonishing duration. This meant that, if our story was to be told, it would have to be in the form of fiction. My friend and brother-in-arms John Bayley, distinguished literary critic and formerly Warton Professor of English at Oxford, got his strike in first with the publication in 1955 of his novel *In Another Country,* in which some of us thought we recognised not only John but also ourselves—transformed, of course.

Release of most of the remaining embargoed material into the National Archive in 2007 stimulated a couple of rather meretricious articles in the press, and consequently the handful of us who had survived the intervening sixty years welcomed the commissioning of a properly researched history of

T-Force from Sean Longden.[1] I gladly gave him all the information I had which could be of use to that end.

In tapping my own resources for him, I had occasion to thumb through the letters which provide the framework for this book. I began to realise that they might form a good chronological skeleton which could be fleshed out with a commentary, elucidating and amplifying, and adding anecdote for which there might well be no suitable place in the historical record. I had no idea when I originally wrote the letters that they might survive. They were meant only to tell my family about my life in the Ruhr, and especially the little town of Kamen on its eastern fringe.

Even so, the tensions which were to surface during the Occupation do come through: the need to reconcile one's own discovery that not all Germans were rabid Nazis with the sentiment still lingering back at home that the only good German was a dead German; the peculiarly shifting circumstances *vis-à-vis* the Russians which gradually rendered the terms 'ally' and 'enemy' meaningless; and the ambivalence between British efforts to acquire assets real or intellectual with which to rebuild their own economy, and those of British officials out in Germany whose function was to kick-start German industry so that the defeated country might begin to pay its own way.

I have chosen the title *Otherwise Occupied* because those of us who were rendered 'supernumerary to establishment' in our own regiments as the army began to run down in the aftermath of war would, pending release perhaps eighteen or twenty-four months hence, need to be just that—otherwise occupied—in the interim. And from the point-of-view of the Germans, they faced not only submission to a conventional army of occupation, but they were to be occupied also by a special force whose task was to strip their prostrate land of the intellectual property and technology of their entire military-industrial complex.

Michael Howard, Sevenoaks, August 2010

---

1 *T- Force: The Race for Nazi War Secrets*, 1945, Constable, September 2009.

List of Illustrations

Illustrations and photographs integrated into the text.

Photographic Credits

Glossary

1RB (2RB, 8RB)	First (Second, Eighth) Battalion the Rifle Brigade
I (VIII,XXX) Corps	First (Eighth, Thirtieth) Corps. Always Roman numerals
2 i/c	Second-in-command
49 Div	49th Division. Divisions and Brigades always use Arabic numerals
60th	King's Royal Rifle Corps
AMG	Allied Military Government
AMGOT	Allied Military Government of Occupied Territory
Bizone	Joint British and US Zones of Occupation
Bn	Battalion
BIOS	British Intelligence Objectives Subcommittee
B o T	Board of Trade
CIGS	Chief of the Imperial General Staff
CIOS	Combined (i.e. US and British) Intelligence Objectives Subcommittee
CB	Companion of the Order of the Bath
CCG	Control Commission for Germany
CO	Commanding Officer (of a battalion, lieutenant-colonel)
CQMS	Company Quartermaster Sergeant
CSM	Company Sergeant-Major
Detachment	Detached unit, of Company strength
DP	Displaced Person
DR	Despatch Rider
DSO	Distinguished Service Order
FIAT	Field Intelligence Agency Technical, our US counterparts
Field Officer	Major (or Lieutenant Colonel)
GHB	Greenjacket Holding Battalion

Greenjackets	Rifle Brigade and King's Royal Rifle Corps
GSO1 (2, 3)	General Staff Officer First (Second, Third) Class, respectively: i.e. Lieutenant Colonel, Major, Captain. (Also G1/2/3, co-terminous)
HMSO	His (Her) Majesty's Stationery Office
IG Farben	*Interessengemeinschaft Farbenindustrie Aktiengesellschaft,* the German chemical combine
IO	Intelligence Officer
KRRC	King's Royal Rifle Corps
Majority	Rank of Major
MBE	Member of the Order of the British Empire
MC/MM	Military Cross/Medal
MT	Motor Transport
Mof	Derogatory name for a German, of Dutch origin
M o S	Ministry of Supply
NAAFI	Navy, Army and Air Force Institute canteen/club/ shop for British troops
NCO	Non-commissioned officer. Ranging from Lance-corporal to RSM
OR	Old Rugbeian; or, as the sense may suggest, Other Ranks
OBE	Officer of the Order of the British Empire
Pip	Junior officer's epaulette insignia of rank, in the form of a star 1 = 2nd Lieutenant, 2 = Lieutenant, 3 = Captain
POW, PW	Prisoner of War
QM	Quartermaster
RB	Rifle Brigade
RDR	Reparations, Deliveries & Research, Division of CCG
Redcoat	Regiment of the Line
RHU	Reinforcement Holding Unit
Rifleman	Private soldier of RB or KRRC, or 1 Bucks; or any member, irrespective of rank, of either regiment
RQMS	Regimental Quartermaster Sergeant
RSM	Regimental Sergeant-Major
SPD	*Sozialdemokratische Partei Deutschlands*
Subaltern	Officer below the rank of Captain
Wren	Member of the Women's Royal Naval Service

About the Maps

Page xviii

Germany, the Allied Occupation Zones.

This map the whole of Germany, along with western Austria, including the occupation zones of the four allied powers in Germany; also the demarcation line between the area of operation of No 1 T-Force—Land North Rhine - Westphalia—and the rest of the British Zone.

Page xix

Rhine-Ruhr Region, conurbation.

The area covered by this map is now described as a Metropolitan Region, which is not a distinct administrative area. The darker shading shows areas of especially high population density. This was characteristic of the region in 1946/7. The population of the region, now eleven million, has not increased much since pre-war levels.

Pages xx-xxi

The Rhine & Western Ruhr, Eastern Ruhr, and Rhine south of Cologne.

This map covers a larger area and shows the two principal highways crossing it, as well as the rivers which give their names to the areas through which they run. Most of the towns and cities mentioned in the text are located on this map.

Germany, Allied Occupation Zones

Flensburg

Kiel

Lübeck

Bremerhaven (US) Hamburg

Geesthacht

Oldenburg

Bremen (US)

UK

Celle

Hanover

Rheine

Minden

Osnabrück

Bad Nenndorf

Bad Oeynhausen

Münster

Helmstedt

Potsdam

BERLIN

USSR

North Rhine / Westphalia

Paderborn

Essen

Kamen

Göttingen

Düsseldorf

Dortmund

Leipzig

Kamenz

Cologne

Siegen

Weimar

Dresden

Bonn

Koblenz

Frankfurt am Main

Prague

FR.

Czech.

Mannheim

Nuremberg

Karlsruhe

USA

Stuttgart

Strasbourg

Baden -Baden

Linz

FR.

Ulm

Augsburg

Munich

Konstanz

Salzburg

Basle

Zurich

Bregenz

Innsbruck

Switz.

Austria

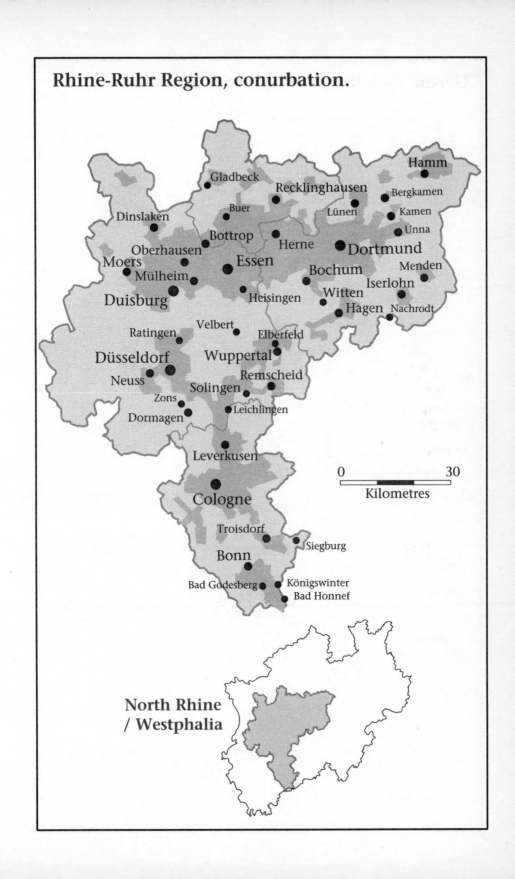

Rhine-Ruhr Region, conurbation.

Hamm
Gladbeck
Recklinghausen
Bergkamen
Buer
Lünen
Kamen
Dinslaken
Unna
Bottrop
Herne
Oberhausen
Essen
Dortmund
Moers
Bochum
Menden
Mülheim
Witten
Iserlohn
Duisburg
Heisingen
Hagen
Nachrodt
Velbert
Ratingen
Elberfeld
Düsseldorf
Wuppertal
Neuss
Remscheid
Solingen
Zons
Dormagen
Leichlingen

Leverkusen

Cologne

0   30
Kilometres

Troisdorf
Siegburg
Bonn
Bad Godesberg
Königswinter
Bad Honnef

North Rhine
/ Westphalia

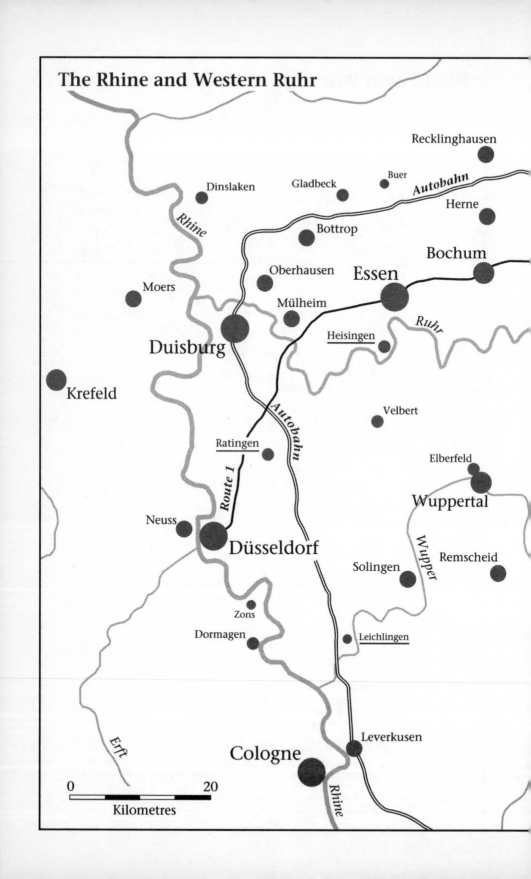

The Rhine and Western Ruhr

Recklinghausen

Dinslaken

Gladbeck

Buer

Autobahn

Herne

Bottrop

Rhine

Bochum

Oberhausen

Essen

Moers

Mülheim

Heisingen

Ruhr

Duisburg

Krefeld

Velbert

Autobahn

Ratingen

Elberfeld

Route 1

Wuppertal

Neuss

Düsseldorf

Solingen

Wupper

Remscheid

Zons

Dormagen

Leichlingen

Leverkusen

Erft

Cologne

Rhine

0   20

Kilometres

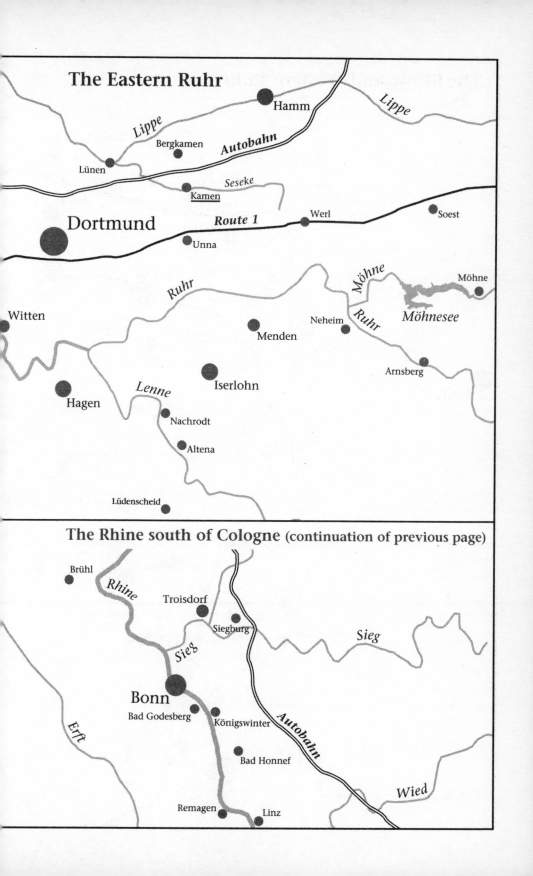

The Eastern Ruhr

Lippe
Hamm
Lippe
Autobahn
Bergkamen
Lünen
Seseke
Kamen
Dortmund
Route 1
Werl
Soest
Unna
Möhne
Möhne
Ruhr
Neheim
Ruhr
Möhnesee
Witten
Menden
Iserlohn
Arnsberg
Lenne
Hagen
Nachrodt
Altena
Lüdenscheid

The Rhine south of Cologne (continuation of previous page)

Brühl
Rhine
Troisdorf
Siegburg
Sieg
Sieg
Bonn
Bad Godesberg
Königswinter
Autobahn
Erft
Bad Honnef
Wied
Remagen
Linz

CHAPTER 1

An heroic action – An awestruck schoolboy – A mysterious posting – A grim little town – Real German girls!

At about half past one in the afternoon of Wednesday 14th January 1943, the day on which the *London Gazette* announced awards for gallantry to twenty members of the 2nd Battalion the Rifle Brigade, the BBC Home Service broadcast the story of the action fought at the end of October at 'Snipe', at the heart of the Battle of Alamein. Sergeant Charles Calistan, commanding the only remaining six-pounder anti-tank gun able to bear on the enemy armour, along with his colonel Vic Turner and his platoon commander Jackie Toms (standing in, in desperate circumstances, for Calistan's dead and wounded crew), brewed up eight enemy tanks with just nine rounds. By nightfall, the enemy armour had withdrawn, leaving fifty-six of their armoured fighting vehicles lying smoking before the battalion position. It was the first time that German tanks had been defeated by a battalion of infantry alone, fighting with just its own battalion weapons, and Rommel would never commit the remainder, as a force, to battle again.

Among those gazetted on that January afternoon were Jackie Toms with his second Military Cross; Tom Bird, the anti-tank company commander, with a Distinguished Service Order to join the two MCs he already had; Charles Calistan with the Distinguished Conduct Medal to add to the Military Medal he had already won; and seventeen others, making it the most

Cadet Howard with his father Major Howard of the Pioneer Corps, 1941.

highly decorated battalion action of the war. Vic Turner's Victoria Cross (which he always maintained should have gone to Calistan) had already been announced at the end of November. I later got to know all these men except for Charles Calistan, who was commissioned in the field and was to die leading his platoon in Italy.

So stirring a story was bound to ignite the imagination of a sixteen-year-old Rugby schoolboy listening to the wireless on holiday at home in Sussex. Lingering even then in the back of my mind was the question of how I would conduct myself under fire. To serve with men of such fortitude would be for me a kind of insurance policy, to show even a vestige of fear in their presence would be the height of bad form, the ultimate disincentive.

Conscription had in fact been introduced in October 1939 for men between eighteen and forty-one, but I was a volunteer. The army accepted young men from their seventeenth birthday, and on my birthday in the summer term of 1943 my house-master gave me permission to cycle over to the recruiting office in Coventry to volunteer my services. I swore the oath of loyalty to His Majesty, accepted the King's Shilling, and asked the sergeant what I should do next. 'Sonny,' he said, 'you go home and we will tell you when we want you.' As it turned out, they did not want me until fifteen months later. In the interim I had been promoted to the rank of corporal in the Home Guard, and cadet officer in the Junior Training Corps. On my eighteenth birthday I could no longer be conscripted. I was a volunteer—a status which I prized.

As such, I could express a preference for an arm of service—army, navy or air force—and even indicate a preference for a particular regiment. Recovering back in England from his head wound, Vic Turner came to Rugby later that summer to recruit for the Regiment. I was not told who was to interview me, he did not introduce himself, and it was not until halfway through that I noticed the little bronze Maltese cross on the purple ribbon on his chest. I asked if I might seek a commission in his regiment, and he gave me the nod. For me there was no doubt: it had to be the Rifle Brigade.

Primary training at Fulford Barracks, York, from September 1944 was followed by pre-OCTU training at Ranby, OCTU at York and Winchester, and then I was commissioned 2nd Lieutenant at Winchester on 1st September 1945. This brought me after twelve months' service to the Greenjacket Holding Battalion, Ogbourne St George, about three miles north of Marlborough in Wiltshire.

> *Officers' Mess, 27 G.H.B., Ogbourne St George*
> *17th February 1946*

Darling Mama,

I am sending home two parcels—the one that is obviously washing should be treated as such, but the other box is just odds and ends and could remain as it is.

I had my last inoculation—it was badly done, but left me no after-effects.

I still don't know what unit I am going to, but I am most inclined to think that it will be with some H.Q. or on some Staff. Nobody here can give me any indication of the possibilities. I have got to report to a transit camp at Tilbury docks by 4 p.m. on Wednesday, but I may easily not sail from there, so it doesn't indicate in any way where I am going to. Quite a lot going to Germany go via Newhaven-Le Havre, thence by train. I am in an all-officer draft consisting almost entirely of majors, so I may be quite comfortable. I would rather go all the way by sea than face the rail journey.

I am well set-up as far as kit is concerned, and I can get it well within the limits of 168 pounds. I am only taking two pounds of coffee and 200 cigarettes, that much is permissible.
All my love,
Michael

This first letter of my cache was written in February, at a time when I and most of the thirty-six who had been commissioned with me in September 1945, either of the Rifle Brigade or the King's Royal Rifle Corps, were awaiting posting at 27 Greenjacket Holding Battalion at Ogbourne St George. My own eyes had turned toward Germany, where 8th Battalion the Rifle Brigade was being disbanded, and both the 1st and 2nd Battalions had remained after VE Day but were unlikely to call for my services. Before Christmas my father, still a serving officer, wrote to the War Office: 'My son, 2nd Lieutenant M H S Howard RB, speaks German. Would it be sensible to post him to Germany?' My implied mastery of the language was grossly overstated but never mind, it was never laid bare and the letter did the trick. Newly-commissioned officers of the Rifle Brigade tended to go only where the Regiment sent them, and individual initiatives of this sort were rare and not always looked upon kindly. But the War Office amazingly took the sensible course, and I was posted.

At 27GHB I had been attached to the Signals Platoon under Wilfred Bourne. Life was a long sequence of mobile signals exercises on '19-Set' wirelesses installed in the back of 15-hundredweight trucks. We quickly established that these exercises were best run from a command vehicle parked on the pavement in the broad High Street in Marlborough, just close enough to those wonderfully welcoming tea-rooms known as the 'Polly' for the cables to be passed through the window to the nearest table. We were served pots of coffee and scones with great attentiveness by nubile young women, invariably of good family. (Why were they not in the Wrens like our sisters, or in the Land Army? Were they too young, or had they flat feet? A mystery. We never asked their age, and I never remember looking at their feet.) From comfortable chairs set cosily before the fireplace, we issued over the air a flow of clues and map references for the direction of our less-agreeably situated comrades as they pursued treasure hunts and the like through the country lanes of Wiltshire.

For me, service with Wilfred Bourne had a particular benefit. In height, girth, length of leg and arm, though probably not in intellect, we shared the same dimensions, and since he was very soon to leave he sold me the 'patrols' which Pulford's the regimental tailors had made for him. Wilfred was certainly some distance into the process of developing and polishing a fine legal mind,[2] though the signals games which he devised lacked the literary and poetic flavour of those conjured up for us as subalterns in 9RB at Ranby, Nottinghamshire, during the previous autumn by the Signals Officer, Captain Laurence Whistler. Whistler's literary gifts as a poet, although considerable, would later be eclipsed by his unmatched genius as an engraver on glass. Between the two of them, and with what I had learned at Officer Cadet Training Unit, I soon had grounds enough to claim to be able to run a signals platoon myself.

Christmas at Ogbourne! After we officers had served the men their dinner, I chanced upon a rifleman outside my hut, stumbling and far from sober, whom I recognised as Patrick Cronin, son of A J 'Keys of the fucking Kingdom' Cronin—as his fellow riflemen had it. (Indeed, the 1944 film featuring Gregory Peck was playing in Swindon at the time). I stretched poor Patrick, who had been teased beyond endurance by his mates into insobriety, out on the spare camp bed in my room, threw a blanket over him, and let him sleep it off until long after dark. We never met again. (Patrick's elder brother Vincent Cronin had been commissioned in the Rifle Brigade a couple of years before, and the later publication of *The Golden Honeycomb* would confirm that the pen rather than the sword was to be his métier.)

---

2 Bourne would later become Clerk of the Crown in Chancery and Permanent Secretary in the Lord Chancellor's Office.

A few days after Christmas 27GHB was inspected by a General Officer Commanding—I forget just what, Southern Command, I suspect—in the most terrible freezing conditions; the roads and the barrack square were like glass. My own contribution to the entertainment of our distinguished guest was graceful but unplanned. Returning to camp just before lunch in my open, red J-Type MG, I surprised everyone, and not least myself, by executing two consecutive 360-degree skids in full view of the General's party at the bottom of the treacherously sloping square. I deemed it prudent rather promptly to find somewhere to hide both my car and myself for the rest of the day. Whether I was too well hidden for anyone to find me, or the General was sufficiently gracious to overlook the incident, I never discovered, but in any event I heard nothing more about it. Perhaps it was as well I was moving on, and by mid-February my movement orders came through.

I really had no idea of what the British Army of the Rhine then consisted. We knew that it was the British Second Army which had raced across the North German plain to the Baltic in April and May 1945. But by August, the British Second Army had lost XII Corps (Army Corps are always numbered in Roman numerals, Divisions and Brigades in Arabic), and been redesignated as the occupation force, the British Army of the Rhine. I cannot for a moment imagine why I thought that I, particularly, was destined for a cushy billet at a headquarters or on the staff. I could just as easily have ended up with a platoon in some redcoat regiment (a fate worse than death), or as a Railway Transport Officer at a station in the middle of nowhere, the standard occupation for a young officer being the command of a platoon of twenty-five or thirty men as one in a thousand subalterns in any of the three Corps Districts.[3] That I should instead find myself involved in the fascinating and half-hidden world of T-Force was a lucky break indeed.

---

3 On March 11th 1946, of the three Army Corps forming BAOR, VIII Corps remained in Schleswig-Holstein, XXX Corps in Lower Saxony, and I Corps in North Rhine & Westphalia. At that time I Corps consisted of four Divisions, each with three Infantry Brigades except for one

I never discovered what happened to that draft consisting 'almost entirely of majors', but I certainly became detached from them. Were they perhaps all destined to be 'Town Majors' in the Military Government? Town Major was the officer responsible for establishing the seat of government in the Stadtkreis or Landkreis (small urban or rural administrative districts) in the British Zone, governed by a major, or in some cases a lieutenant-colonel, for whom there was to be no future in regimental soldiering in the post-war army, and for whom this would be their last posting. They would all be men of a certain age and experience, many of them having in pre-war days been District Commissioners in the Colonial Administrative Service, a position which would have prepared them for almost anything. Some never really progressed beyond treating German civilians as anything other than natives, but overall the Town Major system was a great success.

Many would have been through a course, initially set up with Italy in mind and run at Wimbledon, for officers for the Allied Military Government of Occupied Territories (AMGOT). With the defeat of Italy, and the consequent Italian declaration of war on Germany, these our gallant allies appearing from the wings had suddenly rendered superfluous any need for British officers to exercise the functions of military government in Italy. We were left with a pool of officers just as well equipped for the task in Germany. They became little viceroys within their immediate sphere, and many of them did marvellous work in getting life, commerce, industry, and, through the appointment of a burgomaster, government moving again at local level, even if at the same time some acquired the reputation of living conspicuously high on the hog.

---

which had four. At three battalions per brigade, that came to about thirty-nine battalions, each say 750 men, a round total of thirty thousand, of which there were perhaps fifteen hundred officers in the field and more on the staff at the headquarters at every level, to say nothing of ancillary troops of all sorts, and other arms of service. This sort of pattern, reproduced in each of the other two Corps, VIII and XXX, presented the possibility that a young unattached infantry officer such as myself might be sent absolutely anywhere.

I am amazed to see that the weight allowance for the kit of a young officer was 168 pounds—twelve stone—and wonder how I might have carried so much had I needed it. And I am equally amazed that I thought it desirable or necessary to take with me 'only' two pounds of coffee and 200 cigarettes, as if I were likely to need either by way of sustenance or luxury. I can only imagine that I had been tipped the wink that both had become a means of exchange in dealings with the civilian population, perhaps not yet realising that this was not an activity in which any officer would care to be caught engaged. I certainly never used the coffee in any transaction, however innocent, nor did I ever brew my own. Perhaps I handed it over to the Mess upon arrival.

I already had an inkling of the extent to which some other commodities had established themselves as a means of exchange in the wake of the victorious armies. During my first leave after commissioning, I found myself at the bridge table with Stormont, second Lord Mancroft, who later served in the administrations of Churchill, Eden and Macmillan. He had been among the first troops into Brussels where he had come across a charming, titled Belgian lady with whom he concluded a bargain which left them both satisfied. He gave her a box of three tablets of Yardley's Old English Lavender soap, and in return she gave him what he wanted, plus two Dutch cheeses as change. I took a tablet of Yardley's when I left (it was what we used at home), but it was part-worn and no longer viable as currency.

Three days later I wrote to my mother again.

Transit Camp, Tilbury
Wednesday, 20th February 1946

Darling Mama,

At any rate I have got this far with all my kit. We shall probably be dug out of bed at 2 o'clock tomorrow and told to be ready to embark in 90 minutes. Then we have a journey to Ostend, Cuxhaven or Hamburg taking from 6–20 hours. When I get over there I may be as long as 10 days in a transit camp awaiting posting, in which case I won't have a perma-nent enough address for you to write to me. It is an all-officer draft which is a relief. I am by far the most junior and youngest officer here, and one of about three without campaign medals, so I count myself very lucky. It is bitterly cold today and I shall be glad of all my warm clothing. I have got my kit into two large but manageable bundles, with the Revelation and all my suits in the bed roll. My immediate needs are in the zipper.

I have a feeling that my demands on my bank balance may have been heavy of late so I wonder if you could enquire, and if it has dropped below £20, could you put in £15 from my account with you, if that is convenient. I should like to feel it was there to tide me over the time until I get settled in Germany.

Let me know when you get into the house, and what the new address is to be.

With all my love,

Michael

I arrived in Tilbury in polar conditions. Scott's description would have done for us: 'Good God, this is an awful place!' It was bleak in the extreme. We were on continuous standby, even when there was to be no imminent depar-ture, no doubt to prevent us from sloping off in search of entertainment. But the crossings to the Hook of Holland, which was now by general con-sent believed to be our destination, were not due to start until morning, and the ships had no sleeping accommodation. If we were still waiting at noon, some of us would walk a mile and a bit to a transport café for a plate of stew, spuds and mushy peas. It broke up the monotony of the day. Then we would trudge back through desultory sleet which somehow did nothing to whiten the grey landscape or the grey river, or indeed to lighten our grey mood. Thus a second and a third day passed with no conviction that we would ever leave Tilbury behind.

The long wait allowed me plenty of time for reflection. I realised that I had not set foot on an ocean-going vessel since returning to England aboard the *MV Waiwera* with my parents and my sister Anne on New Year's Day in 1935. We had come indirectly from Fiji, where my father A E S ('Tim') Howard made a career in the Colonial Administrative Service in an epoch when such service was still regarded as a respectable and honourable way of making your living. Born in Dungannon, County Tyrone, he went to the Royal School Dungannon, one of the best in the country, where he excelled at cricket and rugby football. He went on to play both games for Trinity College Dublin to the point of making graduation not merely an unlikelihood but an irrelevance, and in 1913 he left without sitting his final exams. Consequently, direct entry into the Colonial Administrative Service was not open to him, so he found his way into the Colonial Police.

A singular occurrence in 1917 earned him much credit. The armed German merchant raider *See Adler* was on the rampage in the Pacific, sinking over a dozen Allied vessels. It became stranded on the island of Mopelia, and the captain, the Graf Felix von Luckner, took the ship's pinnace with a crew of armed men and made for Fiji. His intention was to overpower another suitable vessel, retrieve the rest of his crew from Mopelia, and continue his piratical operations therefrom. The plan was foiled by a stratagem involving my father and his sub-inspector, supported by a Fijian sergeant and seven constables. Persuading von Luckner and his men that they were covered by weapons concealed on another vessel carrying cattle, my father accepted the surrender of their arms. This exploit earned the formal thanks of the Legislative Council and lent my father an aura of heroism in the public perception.

It was in 1921, as my father sailed home on leave, that a colleague of his informed a fellow passenger, who happened to be a member of the Committee of Lloyd's of London, of my father's role in the von Luckner affair. Some four years *ex post facto* therefore, Lloyd's awarded their Silver Medal for Meritorious Service plus a handsome bounty of £100 to both my father and the sub-inspector who was with him at the time of the incident. The award and the act which gave rise to it were reported widely in the Antipodean press, and again my father's name came to the fore in the colony. In due course this, coupled with his proficiency in his duties as Inspector of Police and success in the relevant examinations, ensured his transfer at last into the Colonial Administrative Service. A further consequence was that he used at least a part of that bounty to purchase my mother's engagement ring, and they were married on New Year's Day, 1923.

My mother Elima, born in Fiji, was then 27, and I think she must have been waiting for him. There is a story, dredged from my memory and which my sister cannot corroborate, that my mother once watched my father play rugby football for Trinity College Dublin, and met him afterwards. If so, it can only have been in the early months of 1913, when he was twenty-one and she would still have been sixteen. But by the end of that year he had become a sub-inspector in the Colonial Police in Fiji. Had that meeting influenced his choice both of profession and destination? Otherwise, why Fiji of all places?

My mother was the daughter of Henry Marks, a man who was playing an increasingly prominent part in the life of the colony, and she would have been seen as a bit of a catch. He was born in 1861 in Melbourne, of British parents, and educated there. When, in 1881, he asked for his future wife's hand in marriage his prospective father-in-law replied, 'Not until you have a thousand pounds.' By my reckoning, the equivalent sum at the time of writing would be seventy-five thousand pounds. So at the age of twenty he took the boat for Fiji. He established his own business as a merchant and 'island trader', and in two years he had his thousand pounds and claimed his bride. Eventually, he became a wealthy man. I am satisfied that the award to him of a CBE in 1918 had much to do with his gift the previous year of ten thousand pounds to cover the cost of recruiting and equipping a hundred men who formed a contingent of the Labour Corps of the Fiji Defence Force to come to England, and on to Marseilles, to provide labour in the docks. Public service from 1913 onwards, as Commissioner for Currency, as Warden and Mayor of Suva (the capital), and on the Legislative and Executive Councils of the colony for many years, led to his knighthood in 1933.

Educated in Melbourne to the age of sixteen, in 1912 my mother was awarded the first driving licence ever issued to a woman in Australia, having learned on her father's three and a half litre Hispano-Suiza. She pursued a more liberal education from then on, travelling in due course with her elder sister on world tours which took her several times to England—and to Ireland—as well as to continental Europe, Japan and Ceylon. She had the usual accomplishments; she spoke French (as well as Fijian), she played a good game of tennis, golf and bridge, she played the piano and sang to her own accompaniment, and she danced—not least with Edward, Prince of Wales at Government House during his 1920 tour—and rather more times than protocol deemed proper, apparently.

My sister Anne and I were born in 1923 and 1926 respectively, and my parents then faced the difficult choice, in an epoch when travel was by sea not plane, whether to educate their children locally or in England with the consequent separation. Not without much heart-searching, they chose the latter—hence the voyage home in 1935. First of all, a 'holiday home' was found for us in Berkshire where we would spend our school vacations. It was run by a widow of a Colonial Service officer with children of her own: a daughter who was head girl of a boarding school, Upper Chine in the Isle of Wight (where Anne, rising twelve, was accepted, and in due course herself became head girl), and a son at Dartmouth Naval College. My parents' choice of public school for me was influenced by their friendship with Maurice Godley, aide-de-camp to the Governor of Fiji, Sir Murchison Fletcher (who was my godfather). Maurice, whose great-uncle the first Lord Kilbracken had been Chairman of Governors of Rugby School, had been in Tudor House. The housemaster of Tudor accepted my entry for the summer term of 1940, and it was on his recommendation that I went first to Rose Hill at Banstead, a preparatory school which sent many of its boys on to Rugby. Toward the end of the summer of 1935 my parents returned to Fiji.

The next four years' separation from our parents was broken only once by my mother coming back for a couple of months in the summer holidays of 1937. Deep down we must have felt that we had been abandoned by our parents, rationalise it how you may. Undeniably, we were cared for in their absence considerately and in comfort, but without love. It was this family dislocation, therefore, and not the advent of war, that first instituted a regime of letter-writing in both directions, with any departure from the weekly norm calling for explanation or exculpation. The perfection of my mother's informative and loving letters, written in her exquisite hand, became for me a little intimidating; later, dissatisfaction with my own by comparison would sometimes make it difficult for me to put them in the post.

So war and its aftermath, and the service it demanded from us all, had scattered the family once more; as the others were about to return home, I was leaving. I had a brown expanding Revelation suitcase, into which I had packed, apparently, all my suits. I wonder what they might 'all' have consisted of. My service dress of barathea, and black leather Sam Browne belt and cross-belt for one. A spare battle-dress, perhaps? Was that all? I left my Rifle-green patrols behind, unsure at first whether I would need them. 'Emergency-only' officers mostly did not bother so to accoutre themselves; patrols were never obligatory, but always a short-term asset. No civvies, except sports kit.

Clearly I didn't feel that a bank balance of £20 was enough, and that £35 would be more comfortable, with pay due at about a pound a day. What would be the right multiple to express it in the coin of today? Forty times? I wonder what opportunities I imagined might exist on which to spend it. At the time of writing, a second lieutenant earns £22,000 per annum, say £60 per day. So my thirty-five days' pay in my bank account would have been the present-day equivalent of at least £2,100, with my keep thrown in. Enough for my mushy peas.

On the Saturday our orders came.

Lt. M. H. S. Howard R.B., Officers' Mess 54 R.H.U., B.A.O.R.
Wednesday, 27th February 1946

Darling Mama,

We sailed early Saturday morning and ran into snow, a gale, and a sand-bank, so when we got free we went back and anchored off Southend for the night. We crossed over on Sunday and arrived at the Hook at 7.00 in the evening, and spent the night in the transit camp there. We made the acquaintance of the Dutchmen in the railway room and sampled the beer in the only pub, but it was really rather a dump. At 10 o'clock on Monday morning we entrained at the Hook into a very warm and comfortable train, and with short stops for food we played bridge for eight hours, and didn't notice the time passing. I won every rubber and ended up 50 points up. We arrived at Osnabrück about 7.30 pm.

The journey was much like any other and rather uninteresting except for the bombing in a place called Rheine of some 20,000 people, where not more than 5 houses were still standing and bombed railway engines were still scattered all over the place with their noses in the ground. This place is not meant to have been really badly hit, but is twice as bad as anything you can see in England. The people are quite well clothed and look quite fit, but will obviously start to feel the pinch now. What is so pathetic are the animals. There are no dogs or cats and all the horses are mere skeletons. The children, thank God, are all seemingly well fed. I don't think I could bear the sight of starving kids.

The Mess here is good but not very lively and the saviour of our lives is the comparatively uncrowded Officers' Club in the town, where you can get awfully good snack meals dirt cheap, and also anything to drink at incredibly cheap prices. A bottle of really good champagne is 21/-, mediocre champagne at 16/-. Double whiskies are 9d, gins 6d, and beer is either free or 2d per pint. All the best liqueurs are 9d per dose. And good Moselle wine is 3/- per bottle. As you can see, whether one stays permanently in an alcoholic stupor or not depends not on one's pocket, but purely on personal whim. For lunch today I had a couple of turkey sandwiches with a cold salad accompanied by two glasses of white Rhine wine. Then two slices of the most delicious chocolate cake, followed by a dose of Cointreau, all for the German equivalent of 3/6. Of course, it seems criminal really, but as long as one realises how false the whole set of values is, it doesn't do any harm. One can live like a king on the proceeds of the sale of a dozen fags per diem. Well, a dozen fags cost 1/- in this spot, so you can see how it all works out.

Tony Lucas & 2 other R.B. officers are here & I'm afraid to say we have more or less already formed a clique. They will probably leave before I get my posting, but it's nice having them now.

I should be posted by 8 days from now and I shall be trying to get a really good job on the A.M.G. Apparently they will recommend you very much for what you want to do, so I shall aim high.

It isn't worth sending anything but letters to the above address, so don't. I should love to hear how the house is progressing, if at all!

Well so long for now. I have had a few chances to speak the lingo, with varying degrees of success, but the barman says I speak well which may or may not be pure flattery.

All my love,

Michael

The trip across to the Hook of Holland was a nightmare. A blizzard blown in on a northerly gale ensured that it was beastly on deck, and the saloons were overcrowded and overheated, and stuffy with cigarette smoke. Our draft had been joined by a party of some three dozen Royal Army Medical Corps lieutenants who had been inducted six weeks previously, and in the interim taught how to return a salute and to treat the pox. When we stuck for several hours with our bottom on a sandbank, conditions became intolerable. The ship lurched violently from side to side, and some of the medicos took the easy way out by the self-administration, either by mouth or hypodermic, of knock-out drops. Having first zipped themselves into their sleeping bags, they lay doggo and well-nigh insensible for the rest of the trip. Eventually, as the tide rose, we floated off and retired to spend an uneasy, not to say queasy, night anchored off Southend. What should have been a six-hour trip stretched out to thirty-six gruelling hours. Our Sunday evening meal at the transit camp at the Hook was a restorative, served to us by a strikingly pretty, tall and fair Dutch girl. We had become sufficiently perky after recovering from our pounding by the sea to regard her as a challenge—until we were warned that she was off limits. She was said to be the preserve of the camp commandant, a colonel in the 60th. Accordingly, we remembered our manners.

Rheine was to be, for most of us, our first experience of bomb-damage. It owed its attentions from the Allied air forces in part to its position on the Dortmund-Ems canal, and in part to its function as a rail communications centre. We realised that stories of witnesses counting the number of buildings left standing on the fingers of one hand were not necessarily exaggeration. Many bomb-damaged houses remained partially occupied, with people living either in the cellar, or in upper rooms with a side open to the weather.

Osnabrück, where six railway lines met, was to be the next stop, but we didn't get there until after dark the next day. Again, its importance as a railway centre had drawn the fire of the heavy bombers of the RAF, and damage was widespread. But it had also been targeted by the medium artillery because an officer-cadet school there had offered sharp and determined resistance. The town bore the distinguishing marks, with much damage inflicted to the roofs and upper storeys, to which the RAF's incendiaries had also contributed.

I wrote on 27th February as 'Lieutenant'. The second pip, promotion to lieutenant, was automatic; it followed at precisely six months from commissioning. We had passed out from the OCTU at the end of August. But I was in limbo, betwixt and between, belonging as yet to no-one, so upon whose published orders could I have appeared? Was I taking a liberty?

The cost of wines and spirits which I reported to my parents opened up vistas of permanent hangover. Not quite Hogarth's *Gin Lane*—'drunk for a penny, blind drunk for twopence'—but in the *'suppression de l'ivresse publique'* price was clearly not going to be a factor. I had merely translated the prices into sterling so that my parents would not have to make the calculation for themselves, but I hadn't thought in advance about the currency in which we were going to be making transactions. In the event, at that time in Germany it was the German Rentenmark (or Reichsmark, both terms were used), for which the British Government had arbitrarily fixed the rate of exchange at forty to the pound—about right for a currency which had been depreciated in real terms by the effect of waging a long war.

Our soldiers were paid in cash in Rentenmarks, the currency in circulation among the civil population, and they used it, for example, in NAAFI shops and canteens. However, they very soon discovered that they could sell their cigarettes to Germans at prices which bore little relation to their cost to the troops—not forgetting their free ration of 50 per week. The Rentenmarks they received in return they brought straight back and spent in the NAAFI, so the proceeds of sale of their cigarettes would buy them, say, ten times their face value in goods from the NAAFI. It was a long time before the stupefied authorities realised what was going on, and by that time there had been, so they calculated, a loss of some £59,000,000 to the Treasury. This led to the introduction in August 1946 of 'Baffs' (BAFSVs, the British Armed Forces Special Vouchers) in which the troops were subsequently paid, which became the means of exchange in the NAAFI. Baffs could be exchanged for sterling only when going on leave, and not into Rentenmarks at all. This did not of course bring to an end the use of cigarettes, so cheaply available to the troops, as a means of exchange for German goods and services.

I found Tony Lucas unexpectedly in Osnabrück. I had known Tony, who was a few months my senior, since 1935 when we were at prep school, where we learned our Latin, French and German together. He and his parents were very good to me, often taking me out of school to have Sunday lunch with them in those years when my parents were abroad. But he had gone on to Stowe and I to Rugby. Our paths crossed again when I joined the Greenjacket OCTU at York in early 1945 and he was already in the senior company there three months ahead of me. He was commissioned in the Rifle Brigade three months before me.

> *Lt. M. Howard R.B., Officers' Mess 54 R.H.U., B.A.O.R.*
> *10th March 1946*

Dear Daddy,

I expect Mummy will have communicated to you all the commonplace news of my journey over. What is of more interest to you is my posting. All reinforcements fill in a form with the Colonel's recommendation on it. This is sent to G.H.Q. 2nd Echelon, and they are responsible for posting you. My Colonel has recommended me for Military Government, which should be interesting. The Colonel seemed to think I had every chance of getting the job, but I don't know how much weight his recommendation carries at G.H.Q. Postings. I have a nasty feeling that they may say we want R.T.O.s and make me one, or something equally uninspiring. Anyway, I will let you know as soon as my posting comes through.

Of course, I have had no news from home for 10 days now, but the last I heard, the 10th was the day the builders gave for Mummy to move into the house. I can only hope there have been no more hitches.

The weather in this Godforsaken country is lousy. I haven't seen the sun since I've been here. There is still a little snow, & the rather dreary land-scape is completely cut out by the fog. They tried to make me Assistant Sports Officer on the Permanent Staff here, but I made my views on the

subject clear in no uncertain manner. It got me a rocket from the Adjutant,
but it also got me posted.
With my love,
Michael

There was little for anyone at a Reinforcement Holding Unit to do. For the reinforcements passing through there was initially an interview to determine where they should be posted, the expression of a personal preference being permitted, or whether they were suitable for any of the jobs for which there were known vacancies. After that there was just the waiting while a recommendation went forward to Postings, GHQ 2nd Echelon, then for a reply, and maybe a further two-way exchange. At least there was sport. These units took part in all the inter-unit competitions with teams composed of their permanent staff, perhaps with the addition of 'guest stars' who might happen to be passing through. If any such guest stars had nothing very fixed in mind as to the posting they desired, there might be an attempt to attract them onto the permanent staff, and thus it was with me. I played a couple of games of hockey at centre-forward and scored a hatful of goals, which at once qualified me for the post of Assistant Sports Officer, an offer which I rejected with a vehemence. This earned me a reprimand, but happily also eliminated me from consideration for a post which would surely have fallen somewhat short of opportunities for adventure.

A fortnight at the Holding Unit in Osnabrück in vile, cold, grey weather and with no certainties about my future had left me rather dispirited. Champagne cocktails were probably the only solace. My news, such as it was, generally went to my mother, who expected a letter from her children once a week. But since I owed to my father the initiative which had resulted in my having the opportunity to get out to Germany, I also kept him directly informed of my progress in achieving an acceptable posting. By now it was out of the hands of both of us. I had asked for a posting to T-Force which the Colonel at 54RHU considered to be 'Military Government' and had recommended; in fact, its only link with Military Government was its consultative function between its commander, the brigadier, and the Deputy Military Governor. Operational directives came from the other side of the Channel.

One of those who had passed through the AMGOT course was my father. He had been on leave from Fiji at the outbreak of war, and was taken into the army early in 1940 with a view to his assuming command on arrival of a Fijian Brigade to be sent as Labour Corps (effectively, Pioneers) to the European theatre of operations. My father spoke fluent Fijian, and had commanded Fijian troops in 1918 when released *ad hoc* by the Colonial Office, and was therefore a natural choice—provided he passed the medical as A1. At the age of forty-eight, he did. In the event the Fijians never came to Europe. The Fijian Labour Corps in Britain and France in the First World War was almost wiped out by a potent cocktail of pneumonia, tuberculosis and 'social diseases', acquired particularly in and around the docks at Marseilles. Perhaps wisely, the War Office opted not to repeat the experiment, and instead the Fijians served with distinction as fighting soldiers in the Pacific, where they were entirely at home with the conditions.

So, after returning from France through St Malo on 16th June 1940, my father commanded a series of 'alien' companies of the Pioneer Corps in the UK, including one known as the 'Millionaires' Company' on account of its remarkable concentration of wealthy, influential, educated and cultivated personnel, mostly of Central European origin. His refusal upon arrival at the unit to allow four or five dozen of his charges to continue to perform as a Palm Court Orchestra in a luxury hotel in Bournemouth, or to keep their Rolls Royces and Bentleys on the barrack square, was reputed to have led to his being the model for the figure of the brutal and insensitive Officer Commanding in a radio play of the time, *The Fingers of Private Spiegel*. Shockingly, the character of Private Spiegel, who played the violin most beautifully (doubtless a Stradivarius), was obliged to abuse his artist's fingers peeling potatoes. One can imagine how fearfully rough and calloused they became.

By the end of the war, my father was within three years of retirement from the Colonial Service, and had decided not to return to Fiji. He had no appetite for prolonging his service whether in Germany or elsewhere, nor did he apply.

With my father's demobilisation looming, and the decision taken not to return to Fiji, my parents had bought a property in Sussex; it was to be their first married home in England. It was quite close to where we had lived in rented accommodation at Forest Row since 1939, and had been requisitioned by the army for an Officers' Mess. It had not entirely escaped the wear and tear which that involved, and the army was due to make good the damage. The renovations were expected to be completed about this time. Though situated beneath three flying bomb flight tracks, two running east-west and one south-north, it had escaped bomb damage. I had not yet seen it, although I knew the area well.

54 R.H.U., B.A.O.R.
11th March 1946

My darling Mama,

I am still here awaiting posting and bored almost to death. I would be were it not for Tony Lucas, Tony Chance and John Kirby, with whom I spend most of my time. We drink in their Mess and eat in mine, using the Officers' Club as a spare for both. Apart from one or two nice types in the Gunners and one crazy Irishman, the other company is inexpressibly dull. The concert hall is 2½ miles away and stinks horribly of Germans and is not really worth the visit. I am playing hockey for the unit today and Tony Lucas is playing for his too. I very much need to exercise to sweat out some of the wine. As a matter of fact I walk a good ten miles a day so I shouldn't be in such bad shape as far as the muscles go. It's my wind I'm worrying about— the food and wine I've had in the last week would keep a family for a month. I haven't worn a greatcoat since I've been here, and that and my walks have kept me fit—I'm about the only one on my draft who hasn't caught a cold as the result of the change in climate. I haven't seen the sun since I sailed from

England. Snow has fallen lightly once and it hasn't all disappeared yet; there
has been a practically permanent fog, completely obscuring the countryside,
which is meant to be rather pleasant round here. If we were to get a fine day
I would visit one or two of the nearer villages, but at the moment it isn't
worth the risk or the effort.
My colonel has put in my name for Mil. Gov. and that is what I should get,
but it won't come through for some days yet.
All my love,
Michael

There was nothing new to add since my letter to my father the day before, but since he was still serving elsewhere, it had to be repeated to my mother to keep the letter count up to the mark. On top of my fortuitous reunion with Tony Lucas, there were two other Rifle Brigade officers apparently kicking their heels with him. In fact, the three of them were taking a large draft of other ranks from England to the 1st Battalion in Glücksburg, but suffering an unaccountable delay at the Reinforcement Holding Unit. It made them nervous lest they might be separated from the draft for which they were responsible and would have to account.

Tony Chance I didn't then know, he being of a slightly earlier vintage; he had followed his father into the regiment. For Tony was the younger son of Sir Roger Chance, 3rd Baronet, who had won an MC and was twice wounded with the Rifle Brigade on the Western Front in the First World War.[4]

John Kirby was the son of Major-General Stanley Kirby who was Deputy Chief of Staff of the Control Commission for Germany, whom John had no

---

4 Having lost his right leg, Sir Roger replaced it with an old-fashioned but sturdy wooden one. Nothing daunted, he raced about the lanes of Sussex in his three-litre Bristol, the pre-war British cousin of the BMW, giving as the reason for his excessive speed his reluctance to shift his wooden leg from the accelerator to the brake. Tony was of a milder disposition. The family company had made the glass for the Crystal Palace, the Houses of Parliament, and the four faces of Big Ben,

inhibitions in telephoning at the drop of a hat. When John reported to me the Major-General's description of T-Force as being occupied in interesting and amusing work, I decided to ask to be posted to them. I had no idea what they did but was told it was secret, and this was in itself enough of an attraction.

To suggest that the concert hall (which we never visited) stank horribly of Germans was an assumption born of blind prejudice. Attributing to the defeated population a particular smell was purely an acknowledgement of fact. Generally pervasive, and not only in confined spaces, the smell I refer to so casually could be detected in the streets of Osnabrück, and indeed, in all the towns of the Ruhr. In due course we all tried to identify its component strains. We agreed that it included the emanations from the low-grade brown coal briquettes which they burned in their stoves, as well as those from the overcooked cabbage invariably found still simmering on top. A particularly distinctive note was added by the cigarettes the populace smoked, made from inadequately cured tobacco grown in their own front gardens. (The Germans considered our 'proper' cigarettes too valuable as currency actually to be smoked.) We felt that the final component was stale sweat, probably issuing from inadequately laundered clothing and bodies in difficult conditions. Whatever its chemical make-up, apparently those out on night patrol in the Western Desert swore by it as being a powerful and reliable warning of the proximity of German positions, and sometimes owed their lives to it.

Lt. M. H. S. Howard R.B., 1 Bucks, B.A.O.R.
13th March 1946

Darling Mama,
Just a note. This is my posting at last. 1 Bucks is a battalion in T-Force, a
rather special unit coming direct under Army command and also under the

---

and pre-eminently for the optical glass of lighthouses. The baronetcy was created in 1900, but later generations were not active in the business; it would never have been Tony's métier, nor that of his father who was Press Attaché in Berlin in 1938.

23

orders of Mil. Gov. Their job is catering for and looking after the people who are taking stock of and removing German heavy machinery in the Ruhr. That is we arrange their messing, travel, protection, security etc. Also the men are used for handling the machinery. Also used for hunting wanted people who have disappeared so we are a mixture of hotel-keepers, pioneers, and security police. There is another R.B. here, and another coming. 1 Bucks wear black buttons and a 60th cap badge and are vaguely affiliated, so it's not too bad.

I am now at Kamen near Unna, between Münster and Neheim, but may be detached to a company anywhere in the Ruhr. Should be interesting. Don't know how confidential the job is so wait until I can let you know.

I passed through the world-famous marshalling yards at Hamm. My God. What a shambles—you need to see to believe. Münster is a ruin—not 1 house in 30 left standing and 1 in 35 with a roof. People don't look underfed but they may be.

Played bridge with the Colonel against Q.M. and 2 i/c and won 15 marks i.e. 30 points. If those truffles arrived you could send them to me here. Also if you can lay hands on a few fags. Also any not too bulky books that you think I might enjoy, as we get no reading matter but day-old papers. I played hockey for 54 R.H.U. in the final of the inter-Unit cup—we won 12–0.

The officers seem a moderate crew. I am the youngest and in the highest release group, but they don't know about my Class B, so I should have a nice summer here. By the way I am due for leave on June 2nd, in time for O.R.[5] post-war celebration and the Victory parade.

Job sounds interesting. Yes sir, I am happy in my work. No time for anything more and so to bed. See what the call of duty does. Are you in your house yet, if not why not?

All my love,

Michael

---

5 Old Rugbeian.

It had been on the previous day, the 12th, that I covered most of the way to Kamen by train, and was then picked up in an open jeep—fortunately wearing my greatcoat—and driven to the Officers' Mess of the 1st Bucks Battalion of the Oxfordshire & Buckinghamshire Light Infantry. I arrived, frozen, in the dark.

Kamen, under the veil of night, had looked much like anywhere else: ill-lit, anonymous—I knew nothing of it. Even today, with about forty-five thousand inhabitants, its name rings no bells until you mention the Kamener Kreuz, the cloverleaf intersection of the country's two principal autobahns. In 1946, with about fourteen thousand inhabitants, it qualified only as an *Ort*, a 'place', a part of the *Kreis* of Unna, which lay five miles to the south. The neighbouring *Ort,* which was hardly more than a continuation of Kamen with no open space between them, was Bergkamen, *'Berg'* denoting the presence of a coal mine within its borders. The twin towns, which had a long history, were known only for two features in the landscape: one was the large twelfth century Evangelical church in Kamen, built of green sand-stone, with its romanesque tower surmounted by a crooked spire. The other was the group of towers for the winding gear at the mine at Bergkamen, the Zeche Monopol. One of the shafts there, the Schacht Grimberg, had given notice of its inherently unstable geology and chemistry with a firedamp explosion in September 1943, killing 107 mostly Russian slave labourers. It had exploded again on 20th February 1946 just before I arrived. In what was Germany's worst ever mining disaster, 405 miners were killed—almost the entire morning shift—and buried with them at a depth of 930 metres were three British officers of the North German Coal Control. Only sixty-four miners escaped. The mine was sealed off with a concrete cap for three years, thus depriving the afternoon shift of their livelihood for the dura-tion. The socio-economic consequences for Kamen and Bergkamen, both of whose populations depended heavily on the mine for their employment, were disastrous. Many homes were left without a man, children without a father, women without a husband. The household would lose the additional ration due to a miner. It created a social situation ripe for exploitation by the troops stationed there.

On my arrival at about ten past six, the Mess Corporal, Corporal Weatherall, took my kit, nodded at the door on the left, and said, 'They're all in there, Sir.' Indeed they were—in the bar, all chatting, and no-one taking the slightest notice of me. So I ordered myself a double Steinhäger and downed it pretty quickly. After about ten minutes Colonel Nicol wandered over and asked, 'Young man, do you play contract bridge?' I replied in the affirmative which prompted a brief confidential discussion with a couple of the others, and then he said, 'In that case, you shall be the Intelligence Officer.' It seems they wished to be quite sure that they would have a four in the Mess at all times; I am convinced that, had my reply been negative, the very next day I would have been in a truck on my way to one of the three outlying detached companies. My claim to play contract bridge was put to the test very early by Colonel Nicol personally, on my second night in fact, and the test was passed in so far as, playing together, we won—at threepence a hundred, or its equivalent in Rentenmarks—seven shillings and sixpence.

The existing Intelligence Officer, Captain R H T 'Dicky' Muir RB, was marked down to become Adjutant in a couple of weeks, so in the meantime I was found a temporary slot in HQ Company, in charge of the Support and Signals Platoons, for which I was deemed to have some qualifications. These platoons were effectively run by a couple of perfectly competent, experienced and good-humoured sergeants, well used to working with young subalterns.

I knew nothing of 1 Bucks. My report to my parents as to the function of T-Force was, after a mere twenty-four hours, fairly wide of the mark, but anyway each member tended to have a different take on it, depending on their own role. I took some comfort from the fact that members of 1 Bucks wore black buttons, their cap badge was a black Maltese Cross very similar to that of the 60th, and their drill movements were the same as those I was used to.

Officers like Dicky from other regiments were not badged as the Bucks Battalion and nor, as it turned out, was I to be. Saying that they were 'vaguely affiliated' was overstating the case, but I later learned that ever since the Peninsular War officers of the Ox & Bucks, and the Rifle Brigade and 60th Rifles (and the Chestnut Troop of the Royal Horse Artillery) had been honorary members of one another's Messes, so were at the least brothers-in-arms.[6]

There was, and still is, a hierarchy among regiments, with certain well-known names rightly or wrongly deemed to be a cut above the rest. Even so, it was insufferably priggish of me to describe the officers as a 'moderate crew', perhaps a reaction to finding a sprinkling of Beds & Herts and other perfectly good county regiments 'of the line'[7] among their number. I had led too rarefied a life, but I would learn. Among those officers whom on such scant evidence I dismissed as moderate were two members of the Beds & Herts who had seen service in Burma where they had a battalion with the Chindits. Captain Ronnie Mayes and Lieutenant Sam Pringle (whose father had been a Liberal MP) had operated deep behind the Japanese lines, and were thought to have gone 'jungle', that is, a bit wild and unpredictable. Having filled me with gin one evening after dinner, they dragged me off into the darkness to meet some actual German females—that is, the ladies of the Grevel family. There was the matriarch Mutti, who retired upstairs and would beat on the floor with her walking stick if we made too much noise, and could soon be silenced by sending her up a slug of gin; Fitti, who appeared dedicated to the entertainment of Ronnie; Tutti, likewise to Sam; and then the strikingly beautiful Marianne. Within a couple of months of my own age, Marianne had suddenly, by the inexorable workings of the demobilisation programme,

---

6 This relationship was to be cemented later with the formation of the Green Jackets, and subsequently Royal Green Jackets, integrated in 2007 into The Rifles as the 2nd and 4th Battalions.

7 That is, not enjoying the distinction of having been taken out of the line and reserved for special duty, as had the Rifle Brigade in 1816 following distinguished service in the field at Waterloo the previous year.

become escort-less. Ronnie and Sam had sought me out to fill that role. I would not have needed the gin; it was no hardship, she was a delightful young woman, and we maintained an agreeable if entirely innocent relationship for nearly a year, conversing in both languages and both seeking to improve. Her English was very good.

This first social encounter with German civilians raised in my mind the question of the status in practice of 'non-fraternisation', though it seemed prudent to avoid exhibiting too keen an interest in it either in the Officers' Mess or in my letters home. In the event, I discovered a certain discrepancy between the code of behaviour expected of the troops, and the attitude tacitly current in the Officers' Mess. I am sure that I was not alone in compounding the double standard by being rather more friendly towards the ordinary German civilian than I would at that time have admitted to my parents. The hard facts were that Montgomery's initial Puritanical edict of March 1945 forbade even so much as a hand-shake with a German. By June the orders were relaxed to the extent of allowing British forces to speak or play with little children (no-one had heard of paedophilia in those days), but not otherwise modified. By July the policy was becoming an anachronism and in danger of being unenforceable. By the end of September it was in tatters, and would be defined merely by forbidding the billeting of British forces on German families, and forbidding marriage with Germans. Other forms of social contact were by inference permitted, subject only to an invocation to soldiers to 'conduct themselves with dignity, and to use their common sense in dealing with Germans'. Since sexual intercourse was no longer specifically excluded, the idea of the soldiery engaging in it 'with dignity' raised interesting questions of technique, while 'common sense' perhaps implied the use of the condom.

Nevertheless, by early 1946 there would be a percentage of older, more senior officers who might now have wives and daughters with them. It would be the wives who would be the most inflexible opponents of any hint of liaisons, particularly sexual, between officers and German women. And some younger officers who had been engaged for instance in one of the episodes of 'no prisoner' fighting found any attitude to 'the Hun' other than implacable detestation unacceptable. We had one such, but as time went by he managed to reconcile his attitude with an affection, indeed a passion, for a particular German lady whom he later married. But he continued to be very harsh in his dealings with other Germans.

M. H. S. Howard R.B., 1 Bucks, B.A.O.R.
14th March 1946

Dear Daddy,

Here I am at my unit and it is more or less what I wanted. This unit is a black button unit, affiliated to the R.B.s. They are what is known as 'T-Force' troops, and the job is to look after and escort and assist the foreign reparations technicians who come round to remove German machinery from the Ruhr. Sometimes we have to hunt out German scientists or specialists who have disappeared. It involves a certain amount of travel, and quite a lot of contact with Germans, and plenty of opportunities to speak the lingo. Later. Cancel none of the above but add the following. I have been made Battalion Signals Officer and also i/c Support Platoon. This means that I have a dozen armoured cars under my control and am also responsible for all wireless and telephone communication in the battalion. It should also mean that I can get about the country a bit, as the companies are on detachment as far as 60 miles away, and they will have to be visited regularly. It is quite a responsible position, but with quite a lot of free time attached. Both platoons are really quite capable of running themselves. I am there in a merely supervisory capacity.

In the case of disturbances I would be in charge of the armoured cars and also a mortar detachment, but that is unlikely.

Kamen is a small and rather dull town. It doesn't even boast an Officers' Club or an Officers' Shop but it has got a cinema, and the Mess is moderate only. The billets are comfortable and I have no real complaints. There are 6 or 7 bridge players in the Mess. It is just at the eastern end of the Ruhr val-ley between Hamm and Unna, not far from the Möhne Dam which Gibson blew up. There are several Officers' Clubs and good sailing facilities there. I shall try to get over there from time to time. The I.O. here is a former R.B. and quite nice. Tony Chance, also of R.B. and a friend of mine, may be coming in a few days.

I have no news from home at all, and for all I know you may be demobbed and at home. At any rate could you ask Mummy to send me some decent writing paper. I forgot when I wrote to her.

With love,

Michael

By the next day I had been able to give my father a better description of what T-Force actually did, without yet getting it quite right. Also, a better description of what my immediate duties were going to be, although I won-der what made me think that we would enjoy so much free time. Our duties were such that there was little training involved, and only enough of military activities, parades and drill, to remind everyone that we were still soldiers even though we didn't always seem to be acting as such. Part of my responsibilities as Support Platoon commander was to see that the relatively inexperienced armoured scout car drivers, some still learners, improved their skills. This took me out with them onto the autobahn and other roads in the Humber scout cars, which gave me a chance to get a look at the locality for twenty or thirty miles around, and to learn to drive on ice, of which there was still plenty.

I had clearly been spoiled in Osnabrück into believing that there would be Officers' Clubs all over the place. In fact, the nearest would be twenty-five miles to the east at Soest, and this became our preferred evening out, and then there was Dortmund, which had been a German Army Officers' Club and had been taken over as such. And there were Officers' Clubs—in the plural—and sailing facilities, by the Möhne Dam about ten miles south of Soest. The destruction of the dam by Guy Gibson and 617 Squadron meant that its name alone was enough to spark an interest, and in my innocence I anticipated happy hours sailing on the re-established lake, perhaps with Tony Chance whom I expected to be posted to T-Force within a matter of days. But I had no idea how hard we were going to have to work.

East of Möhne and Soest lay Paderborn, very much in the centre of good tank country, and the young officers of the tank regiments stationed there often took their recreation dinghy-sailing at Möhne. Most of them were as inexpert as I, but they had the habit of going sailing in their heavy tank boots which needed a good deal of doing-up and undoing. As may happen with land-locked lakes surrounded by wooded hills, the wind seldom came from the same quarter for ten minutes at a time, with the consequence that a capsize was not an infrequent occurrence for the unwary or unpractised. A number of drownings among the booted and spurred subalterns of the RTR persuaded us that it would be less dispiriting to do our sailing in the arm of the lake from which we could not see the black flag hoisted at the Yacht Club calling us in when one of these incidents occurred. Gradually, cause and effect were linked, and fatalities were reduced.

Lt. M. H. S. Howard R.B., 1 Bucks, B.A.O.R.
21st March 1946

Darling Mama,
Here I am well and happy and fit, but no news from you yet. I expect my fan mail has been following me round Europe, and not quite catching me anywhere. As O.C. Support Platoon I have my own Humber scout car and a motor-bike at my disposal whenever I like. The other day I ran down to Iserlohn about 25 miles to the south and went to the Officers' Shop there. We can get good kit and clothing there without surrendering coupons and at a very reasonable price, so I shall stock myself well before leaving Germany.

I have just a pleasant amount of work and responsibility. Today a section of my armoured cars is doing a reconnaissance of the Möhne Dam area to see what Officers' Clubs there are in the area. Later on in the summer I shall join the Yacht Club there and do a little sailing in a sailing dinghy.

I'm afraid to say that this Battalion is leaving T-Force during the summer, so if I am to stay in T-Force I shall have to join some other unit. The Intelligence Officer here, one Dicky Muir of the Rifle Brigade, has much the same ideas and I shall be guided by him and circumstances.

I have played bridge here for four evenings and have won 29, 18, and 9 hundred, and lost 2 hundred, so at that rate I shall pay my Mess bill.

This letter counts as just a routine effort to let you know that I am O.K.—I will try to do something more detailed at the weekend—if I'm not too busy enjoying myself at Möhne.

All my love,

Michael

A Humber scout car was not the most refined form of personal transport, but at least it gave the impression that it was engaged in some sort of mission and should not be hindered or subject to questioning. Thus it was quite adequate as a vehicle in which to travel twenty-five miles to visit the Officers' Shop where I bought a pair of tank boots (not to go sailing in). The Humber could be overdriven and, downhill and with the wind behind it, it would do seventy miles per hour down the autobahn, but on one occasion I blew the cooling system and limped home only after plugging the hole with the sawn-off butt-end of a broom handle scrounged from the petrol station at Wiedenbruck.

The fact that 1 Bucks was soon to quit the T-Force role (in the summer, I thought, but in fact much sooner) did not mean that I myself would be leaving. Colonel Nicol asked both Dicky Muir and myself—both of us bridge-players—whether we would go with them, but by then we represented the nub of the T-Force intelligence operation in I Corps District in the western half of the British Zone. Apart from our being personally strongly disinclined to accept, HQ T-Force would not have agreed to it. 1 Bucks was disbanded not long thereafter, and the Colonel retired at around the same time.

Short of going out to one or other of the clubs to dine, bridge was the way in which we passed most evenings after dinner, and in a week I had played four times. My winnings during the week totalled thirteen shillings and sixpence, quite enough to cover my bar bill. As elsewhere, bridge was an agreeable way of passing the time with people into whose company one is forced by circumstance, but with whom one might have almost nothing else in common. Not that that was by any means true of all my companions at that time.

Lt. M. H. S. Howard R.B., 1 Bucks, B.A.O.R.

22nd March 1946

Darling Mama,

No news from you yet [25.3.46—2 letters just come—am writing], but I am told that that is nothing out of the ordinary, so I am not worrying. I am just hoping that by now you are safely installed in the house, and that Daddy has shaken the dust of the Army from off his boots. Talking of boots—on February 15th I left a pair of black ones at the cobblers next to the P.O. in Forest Row. I think I asked you to collect them for me, but in case I didn't, could you chase them up.

For the first time since last September I woke up with a full day's work in front of me if I want it. It's practical maintenance on the trucks with my platoon, and I thoroughly enjoyed it. Luckily both the signals and support platoon sergeants are charming fellows, easy to work with and reliable, so it makes my job much more pleasant.

The G.1, the chief staff officer, Lieutenant-Colonel David Edwardes from H.Q. T-Force was down last night, and has been chatting over the future of T-Force with the Colonel, and as far as I can see I am going to stay in

T-Force with the Colonel, though what my new role is to be I cannot tell. I shall be very happy to carry on in this job for a month or two anyway. We had a bit of a hectic party which wound up eventually at 3 o'clock. I seem to have more or less escaped damage except for loss of sleep which can be easily made up.

You might try to check up for me on Phyllis Walker's sister in Minden. Could you let me know her full name and what she does. I know she lives at a naval barracks in Minden, and wears a sort of Wren uniform, and that her name is Leigh or Lee Walker, but whether or not that is her sur- or Christian name I don't know. I would like to know this as we are trying to get up a Mess dance, and she might easily be able to help. On Monday the P.M.C. and I are going to Minden to try and get hold of something but with that rather scanty information we may not manage. It should be a nice run anyway about 110 miles down the Cologne-Berlin autobahn, a lovely road.

I shall not close this letter until today's post arrives, as I really should be getting something through by now. I shall be listening to the broadcast of the Varsity Mile, as Gordon Wilson has quite a chance of winning.

Recreation in Kamen itself boils down to bridge and ping-pong, but hockey is played and badminton and cricket are about to begin, so that is not too bad. Other entertainments of a more abstract nature are almost entirely lacking and have to be sought in such places as Dortmund, Essen etc, which are all really too far away to make it worth while.

It is an experience just being in this country as long as you keep your eyes open. The problem of entertainment for the men in a place like this is extraordinarily difficult, and of course the answer as far as they are concerned is German women: an awful lot of the men do want to marry Germans, which makes the situation difficult. The food situation here seems not too bad: as far as I can see the disturbances so far amount to large scale pilfering of food-stocks, but nothing serious, and nothing in this area.

5.00 p.m. I hope to goodness that you are in the house by now—I have as yet no means of telling.

I gather that the address is to be: Cat Street House, Upper Hartfield, Sussex.

With all my love,

Michael

The GSO1 from HQ T-Force who came down to talk with Colonel Nicol about the future of T-Force, David Edwardes, was a very charming man, handsome behind his suitably Edwardian moustache. By the end of the evening his wish that Dicky and I should both stay with T-Force was made clear, and he had pencilled me in as Intelligence Officer. Later ill-conceived attempts to make me Adjutant—a post which nominally carried more prestige and which I should by rights have coveted—failed because, at the end of the day, it was his word that counted. From time to time I did stand in briefly when the incumbent went on leave, in order that successive colonels should not feel neglected and Adjutant-less. Edwardes left the army in the second half of 1947 and went on to become personnel director of the disastrous groundnut scheme in Tanganyika.[8]

By that time, many of the men who had been stationed in Germany for some while had established relationships with local women. For a newly-arrived innocent like me, however, access to attractive and unthreatening English female company seemed a desirable objective. Phyllis Walker was a pleasant friend of some fifty summers, who had been a colleague of my mother's at the WVS canteen in Forest Row at the end of the war. She gave me a collection of gramophone records, seventy-eights of course, which had been in the possession of

---

8 When I was leaving Cambridge three years later I asked him to give me a reference. This he did in glowing terms, and said that if my prospective employers did not give me a job, he would offer me employment himself—something I would have given anything to avoid. I was relieved not to have to offend him.

WVS canteen, Forest Row: canon shell damage from attack by Focke Wulf 190s.

her uncle, Howard Carter, the Egyptologist and discoverer of Tutankhamun's tomb. The collection included notably the 1928 recording of Beethoven's Opus 97, the 'Archduke' trio, performed by Cortot, Thibaut and Casals. The records were somewhat worn, which affected mostly the upper register of the violin part. Phyllis said her half-sister Lee was some fifteen years younger than herself, which would still have left room for her to be quite a bit older than me. She was described simply as being a Wren at Minden, as if that would be address enough, and I was encouraged to look her up.

In those days the BBC gave more attention to the 'Varsity sports' than they would dream of doing today. After all, it was a competition between the only two universities they had ever heard of. Gordon Wilson was a younger contemporary in my house at Rugby and a Cadet Officer in the Junior Training Corps with me. A gifted and dedicated athlete, who set a record for the Freshman's Mile at Cambridge. Later Surgeon-Captain to the Royal Horse Guards, he was killed in Cyprus in September 1956 by an EOKA sniper while attending to the wounds of a civilian woman in an open square.

At the time of this letter, a combination of the continental climate and the winter weather made outdoor team sports a doubtful proposition, but the nature of the duties of the ordinary rifleman allowed participation in them to be frequent once spring came. Badminton was an indoor pursuit, and the arena for that was a large public hall, the *'Turnhalle'* in the town of Kamen, where we were able to reserve time for ourselves in the evening as long as we did not mind playing under the curious gaze of the public.

On 22nd March I heard that my parents had at last moved into Cat Street House. It owed its name to the fact that the traces of an old pilgrim road, St Catherine's Street, passed at an angle through the property in the general direction of Canterbury. The road was by then no more than a shallow continuous depression in the soil, under which I assumed it would be possible to uncover a stone surface sufficient at least to bear an ox-cart. I promised to excavate enough to find out and, who knows, one might even have made a feature of it. Twenty-six years later, when my sister and I sold the property, I had failed even to scratch the surface. The house was on the crest of a ridge running from east to west on the northern fringe of the Ashdown Forest. Apart from the two servants' bedrooms, which of course faced north, all the bedrooms and one of the bathrooms faced south and had views over the forest to the clump of trees known as the Camel, or more formally as Gill's Lap, or Leap, a forty-minute walk from the gate at the bottom of the property. From the windows in the summer we could see no other house. Long and low, the house had started life as a cottage with a narrow staircase. The architect Clough Williams-Ellis, who later designed the Italianate fantasy village of Portmeirion on the coast of Wales, had extended it at both ends for his own use, but it created the problem of pumping hot water from the boiler at one end to the radiators in the drawing-room at the other end. It was an expensive affair.

The first letters from home arrived while I was in the course of writing the following letter, on the 25th.

Lt. M. Howard R.B., 1 Bucks, B.A.O.R.
25th March 1946

Darling Mama,
My first letters have arrived today. The one that you wrote to me at Osnabrück had been all over Europe. The one you wrote on the 21st therefore took 4 days to get here.

I think that the least they can do is to let Daddy out when he wants to. Has he no redress? What about Colonel R. Stephenson Clarke—you might make him justify his existence.

Just like Brian.[9] *He has me whacked for sheer bloody casualness and he always will be like it. He is without exception the most selfish person I know, but quite good company and very amusing.*

Glad you've got a cook. This arrangement sounds more satisfactory than your two gentlewomen.

I tried today to get to Minden and see Phyllis Walkers' sister, but I was in an open jeep and by the time I had gone 75 miles and stopped at Herford for lunch and rested a bit, it was 3 o'clock, and if I had gone on the last 20 miles, it would have entailed coming back in the dark, and the jeep wasn't too reliable. One day I shall set off after breakfast in one of my armoured cars, and should do it quite easily. The whole journey is along the auto-bahn—through lovely countryside—huge stretches rather like the Ashdown Forest, with lashings of coniferous trees. The road is wonderful, three lanes in each direction for hundreds of miles, with clover leaf branch-offs.

The new establishment has been settled—I am to be Liaison Officer of T-Force Intelligence. It should be interesting and give me more chances of speaking German, which I am doing quite a bit anyway. It does not ostensibly carry a captaincy but I shall see what I can do when the new colonel arrives. I believe he is to be a Rifle Brigade fellow. With any luck and a little assistance from Dicky Muir (R.B.), who is to be Adjutant in the new T-Force, we may be able to arrange for such as Michael Corbett and Robin Smyth to be posted to the unit, and make quite a clique out of the whole affair.

I went to Möhne on Sunday, and it was simply lovely. Rather like Winder-mere, but nicer. The area is covered by pine-trees. There is an Officers' Yacht Club there, which I am joining, and also a mixed officers' residential club, and I shall spend quite a lot of time there in the summer. The clubs will be

---

9 Brian Lascelles, the butt of much affectionate abuse.

crowded no doubt, so I shall try to arrange with one of the peasants who live round the lake to let me have a room permanently at my disposal. I would eat at the Officers' Club. That is of course provided that our H.Q. remains at Kamen. We may possibly move to a spot called Leichlingen between Cologne and Düsseldorf, both of which are good towns, and Leichlingen is a lovely spot not many miles from the Rhine.

I had given thought to the idea of calling Mrs. Scott 'Aunt Primrose' and had decided that it would be easier to come fresh to it on my next leave.

All my love,

Michael

P.S. Later—I gather that my new job may quite easily carry a captaincy, which would be pleasant.

So! I thought the new establishment had been settled and I was to be 'Liaison Officer' of T-Force Intelligence—a designation I never heard of again. Another day, another title. There was already a Liaison Officer from HQ T-Force to the office of the Intelligence Officer of 1 Bucks, in the corner of whose office he had a desk, but he was due for demobilisation within a couple of months. He was a GSO2, a major. Was I to replace him? His job was really to interpret policy as it evolved—as it did fairly continuously, if not always with clarity—not to implement it. That was the Intelligence Officer's responsibility.

These were the beginnings of my preoccupation with the rank which went with the job. There was nothing to say that the IO of an infantry battalion like 1 Bucks had to be a captain, though he might be, and Dicky Muir was. The IO had to deal in the course of business with many officers of senior rank in Military Government and the Control Commission, and to exercise an authority far above his apparent level. It would make his dealings with outsiders easier if he held the rank of captain. But I would not be twenty for a couple of months, and had only been promoted from second lieutenant to lieutenant at the beginning of the month. There was the suspicion that, since the incoming colonel (as yet unnamed) was to be a Rifleman, he might be persuaded that the officers around him at the new Unit HQ should as far as possible be Riflemen, and that they should wield the added authority of an extra pip. The condescension of my word 'fellow' proved, once we met the man, to be hugely inappropriate. It was to be Peter Brush. He was a proper soldier with a magnificent fighting record, and a decoration to show for it—and a record for sterling defiance as a prisoner of war, with a decoration to show for that too. Besides, he was a lovely man.

Since we would at first be desperately short of officers to carry out the intelligence side of the work, Dicky and I hoped to acquire Riflemen whom we (a) knew to be available, and (b) knew would do a good job of work. My first choice fell upon two who, each in their way, stood out among those who had been commissioned with me and were still at 27GHB at Ogbourne St George: Michael Corbett and Robin Smyth. Michael had been, *inter alia*, the leading schoolboy athlete and games player of his generation and, more importantly, his wry humour enlivened even the direst situation. Robin had been at Ampleforth and had won the senior history scholarship at Trinity College Oxford; he was the most profoundly educated and civilised member of our intake. Youngest son of Brigadier John 'Jackie' Smyth, VC, MC (later MP for Norwood and 1st Baronet Smyth of Teignmouth in the County of Devon, who had commanded a brigade at Dunkirk and a division in Burma), Robin was not himself instinctively soldierly, but would be a great social asset.

My attempt to locate Lee Walker was laughable, and a three-course lunch at the T-Force Transit Mess at Herford didn't help. The excessively relaxed attempt was doomed to failure.

The comparison of Windermere with the Möhne See to the advantage of the latter was one which I would not now support. Windermere is longer (ten miles as against six) and wider (two-thirds of a mile as against half a mile), and is bounded on the north side by peaks rising to over 900 metres, compared with the hills of the Arnsberger Wald at a little distance to the south of Möhne of up to 550. As to grandeur—not a word to apply to the Möhne See—Windermere has it. However, the slopes down to the Möhne See are covered with pines, and having an accessible green lung to which to retire from the grey, crowded ruins of the Ruhr was a great boon. With the housing situation as it was in Westphalia and the Ruhr, the idea that I might find a 'peasant' who would put a room in the vicinity of the lake permanently at my disposal was a fantasy. In the event, I went sailing only a handful of times.

There had been some talk of moving the unit HQ from Kamen to join D Company at Leichlingen, a pleasant little town set in agreeable countryside with easy access to both Cologne and Düsseldorf. We had already requisitioned the Schloss as a Mess for investigators. However, from an operational point of view Kamen, as first stop down the autobahn from Army—and T-Force—Headquarters, was better placed for the despatch of machinery and equipment to the T-Force Evacuation Depot on the Elbe near Hamburg, and to control the flow of investigators in both directions. It was after all decided that we would stay in our dull little mining town.

Lt. M. Howard R.B., 1 Bucks, B.A.O.R.
26th March 1946

Dear Mama,

Letters yesterday from Anne and Daddy with quite a lot of news from each in their respective spheres. The Army don't seem to be playing quite fair with Daddy, but I gather that he is pulling a fast one for the 240 days following April 1st (All Fools' Day) to help you get straightened up. Your packing cases from Fiji arrived at a timely moment. I'm glad there is so much that will be of use. Is the photograph album amongst the things? I couldn't bear that not to be there.

The letter I got from Anne was posted in Wales on the 20th and only took three days, which is quite good going. I gather she saw Marmaduke Hussey at Betsy's 21st, and dancing too. He was a fine athlete and all that is lost to him now. I regard that sort of thing as one of the tragedies of war. Luckily he has quite a good brain.

Daddy and Anne both said that the two portraits came out quite nicely or even better. You might send me a little one between thick cardboard. I hope I am being included in the list for half-size ones, but I wouldn't risk having it sent out here. I gather Anne is spending her last days in the Wrens in traditional manner, and will play out to the tune of 'Dangerous Corner'.

Dicky Muir and I went out to dinner at Soest last night. We dressed up in Service Dress and Sam Blacks and were thoroughly Rifle Brigade. It makes a change from the Mess atmosphere and though I should hate to be thought a snob, he talks the same lingo as I do, which is more than can be said of some of my Mess mates, not that I hold it against them. It is just pleasant from time to time to escape to a land of pure vowels and something higher in the way of conversation than mere coarse cracks. He is an Uppinghamian and some 3 years my senior. Rather like Robin Smyth—only slightly less intelligent and more suave. He is going up to King's after the war. After dinner (4 courses with turkey and fizz off the ice) we drove over to Möhne to find the club almost deserted, so we sipped at Cointreau and chatted until 10.40, then home and in bed by midnight. At Möhne I ran into a fellow called Swindells who was in H.J.H.[10] and whom I knew fairly well. He is in Recce at Neheim but is going on a War Graves Commission romp, so I shan't see much of him.

As the new Colonel is to be an R.B., I am frantically writing to all my friends to see if they want to come out here, and if they do I will (with great tact) tackle the Colonel on the subject, as he has only to snap his fingers to get them posted. A few of the 'old gang' in this spot would make it complete.

Yours ever,

Michael

---

10 H J Harris' House, Rugby School.

One thing the packing cases from Fiji did not bring was the metal-framed tropicalised upright piano which my grandfather had ordered for my mother from Blüthner of Leipzig between the wars, and which held its pitch wonderfully in an often hot and humid climate. I now rather regret it.

My sister Anne had written to tell me that she had seen Marmaduke Hussey at her friend Betsy Dawson's dance for her 21st. I had known 'Dukey' in my house at Rugby, although he was nearly three years older than I was, and our mothers played bridge together. He was a great athlete who had won the high jump and hurdles at school, captained the rugby football XV and played for the cricket XI, and went on to win a wartime blue in 1942 at Oxford where he spent a year before going into the Grenadier Guards. He was wounded in Italy and lost a leg, but it did not keep him off the dance floor. He had won a scholarship to Trinity College Oxford, where he later read for his degree around spells in hospital. He went on to become chief executive officer and a director of Times Newspapers, and subsequently chairman of governors at the BBC. I was about right, then, when I said he

had quite a good brain. Betsy's father Geoffrey Dawson had been editor of the *Times* until 1941, but I don't think that played any part in drawing Dukey there.

My sister Anne and I had both sat for portraits on our mother's insistence by a lady known as 'Georgie' Lyon, an artist reasonably well-known at the time. I sat for mine in uniform during my first leave after commissioning. She drew in pencil, and the drawing was then photographed, and reproduced half-size and postcard size. The original and larger copies were then tinted. She did me from my 'better side', which she said was

The author, by Georgie Lyon, September 1945, from his 'better side'.

43

usually the side toward which one's face leaned. It was a comfort to think that one had a better side.

Going out to dinner at the club, it was nice to get out of battledress and into service dress, and to wear the insignia which, added to our black buttons, differentiated us from the common herd. We wore black 'Sam Browne' belts with silver buckles, black shoes instead of brown, and black gloves. We were proud to emphasise these distinctions, which had their roots in the history of our regiment—a regiment we naturally believed to be both different and better. Later, when I had sent for my dark Rifle-green patrols which did up at the neck like a bellhop's, I would dress up in those both for going out and for Mess nights.

I am not sure that Dicky's vowels were not a fraction too far on the cut-glass side, but it is a matter of aesthetics, and aesthetics may be a matter of what one is used to. Regional accents may be very attractive, though some of them are more euphonious than others, but what I detest is any of them gentrified. Some of my companions in arms, finding themselves officers and by definition gentlemen, felt that their new status called for gentrification. It lacked authenticity: it grated.

My confidence that the new colonel, being a Rifleman, would have only to snap his fingers to get my pals posted in would soon be put to the test.

Lt. M. Howard R.B., 1 Bucks, B.A.O.R.
27th March 1946

Dear Daddy,
Just a note to thank you for your letter and to let you know that things have turned out better than I had ever hoped or imagined.
T-Force is a unit of which there are roughly two battalions in the whole of Germany—one in 30 Corps area, and this one in 1 Corps area, which includes the whole of the Ruhr, and in fact most of industrial Germany. The job of T-Force is to remove everything from Germany of military or industrial or scientific importance, by way of reparations—to the various

countries concerned. The person responsible for the evacuation of equipment and the general smooth-running of the scheme is the T-Force Intelligence Officer. So you can see that thanks to your initiative in the first place, and a little judicious playing of cards (metaphorically) on subsequent occasions, I have hooked quite a job. It should keep me interested and the experience should prove invaluable. I have to go round to factories quite a bit, and normally an interpreter is taken, but I shall dispense with that, and so I shall force myself to speak the lingo. I shall be hurt if they decide that I am too young for a captaincy, but not surprised. I learn now that it is a captain's job, so shall have to be on my toes all right.

The new Colonel is an R.B. called Brush, but I don't know anything about him—he hasn't been with any of the battalions during the war. At any rate I hope he is amenable to such as Michael Corbett and Robin Smyth being posted out here.

Our billets are in what used to be the Burgomaster's house; a nice spot, well furnished, pleasant garden, and quite a lot of soft fruit. We should be quite comfortable during the summer when there are only 6 officers in H.Q.

It is a pleasant life, and it affords the opportunity of getting round the country a bit. I am hoping to go as far afield as Hanover and Frankfurt in the not-too-distant future.

Thank you—a few fags would be welcome. I won't turn up my nose at the humble 'Player'.

I'm sure all this responsibility is good for me, and it will be quite nice to have as much work as I am able to cope with. (Don't think that I am taking myself too seriously!)

Yours ever,

Michael

By this time I was getting better at understanding just what our role was, and at explaining it to my family. I overstated it a bit, playing down the role played by 5 Kings who, with B and D Companies 1 Bucks under command, had been in the lead in the April/May 1945 helter-skelter across North Germany intended to deprive the Red Army of possession of the Baltic ports. However, now the attention of HQ T-Force, and of the British Intelligence Objectives Sub-Committee who were ultimately their masters, was focussing more upon the industrial riches of the Ruhr and its environs, which was our bailiwick, and where eighty-six per cent of the heavy industry of the British Zone was concentrated. Perhaps it was this shift of emphasis which led to our being referred to as No 1 T-Force Unit, and them as No 2.

I was keen to impress upon my father my attempts to improve my grasp of the German language, because it was that which had prompted him to stimulate the War Office into posting me there. As things developed more and more to my liking and advantage, I found myself becoming increasingly grateful for his intervention.

Hardly a week before Peter Brush was to arrive, I knew nothing about him or his record, and he was certainly not the sort of person given to self-advertisement. As recruits in the regiment we were made well aware that it was the 1st Battalion who, along with other Green Jackets, had fought in the Defence of Calais, buying the necessary time in the face of an onslaught from two Panzer Divisions to make the evacuation of Dunkirk possible. But when the Calais decorations were gazetted after the war, very little actual detail was given and they received scant publicity, so I had not at that time heard Peter's name associated with the exploit, as profoundly it was.

In March and at the beginning of April, there was room for us all to sleep in the Mess building, which had been the Burgomaster's house. Kamen had been taken in April 1945 and occupied by the US Army. They had made a point of principle, there as elsewhere, of requisitioning for themselves the properties of prominent citizens and officials, particularly where the owners were known to be active members of the Nazi Party. The Burgomaster of Kamen, Rolf Berensmann, who was such a one, had been removed from office. His house was large and imposing. Built between the wars, it was set slightly apart on the fringe of the town as one of a group of four. The little enclave proved convenient as officers' quarters, first for the US Army and then for the British. There was enough space to provide a degree of security since anyone wandering around would be very noticeable, and all the houses stood in good-sized gardens.

In addition, and just as large but less imposing in character, there was the house of the Kunsemüller family. Dr Kunsemüller was the best-known of the doctors in the town, with a senior post at the hospital. He also had his own practice which he ran from home. The house had a separate entrance, a waiting room, consulting-room and surgery with the usual offices. As such, the premises should have been exempt from requisition, but requisitioned it was nevertheless, and any complaints and appeals went unheard. The mine at Bergkamen kept him busy, and his specialisms were in the ailments to which miners are prey: pneumoconiosis and crushed limbs. Dealings over the use of these premises were to become an ongoing cause of argument and annoyance. The family had been found meagre but ill-spared accommodation in the hospital.

I am surprised to discover that I accepted my father's offer of cigarettes, because at that time I hardly smoked seven a day, and there was the general free issue of fifty per week. Ours were 'Craven A'. 'Oh God,' I declared loudly in the bar one evening, 'the only brand known to be positively injurious to the health.' I received a quiet word of warning; Colonel Nicol was said to be a substantial shareholder, and it was he who had selected the brand. I don't think anybody had yet told me that I was entitled to buy up to 200 per week at a ridiculously cheap price. I did so later, keeping them in a zinc-lined tin trunk of a design well-known to officers of the Colonial Service as a protection against humidity. It must have been my father's.

Lt. M. Howard R.B., 1 Bucks, B.A.O.R.

2nd April 1946

Darling Mama,

Thanks for writing paper which I am using, and for the cigarettes, which arrived untouched today, also a letter, posted on the 29th March. Thank Phyllis for her step-sister's address—I wonder what she is like. I am going over to see her tomorrow or the next day and see if she can come to a week-end party at Leichlingen—I hope she is slightly less staid than Phyllis—though I don't see why Phyllis couldn't have been good fun when younger if treated the right way.

Before the letter arrived today telling me of her new address I had decided to go and try to look her up at Minden this afternoon: so I duly hopped into a Humber and batted off down the autobahn, lunching at Herford and arriving at Minden about 2.30. (Incidentally the scenery round there is quite superb.) I wandered into the W.R.N.S. quarters in the naval compound in my armoured car, until I saw a Wren darning her stocking, who was quite sweet and to type and very helpful. We looked up someone called Walker who was not the right one. From there to one called Lee-Warner who was also quite sweet but not the right one: so what better could I do than to issue to them invitations to a dance in the near future. By this time I was so embarrassed, what with trying to chase somebody I didn't really know in a place I didn't expect her to be, that I refused a kind offer of tea and batted off down the autobahn again—still they were nice types, and as long as I don't lose sight of them the time won't have been wasted. The trouble about next weekend is if the party becomes rowdier than I bargained for, whatever my personal standard of behaviour may be I don't want to put Phyllis's sister off at the first meeting—so I shall have to do a bit of quick summing-up as to her 'broad-mindedness' when I go and see her, compare that with what I think the party is likely to run to, and do a quick bit of arithmetic. Essen I can reach.

Having unburdened myself of the problem of the moment, here is a little more general news. I have written to various people in England asking them if they want jobs here (Brian not included). To Brian I have addressed a screed of horrible abuse, and if that fails, all else fails until I see the miserable worm again.

At the moment I am understudying the I.O. which allows me considerable freedom of action—as I told you, I went the odd 95 miles to Minden today—I shall go to Essen tomorrow and probably look round what was Krupp's.

I am glad that Anne has got her date fixed, although as you say, it does bring other problems in its wake. I can only agree that a long separation is a hard beginning to married life, and knowing them both I would say that they will do what is in the long run the best, and whatever it is they will make the best of it.

Yes. I always said that Peter Bickersteth was a delightful person; a mass of charm if not of brain, always infectiously cheerful. I have a feeling the other Bickersteth was a cousin.

Thank you, but please keep my boots as I don't really want them. It would be stupid to have them out here.

Dinner suit a v. good idea. I am keeping my patrols long enough to be able to practice archery in the Petty Cury when at Cambridge.

Life out here is proving to be an experience in every respect, a beneficial one I hope, as long as one realises where the change of values exists.

I have not yet been able to pin down the Ballets Jooss, though I think they are up in the north at the moment. They are certainly not in I Corps area at the moment. I only saw Pat for a few minutes and she seemed awfully nice. I expect she gets all the entertainment she wants, but it's worth trying.

I get plenty of opportunity to drive around and switch from left- to right-hand drive with the gayest abandon. The driving on the right is really not difficult at all—everybody else does it! One merely has to conform to type or one is soon forcibly advised to. I have driven a good 500 miles without hitting anything yet.

If I come on leave on June 2nd I shall go to the O.R. reunion on the 6th and probably to a Rifle Brigade dinner at Claridges on the 4th, but that depends on who else is going rather.

I am v. well and not yet as fit as I shall be when I have ridded myself of the alcoholic hangover from 14 days' ennui at Osnabrück.

All my love,

Michael

I continued to make strenuous and more than slightly ridiculous efforts, motoring round the WRNS compound at Minden in my armoured car, issuing invitations left and right to 'quite sweet' Wrens, in my attempt to invite Lee Walker—who, alas, was now in Essen—to a weekend party in Leichlingen. This was the sort of function which later pretty well disappeared from the social calendar of No 1 T-Force (with one exception, which I was to remember all too clearly). It was probably sparked by the certainty that 1 Bucks were very soon pulling out, and would have some goodbyes to say that might best be said over breakfast. My brief experience, in less than a month in T-Force, had clearly made me nervous about the possibility of these parties getting out of hand.

Specific pretexts for making day trips from Kamen, for example to Minden, were in my vestigial capacity as Officer Commanding Support Platoon, not really necessary. But Minden, as the location of the headquarters of the Control Commission for Germany, could always provide a pretext, however slight. Its location where the River Weser cuts through the line of hills at the 'Minden Gap' and known to the Germans as 'Porta Westfalica', the Gate to Westphalia, is really quite spectacular.

Peter Bickersteth was another Rifle Brigade officer with whom I had been at Rugby, where he too had been a Cadet Officer, but two years my senior. His family home was at East Grinstead, only four miles from Forest Row where my mother will have met him. The 'other Bickersteth' was John, an older cousin of Peter's who, in due course, became Bishop of Bath and Wells, later Clerk of the Closet to the Queen and knighted KCVO.

My sister Anne was in the WRNS stationed in Pembrokeshire, and the date referred to was that of her release. Her fiancé David Scott was a Royal Navy lieutenant. They had never served together, the connection was a local one in Sussex, which was our wartime home. The dilemma was merely that he was due to be posted abroad to Malta, and Anne could not go with him unless they married. It was considered rather soon after their engagement for marriage; after the war, longer engagements were catching on again.

My interest in the Ballets Jooss was on account of one Pat Hallett, a ballerina I think, rather than one of the *corps de ballet*. I seem to have been in that period chasing anything in a skirt or, even better, a tutu. She was to become a connexion of my sister's, for Pat's father had married, as her second husband, Anne's prospective mother-in-law. Had the ballet been in I Corps District, they would have come to perform for the troops at Iserlohn, the Corps headquarters, twenty miles to the south of us, where the bomb-damaged theatre's roof had been more or less repaired. Pat was actually a married woman, having married an officer in the Norfolks with whom she had corresponded for some years as a pen-friend while he was a prisoner of war. Later she was to be my niece's godmother.

I had planned with Dicky, that we would deploy our 'patrols'—our Riflegreen Mess kit—in order to have a little fun when we both eventually got to Cambridge. Our intention was to take advantage of a (probably apocryphal) Cambridge city statute which supposedly extended certain privileges to scholars of the university if suitably clad. One summer evening in 1948, by which time I was up at Peterhouse and Dicky at King's, and having purchased toy bows and arrows from Woolworth's that afternoon, we set off to fulfil our mission. The statute declared that 'Scholars of the University, when dressed in a suiting of Lincoln green' as provided, might 'Repair to the Petty Cury, and there require the Constable to detain the Traffic, in order to practice Archery.' Having ensured with the help of friends that there was a policeman in the Petty Cury, we greeted him: 'Officer, we are scholars of the university dressed, as you see, in our suitings of Lincoln green. Kindly stop the traffic; we propose to practice archery.' He gave us a weary look, and took absolutely no notice. Ignorant fellow. We fired off a volley of suction-cup tipped arrows anyway, and went for a drink.

CHAPTER 2

A box of 'wodges' – A Nazi palace amid the ruins – An OBE at breakfast – A Communist threat – A list of the local 'ladies'

Lt. M. Howard R.B., 1 Bucks, B.A.O.R.

5th April 1946

Darling Mama,

This is as much to practise my typing as to tell you anything, but there are a few odd items of news that I can deal with. Firstly, parcels to acknowledge—a packet of cigarettes from you and from Daddy, and also that box of Auntie Miriam's wodges, in very good condition. I shall be writing to thank her in the near future.

Could you send me some black darning wool as holes are gradually consuming more and more of my socks. Otherwise there is nothing I can think of that I want.

Yesterday I went over to do a job of work in Düsseldorf. The whole business was carried out in German and it really stood up to the strain quite well. On the way back I dropped in and saw Lee Walker, who was really very nice. She is tallish, and fair, and rather good-looking in a strong sort of way. She has got the same sort of mouth as Phyllis and was quite easily recognisable. I have asked her to come to our dance which she accepted with every show of pleasure. I think she is P.A. to practically the king-pin of North German

Coal, which is a very good job. They work in what used to be Krupp's private house—a lovely spot. There is a squash court there and I have been offered the use of it, for which I am very grateful. She asked me to spend the weekend there, which seemed a friendly act, and although I was not able to accept, as I am to take over my new department by Monday, I might reciprocate by asking her over to Möhne one weekend in the near future.

I am almost counting on having my leave from June 1–14th. I would like to go to the O.R. reunion on the 6th, but I don't think I will bother to go to the R.B. regimental dinner at Claridges on the 4th unless I find that a lot of my friends are going too. I think you can base all your calculations on those dates, but you know from past experience how likely they are to be changed. This is really a lovely country, with a completely different character from anything in England. Bits of it are duller than anything at home, but some of it takes a lot of beating. I am going to look at the Harz Mountains in the near future. I am angling for 72 hours in Paris or Copenhagen or both, but that depends a great deal on where our assessors want to go to.

My route yesterday took me right through the Ruhr and it is an amazing sight. Literally there is hardly a street for 50 miles in which at least 25 per cent of the houses are bombed, and you can drive for miles through large towns without seeing signs of human habitation. Acres of factories, rusting away, and covered in weeds. My opinion for what it's worth is that Germany won't be able to wage war by herself for some 40 years.

No more news, I think.

My typing hasn't been too bad.

With all my love,

Michael

Written communications from our office had to be typewritten. We had half a dozen typewriters of various makes in the section, all with English keyboards, and one stood habitually on my desk, offering me a strong incentive to learn to type—with two fingers as training in touch-typing was not available—faster than I could write by hand. All our letters were signed by the Intelligence Officer until, many months later, the Colonel had a sudden rush of blood to the head and ordered that he should sign all correspondence leaving the unit, a practice in which he persisted for the better part of eighteen hours before giving it up.

'Wodges' were a wartime utility imitation of chocolate truffles, and although they clearly contained both sugar and cocoa powder, they were not covered by the sweet rationing which was to last for another six years. My aunt's source of wodges was the concierge at the Chatsworth Court Hotel in London where she resided. I wouldn't go so far as to say that there was a black market in wodges, but scarcity would have determined the price at which they were traded. Not that I recall our being much constrained by sweet rationing in the army in Germany, and nor were our brothers-in-arms in the US Zone of Occupation, for whom the Hershey Bar became a potent element as a means of exchange in the commerce between the sexes. For our soldiers the equivalent was the two-ounce bar of Cadbury's Dairy Milk and, more rarely, the plain Bournville chocolate bar, free from adulteration with powdered milk. One evening an unusually spruced-up Rifleman Barran passed my open office door on the way out of the headquarters building. 'Barran, where are you off to?' He turned to me, took a chocolate bar out of his battledress breast pocket and waved it at me, then put it back and went on his way. Words were superfluous. I wonder whether the rather straight-laced Quaker Cadbury family were aware of the extent to which their innocent product was being used to oil the wheels of social and sexual intercourse?

Regimental dress practice required all visible accessories to meet the colour code, and this extended to socks. As with footwear and gloves, these had to be black. Metal objects, badges, buckles, etc, had to be silver. The Mess Corporal had control of a small coven of local 'ladies who darn', but they had to be provided with suitable wool, hence my request to my mother.

I was clearly preoccupied with the desirability of finding a suitable and presentable partner to bring to the dance, which had been mooted at a time when 1 Bucks first knew that they were to be moving on: an opportunity to say a few fond farewells. Lee Walker, whom I had still not met, suggested herself as a suitable target and I had no hesitation in inviting her at first meeting. My invitation was accepted and immediately countered by her inviting me to spend that weekend at the Villa Hügel, the headquarters of the North German Coal Control where she worked and lived. That was Thursday, so was I to be back there on Saturday? I was probably frightened to death by so swift and eager a response, and perhaps took refuge in the pretext that I was having to prepare to take up my new appointment on the Monday—an excuse which had the advantage of being true.

The Villa Hügel had been the home of Alfried Krupp von Bohlen und Halbach, one of Germany's leading industrialists and head of the Krupp industrial empire. Krupp had been classified as a major war criminal for his use of Jewish slave labour from the concentration camps in the Krupp factories, where he had earned Hitler's favour for designing and producing ordnance and tanks for the German army. In April 1946 he was awaiting trial, and would eventually be sentenced at Nuremberg in 1948 to twelve years' imprisonment, and forfeiture of all his property. Pardoned and restored to his property after three years, Krupp later reinvented himself as a leading philanthropist. But in 1946 his villa was still a prime target for requisitioning—indeed for confiscation. Built in an Essen suburb in 1873, it was a huge and imposing building standing in seventy acres, and was manifestly the fruits for the Krupp family of the Franco-Prussian war. Chiefly following the conventional classical style, three otherwise blameless floors were topped by a fourth resembling a small-scale imitation of the Parthenon, rather as if the Prussian army had as an afterthought gone on to defeat Greece and occupy Athens. In the grounds to the side of the Villa were the stables and the huge indoor riding-school where, in one small corner, the British Army had built a squash court. Attached to the staff at the Villa Hügel was a senior Rifleman, Colonel Pat Curtis, who gave us the run of the place, and we were all to make good use of the squash court from then on.

Within a month of arriving in Kamen, and before I had even taken up my appointment, I was already worrying about where I was going to take the short, 72-hour leaves due to me, and had identified Paris and Copenhagen as likely targets. Brussels and Prague also came under consideration. I got to Paris with Tony Lucas, but not until the summer of 1947, and I never made it to Copenhagen. It would take about a year before I began to feel comfortable about leaving my desk, other than to go home to visit my family.

My trip that day to Düsseldorf gave me my first view of the heart of the Ruhr from ground level, and I returned along Route 1 which ran west-east bang through the middle. I must have meant that there was hardly a street for fifty miles which did not have at least one in four of its houses bombed or bomb-damaged. There were of course areas not bordering Route 1 which provided an exception, but as a general impression it was no exaggeration. And I had not yet clapped eyes on the suburbs of Cologne on the eastern bank of the Rhine, more like moonscapes than anywhere else in the battered Ruhr except, perhaps, for some bits of Bochum. Horror at the sight of these suburbs of Cologne drove Solly (later Lord) Zuckerman to abandon his project of writing a book about the bombing; he concluded that he was simply not able to face doing it. His proposed title, *On the Natural History of Destruction*, therefore remained available for W G (Max) Sebald to deploy fifty-five years later for his set of essays examining the persistent failure of German writers to tackle the subject.

Route 1 took me, on the eastern side of Dortmund, past a bombed church whose two square towers alone still stood, leaning toward each other a bit, with the hands of the clock on the south wall standing at ten to three—which they did to my certain knowledge for at least the next eighteen months. It was a useful landmark amongst the rubble: there, on the way home, you turned left. Grantchester it was not.

Lt. M. Howard R.B., 1 Bucks, B.A.O.R.
8th April 1946
[Posting delayed until 12/4/46]

Darling Mama,

Thanks for your letter—no, I have not yet got Anne's photo, but I expect it will arrive today. At any rate I shall not send this off until it has come. Don't worry about Anne; as far as I am concerned, I think it would be better if they decide to wait, but I can see that they might feel that it was just two years wasted, and there is a hell of a lot in that. In any case I would not dare to express an opinion either way to either of them, and I am sure they will do what is best.

I'm sorry you are not yet in the house but I do feel that nothing much can hold you up now from going in on the 15th. I'm sure the place is looking lovely, and I hate to miss it. Spring is well upon us here, and we have had sun for a good fortnight now. The road where our Mess buildings are has two rows of small trees down either side, all coming into bud—and lots of blossom out too. In our own garden we have got fruit trees of all sorts, and most kinds of soft fruits too. There are many more trees in Germany as a whole—they went in for reafforestation on a large scale and the result at this time of year is quite superb—everybody seems to plant trees on the slightest provocation, and it adds to the character of even the dullest piece of country.

I am now sitting in the I.O.'s seat and trying to do his job—I have grasped most of the relevant facts, and I am sure that it is within my capabilities, such as they are. I will be rather more tied to my desk than before, but there will still be plenty of opportunities of getting out and about. I am hoping to go up to Hamburg in the near future to inspect a warehouse, and I shall be able to look up the 1st Battalion R.B., who with the 2nd Battalion are moving much nearer here in the early summer.

Depending of course on what happens next, I think that I wouldn't really mind if my Class B demob didn't come off until next year. I still have not the slightest intention of postponing my Class B, but if you see what I mean, I wouldn't feel that I had a grievance if it didn't come through for a year.

How long is Mrs. T. going to work per day when you move in? Just a morning's work or is it going to be more or less full time?

By the way, the photo did not arrive by this morning's post, so I shall send this off without waiting.

There does not seem to be very much news, so I shall leave it there.

All my love,

Michael

Now that I was 'sitting in the IO's seat', entirely unencumbered by any relevant experience, one might imagine that all I needed to do was to open the top right-hand drawer of my desk and take out a large ring-binder carefully inscribed 'Manual for the Instruction and Guidance of Intelligence Officers of T-Force in the Proper Performance of their Duties'. There was no such manual.

Before operations had commenced in 1945, some manuals had been written, for instance for the correct layout of a T-Force camp, the only definite consequence of which was that no encampment, temporary or permanent, was ever constructed or organised in accordance with those guidelines. Guidance was also offered to cover a number of eventualities. For example, at that time Britain was still at war with Japan, so any Japanese encountered were at once to be apprehended. To distinguish a Japanese from any other person of oriental appearance, soldiers of T-Force were instructed to oblige them, by whatever means, to say 'hello'. If they said 'hurro' they were at once to be taken into custody as an enemy alien. No such occasion ever arose. Manuals for correct procedure were not always useful.

By 8th April I had been in Kamen a month. The general area in which I was to function had been sketched in since the visit of David Edwardes from HQ T-Force on 21st March, and I had since then missed few opportunities to discuss with my brother officers in the Mess, and particularly with the sitting IO Dicky Muir, the part played by the intelligence office in the unit. Since my initial duties with the Signals and Scout Car platoons did not fully occupy me, I sometimes even sat in Dicky's office and listened to his phone conversations with HQ T-Force, which enabled me to gauge the nature of the relationship. With the guidance of the brilliant Sergeant Wigg, who had established a smooth routine, and of Jim Quick the liaison officer from HQ, I slipped quickly into the mode of 'learning by doing' and in under a month I felt able to act autonomously and with confidence.

As early as my first day in office, HQ T-Force expressed the thought that it would be useful for me to go and see what went on at the T-Force Evacuation Depot at Geesthacht on the Elbe a few miles upstream from Hamburg, to which I would be sending almost all the heavy equipment we took out. The 1st Battalion the Rifle Brigade were at that time at Glückstadt in Schleswig-Holstein, also on the Elbe, some miles downstream from Hamburg. While it seemed just round the corner, a visit to Glückstadt would have cost another day away from my desk, which at that point I could hardly afford or justify. Instead all I could hope for was a night at the officers' transit hotel, the Atlantic in Hamburg. The long bar at the Atlantic was a shambles always some distance removed from sobriety; and keeping a semblance of order there was a continuing problem, and not just among the junior officers. The story is told of the RAF squadron leader on the fifth floor (somehow it always is the fifth floor, whether of the Crillon in Paris, the Excelsior in Rome, or wherever) who was caught stark naked in the corridor, chasing a lady also in a state of nature. Charged with the offence of being improperly dressed, he was said to have got off the charge on the grounds that he was 'properly dressed for the sport in which he was engaged'. My room was on the fourth floor. I learned nothing important or useful at the Depot at Geesthacht.

When I had first arrived in Germany, and before all the attractions of a really fulfilling appointment had made themselves apparent to me, the question of the prospect of 'Class B Release' was much in my mind, holding out as it did the possibility of early release from the army to go up to university. As it was now evident that I would not be required to play any part in a shooting war, picking up my degree was, on the face of it, my next priority. Under the Class B Scheme, it was open to the university—or rather the individual college—if it so wished, to apply to the War Office for the early release of any serviceman to whom that college had awarded a scholarship and for whom they had reserved a place. Hence my exhibition at Peterhouse Cambridge made me nominally eligible. Without much in the way of valid grounds, my expectation of special favour was lively, but I had not stopped to consider the position of those scholars of 1940–1942 who by virtue of longer service would have a prior claim, and they could well account for all the places that the college had available in 1946, and indeed in 1947 too. In the event Peterhouse, the smallest as well as the oldest college, promised no more than that they would do their best, warning me that pressure on space remained high. They did, however, point out that there might well be a number of scholars who, when it came to the point after three or four years' service, might wish to forego their place and remain in the service as regulars, and others who might in any case not care to return to academic pursuits. But, after so short an experience, I was already getting a taste for the life, and here I was admitting to my family that if I were not to be demobilised until September 1947 at the latest, so as to go up to Cambridge that October, I wouldn't feel too hard done by. While not renouncing my claim, which lent me a little prestige as belonging in an apparently superior category, I was now entirely prepared to let matters take their course.

Mrs T—I don't think we knew, and certainly never used, her first name—was the wife of Bob Tailbury, who before the war had been gentleman's gentleman to the surgeon Lacon Sibley at his London home. Rejected for active service on account of flat feet, he had learned the rudiments of horticulture during the war and then came to work full-time as gardener for my father. The kitchen garden at Cat Street alone approached an acre, and there was at least another acre of lawn to be mown, and a small orchard and a field, all with hedges. About this time the Tailburys were given a council house in Forest Row. Mrs T had worked for my mother in our rented accommodation from quite early in the war. She suffered intermittently from agoraphobia, with the occasional panic attack and suicidal fears. The 91 bus, which plied with a frequency of thirty minutes between East Grinstead and Tunbridge Wells, stopped near their front door and then at the end of our drive, so the arrangement was able to survive our move to Upper Hartfield. My mother's years of wartime housekeeping, and of work as another pair of hands at the WVS canteen in Forest Row, had already divorced her from the norm to which she had become accustomed in Fiji. There, passable Indian cooks (whose parents' generation had come to the colony as indentured labourers in the cane fields) could be taught to cook by my mother in the English manner, sweet-natured Fijian girls were there to help look after my sister and myself— along with an English nanny for some years—and there were others to do the housework. Prison labour was available to the District Commissioner to do the heavy work in the garden and around the place.

Lt. M. H. S. Howard R.B., 1 Bucks, B.A.O.R.
12th April 1946

Darling Mama,

Thanks for your letter, and could you thank Dad for me for another parcel of cigarettes, which were very welcome. I am afraid to say that Anne's photo has not yet come but if it was done up in anything like parcel form, that is not surprising, as parcels take immeasurably longer than letters.

You misunderstood what I said about changing from right hand drive to left hand drive; you always go on the same side of the road, the variation is on which side of the vehicle the steering wheel is—so 'Dear Mom, in Yurrup they drive on both sides of the car.' I break into pen as the typewriter is being put to more urgent use.

My big moment as I.O. is arriving. The new C.O. is arriving tomorrow, and I am meant to be working efficiently by then. Some of the work is purely Intelligence and that is by far the most interesting side of it. I am going out to interrogate an odd scientist tomorrow, which should be entertaining, and then we are always having a member of some political party in, who wants to split on one of the other parties, and who accuses all the others of being Nazi—merely to gain our favour, and get influence thereby.

Yesterday Dicky and I went to play squash at Villa Hügel; it was most enjoyable, and I won by the odd game in nine. We were able to get a good hot bath afterwards—and decided to have dinner at the Officers' Club in Dortmund. Unfortunately we spent the next two hours wandering aimlessly round the Ruhr in a jeep, quite hopelessly lost, which rather ruined our tempers and the evening as a whole, but we found the place in the end, a nice spot in a large country house, and in spite of arriving at nine o'clock we got a good meal, and enough champagne to make us feel vaguely benevolent—and we got back home at midnight and went to bed dog-tired. It was the first real exercise that I have had for four months.

My immediate senior here is a G.S.O.2—a major called Jim Quick, and I never hope to work with anybody more pleasant. He has a very keen sense of humour, which makes the most humdrum of jobs seem more entertaining. If I am away for an hour or two, my 'in' tray is always empty, and he never tells me he has done it, and doesn't expect any thanks in return; he just does it because he likes to do kind acts. He was a schoolmaster in peace time, and is going back to it. Never a cross word is spoken, and nothing ever ruffles him. To my intense relief he signed on for another two months, and now leaves the army in August; that obviates the unpleasant necessity of working with a new G.2 before I know my own job backwards. My own 'I' sergeant and the interpreter sergeant are both delightful, so ours is a happy little concern. There is the hell of a lot of work done here, believe it or not, so it is just as well that tempers remain unfrayed.

I count myself incredibly lucky to have got this job because it gives one a picture of what is going on at quite a high level, which does not happen in ordinary stooge jobs. Also it is a satisfactory feeling to be able with a stroke of my pen to send convoys scuttling from Frankfurt or Munich to Hamburg, or to put my hand into the Ruhr and pick out sundry scientists with an airiness that comes from being (very nearly) one's own master. If a really interesting job comes along I can almost always do it myself instead of delegating it to one of the others. I tried to go on the last job to Munich, but it would have entailed being away 6 days.

I have heard from Michael Corbett asking if I can get him out here, which I shall most certainly try to do.

As for my washing from Brian—I think that we will have to be content with what we have until I can get my hands on him. The sheet was one I inadvertently swapped with Michael while we were sharing room—he had one of mine.

Nothing more for the moment.

With all my love,

Michael

Both 1 Bucks and T-Force had a mixture of British (right-hand-drive) and German (left-hand-drive) vehicles, and we commonly found ourselves swapping from one to the other in the course of the day—or even in the course of half-an-hour. It could, on the face of it, appear confusing; in practice one adapted almost without thinking. Clearly, I had not made myself plain to my mother who had only ever driven on the left in right-hand-drive cars. Conformity with local practice, the first and last rule of the road, was then, as now, necessary for survival, but the German roads were blessedly free of traffic, so a moment of forgetfulness did not necessarily exact a violent penalty.

So I was back almost at once, taking up the licence to use the squash court at the Villa Hügel—and the comforting hot baths. If Dicky and I were good enough for either of us to win by the odd game in nine, then the games will have been pretty even too, and I am amazed by the thought of playing as many as nine games in a row. We must have been exhausted. Championships and club competitions are played as the best of five, and that is quite enough, but I was glad of the opportunity to work up a good sweat. My few games of hockey at Osnabrück had not achieved the same effect and there will have been quite a lot of nicotine and Steinhäger to work out of the system, as well as muscles to be toned up.

The decision to dine at the Dortmund Officers' Club was taken on the spur of the moment, and without precise directions. Signs to it were non-existent, except in its immediate vicinity, and predictably any soldiers we asked by the way had never even heard of it, not even at the two barracks we passed. We persisted because we had signed ourselves out of dinner in the Mess. We stumbled across the club almost by chance, and by then in the dark. During dinner there was a floor show, and one of the acts was performed on one of the round dining-tables. There a lady contortionist performed a routine which seemingly could only have been attempted by someone lacking verte-brae. She bent so far backwards that her face reappeared, smiling, between her knees. At this magnificent climax of her routine an excessively fat officer of the Control Commission, dining alone at the nearest table with his face hardly six feet from that of the contortionist, turned his eyes up toward her from his now empty plate for the first time. 'Ow,' he said loudly, 'take 'er away. I've 'ad me dinner.'

In its time the place had been a German Officers' Club, and in the down-stairs loo we were faced with a piece of equipment which had us nonplussed for a moment. Set on the wall at about waist height, with a pair of handles on the wall on either side, were round basins not unlike urinals in shape and size, flushing on demand by the press of a button: vomitoires. The fact that there were as many vomitoires as there were urinals revealed something about the habits of the German officer on his evening out, his capacity and determination to return to the fray. The thought was almost enough to give rise to their immediate and involuntary use.

Jim Quick was not in fact my immediate senior in the sense that I took no orders from him. A Lancastrian, he was a major in the Royal Artillery on the staff of HQ T-Force, attached to what had become my office as Intelligence Officer, not his. Since I was by two ranks his junior, this was a most unusual arrangement, and it worked only because he was a tolerant, experienced, relaxed and very nice man. His function was more the interpretation of policy in an ill-defined and continuously evolving situation, as it applied to an activity which was often considered suspect in the Military Government environment in which we operated. Nominally, he had nothing to do with, and no responsibility for the evacuation operation, which had become mine. His desk was positioned in a corner of my office, and when visiting officers of whatever rank entered they saluted 'the desk', as was the custom, but my desk, not his. And I returned the salute by standing. As an older and more senior officer, Jim's ability to work within an environment created by the section of young clerks and interpreters under my inexperienced command (mostly NCOs) was exceptional, and I grew to like and respect him very much. It was his habit, when in doubt, to whistle snatches of the Mendelssohn violin concerto, with which I also was very familiar. After a little informal coaching from some 78 rpm records, we managed on one quiet occasion between us to whistle our way through the whole concerto in twelve minutes without interruption. We were quietly triumphant. I considered myself lucky that he decided to sign on for an extra couple of months.

Of all my friends, other perhaps than Robin Smyth who was to join me later, Michael Corbett was the one I most wished to get into No 1 T-Force. At

Downside, he had been the outstanding schoolboy athlete as a team games player of his or perhaps any other era. For four years, the whole of his time there, he represented the school at hockey, rugby football and cricket (captaining them at the latter two) and for the English Schools as wicketkeeper. He was, as I have said, a great athlete and sportsman, but it was for his charm and humour that I valued his company, and for his tenacity, reliability and native intelligence when things became difficult, as they had sometimes done in the course of our training.

Lt. M. Howard R.B., 1 Bucks T-Force, B.A.O.R.
14th April 1946

Dear Daddy,

Thanks for another parcel of fags which arrived a few days ago: I asked Mum in my last letter to thank you, but here am I to do it in person.

I am now duly installed as I.O. and have been doing the job alone for some days now—I think with adequate competence. The new C.O. has arrived, an R.B. called Brush, with a D.S.O. he got in '40. Since then he has been doing high level A.D.C. and staff jobs. He comes from commanding the now defunct 8th R.B. Very pleasant, and I suspect, pretty shrewd. Dick and I played bridge with him and Colonel Nicol last night, always a good start. In the last 4 weeks I am up 95 points on my bridge—it pays a third of my Mess bill, which is convenient.

My job really is very interesting, and there is as much work as I am pleasantly able to do, allowing for a certain amount of entertainment. Of course quite a lot of the work is great fun, and work and play are liberally intermixed—always a good thing. I am gradually getting used to all the bumph, but difficulties still crop up, for which I can find no answer myself, and have to go running off to the former I.O. Luckily the G.2 with whom I work is a delightful person and most easy to get on with, and we can always have a good laugh about the work.

No more special news—Mummy probably keeps you up to date in that respect.
Love,
Michael

My father would have been interested to hear of our newly-arrived command-ing officer, who had joined us on Saturday 13th April. Relatively isolated from normal regimental sources as Dicky and I were, hard information about Peter Brush's history was sketchy, and he was certainly not the type of man to spill the beans except under the sort of tactful questioning that we were not yet ready to attempt. Given a little more time, we would discover other virtues in him, but we could sense at once that in Peter we had been really fortunate in our pleasant and shrewd new colonel. Both Dicky and I would enjoy playing bridge and squash with him, and the traditionally relaxed relations between colonels of the regiment and their young officers were very much a factor in setting an informal tone in our otherwise rather mongrel Mess.

The volume of work at that time was manageable, although it had not yet approached its zenith, when the strain would increase markedly. But that was how we liked it.

Lt. M. H. S. Howard R.B., H.Q. T-Force, I Corps District, B.A.O.R.
16th April 1946

Darling Mama,
[Please a decent comb if Clark has one. Also please be prepared to dig up a squash racquet.]
The photo of Anne's portrait arrived yesterday—at first I did not like it but it is growing on me, and now I think it really is quite good. Is it from the same angle from which she started to draw? I have a feeling that the angle has been changed. Anyway we are looking in different directions. Also please thank Daddy for another parcel of cigarettes, which arrived today—they are

very welcome as we don't get much of a ration, and one has to use fags to pay for laundry and other sundry items.

We have had the most marvellous weather for about a month now—we have had a succession of the most lovely days, and it looks like going on indefinitely. Unfortunately I have been very busy and had not been able to take advantage of it to the full, but I should be able to get away this weekend (Easter). I think I shall go up to the Möhne See on Friday afternoon, play squash on Saturday, listen to Bach's Passion in Dortmund cathedral on Sunday, and hope to take part in the Div. Hockey six-a-side on Monday, and return exhausted to face a huge pile of paper on Tuesday.

I am in the process of agitating to get Michael Corbett out here for a start, and will try for any others who feel like coming later. I think that the new Colonel is all in favour of filling the place with R.B. officers, and should be able to work it all right. He is a very nice fellow by the name of Brush, who was captured in France in 1940, and who has recently been given a well-deserved D.S.O. for his part in the defence of Calais. He is a charming person, a regular soldier of the best type, and a worthy successor to Nicol, also a delightful person, whose place it would be difficult for anybody to fill. Nicol, also a regular soldier is leaving the Army in June at the age of 34 with a D.S.O., to go and get married and manage an estate he has been left in Scotland.

The countryside here is really looking a treat, with all the trees just getting their leaves, and packets of blossom all over the place. There is a peculiar sort of lime which grows in this country, which has light copper-coloured leaves, and looks quite superb; anyway, whatever it is there is a long avenue of them outside the Officers' Mess. The Mess is the last building in Kamen, and we at least have an uninterrupted view out over the surrounding farmland, which is flat and uninteresting, but pleasantly green.

In case you didn't realise it I am due for U.K. leave in six weeks, so it is never too early to start theatre bookings, etc. Not that I want a frantically

busy leave, but I don't want to miss anything really good that may be on at the time. If I can bear the idea of cutting my luggage down to 65 lbs I shall ask for an escort duty by plane at the end of May and thus gain a few days in England before my leave is due to start, but I shall see how it pans out nearer the time. I want to go up to Rugby on the 6th and 7th, spend a day at Cambridge and one looking up the R.B. types, probably in London, and the rest in peace and quiet at home; who knows, I may even dig that path through into the orchard. And even a spot of weeding on the tennis lawn.
No more news for the moment I think; I am having a grand time out here.
P.S. I am on the track of the Ballets Jooss. They are not in this area at the moment.
All my love,
Michael

There was a lot of fuss about getting a copy of my sister's portrait to me. Neither 'Georgie' Lyon, the portraitist, nor the family felt that the first one had entirely caught her likeness, so this was a second attempt which they all liked better.

I seem still to have been partially dependent upon my father for my supply of cigarettes. This surprises me because, by the time I was demobilised at the end of the following year, I had accumulated an enormous unsmoked cache which I kept in the airtight tin trunk. I am sure there was a free issue of fifty cigarettes per week, which I recall as having been Senior Service, packed in a round airtight tin. But at some point we acquired the right to purchase up to two hundred more per week at an absurdly low price which I could well afford. They were of course, *inter alia,* the small change with which we paid for little local services like laundry and darning, but what was left after that would have supported a nicotine habit of, say, thirty a day. As yet we were unaware of smoking creating any health hazard, although one or two of the more determined practitioners had developed a habitual smoker's cough which tended to resonate in particular at the breakfast table, where Dicky smoked Egyptian to go with his black coffee. A motion in the suggestions book for him to be asked to switch to the less malodorous Virginian was ignored.

My plans for the Easter weekend were fairly comprehensive. We were up to date and all other offices would be empty, so we could afford some recreation. A visit to the Möhne See at that stage meant some relaxation at the club and a drive round the lake. Later, in the company of friends with a measure of competence in sailing dinghies, I might risk a spin on the lake. On the Mere at Thorpeness, where the water was a uniform three foot six inches deep, a moment of rashness was punished at worst by a walk home in water up to the waist. With only the rudiments of sailing acquired there under my belt, I was not going to risk the Möhne See which exacted penalties of a quite different order for sailing too close to its ever-shifting wind.

My musical education at that point, always informal and mostly autodidactic, had not taught me that Bach, whose austerity intimidated me a little, had more than one Passion to his credit. In the event, no one was interested in coming with me to the cathedral at Dortmund, and I was reluctant to go alone. As to the hockey, we had inherited from 1 Bucks a slot in the 49 Division six-a-side competition, and my confidence must have allowed me, sight unseen, to talk myself into the side. Nobody there can ever have seen me play; I can only conclude that they must have been short of volunteers.

My earlier prediction that Peter Brush would have merely to snap his fingers to get some of my closer friends posted in proved over-optimistic, although I had letters from them detailing how under-occupied and bored they were at Ogbourne. I got the feeling that the Regiment began to harbour a suspicion that Peter was trying to pick off the better candidates for himself, and this concentrated their mind on using them to fill vacancies arising in the two regular battalions as demobilisation of those with longer service worked its inexorable effects.

Any early doubts I might have harboured about Peter Brush's capacity to fill John Nicol's shoes were soon dispelled, and the problem would in time become rather the one of finding a successor to fill his. John Nicol, born Warner, had been the beneficiary of an inheritance involving taking the name of Nicol, and with that went the estate of Ballogie in Aberdeenshire. On leaving the service, he married and settled at Ballogie where he was to live for the next sixty-two years. His own account of his service as a soldier makes little mention of his time as CO of 1 Bucks acting in the T-Force role; for him it was not a proper occupation for a soldier. It was irksome, he felt it demeaning and furthermore he considered the policy T-Force was responsible for executing was a mistaken one. In his later years he had rather wiped it from his memory, and didn't much care to be asked to revisit it.

I had been planning all sorts of things to occupy my time on my first home leave due in June. Flaunting my prized black pips at Rugby was obligatory, and a priority was a trip to Cambridge to sound out the prospects for Class B release at Peterhouse. But the nearer the date came, the more certain I was that I wanted to do little but enjoy exploring my new home at Cat Street and its immediate surroundings, and then get back to the job which now so absorbed me. My threat to excavate St Catherine's Street, the pilgrim road which ran diagonally past our front door, was always an empty one. I could only ever have made the merest dent in it.

Lt. M. H. S. Howard R.B., H.Q. T-Force 1 Corps, B.A.O.R.
18th April 1946

Darling Mama,

I have not written for some days as I have been rather busy. I know it is not yet a week so I have no cause to scold myself. I enclose a letter to Auntie Miriam which please forward. I never can remember the address. I know the word Chatsworth comes in somewhere. I have also written to Auntie Nan for her birthday.

I have heard from Michael C., Robin, Ian, Barry Smith and John Marshall that they all want to come over here, so I have applied for the lot of them to be posted to this unit, but I don't know how the application will be received by the various departments concerned with the postings. I would love to have them out here, so I can but hope.

When your daughter returns from the Navy and gadabout, I should go to bed for 48 hours and make her wait on you. I am only afraid it may be the other way round. Just you take it as easy as you can for a bit. I'm glad the cook seems to be more or less the right sort. As long as she is willing, you can direct her much as you directed the Indians. I'm sorry to hear about Oliver for your sake—just another additional hold-up.

Life goes on more or less as usual. Yesterday Dicky and I took Colonels Nicol and Brush over to Villa Hügel and we had a good 80 minutes' squash. I was so tactless as to beat the lot. Then we had hot baths and went to the Dortmund Officers' Club for dinner to which we sat down after a gin or two, at a quarter to nine. When we rose at 10.55 we had consumed enough wine for the two colonels to be reminiscing furiously, which as they are both delightful people, was most entertaining. We were back here in Kamen by midnight after a most pleasant afternoon.

If you can arrange for Tosca[11] to be greased and overhauled so much the better. Battery topped up, tappets adjusted, oil changed in the sump, gearbox and differential.

I am longing to get home and see the house—I expect that when I come home on leave I shall ask one or two people down for a couple of days—O.K.?
With all my love,
Michael

Letters from all five of those whom I had singled out for posting to T-Force confirming that they wished to come strengthened my hand in discussing the matter with Peter Brush, and his in going to Army HQ requesting the postings. Goodness knows to which detachments we would have sent them had they all

---

11 My scarlet J-type MG.

come, and how we would have paired them off. Distances were not so great that getting together socially, for sport and otherwise, would have been any difficulty.

My sister was on the point of being demobilised from the Wrens, and she was celebrating by going round to make her farewells in her second-hand Triumph, 'Gloria'. Anne had for a while been one of a close-knit party of eight ordinary ratings at the Fleet Air Arm Station at Yeovilton, where they trained the FDOs, Fighter Direction Officers of the fleet. Most of them were, like Anne, recent university graduates on pay of sixteen shillings per week. The officers under training cycled round on tricycles like those of Walls ice-cream vendors ('Stop me and buy one'), simulating the conditions of naval air warfare. The increasing speed of aircraft eventually made this practice obsolete.

My mother must have had some slight indisposition for me to tell her to take it easy, and to give her cook instructions much as she had in Fiji seven years before—the last time she had had a cook. The only one I remember was Ragu, a very dark Madrasi who had worked for us in Navua, and at Nukua-lofa in Tonga. In 1934 my father spent ten months in Tonga as His Britannic Majesty's Agent and Consul. Having previously dined at the royal palace next door, my parents returned Queen Salote's hospitality by directing Ragu to prepare an eye-wateringly hot curry of giant clam, the Queen's favourite dish. She and my father devoured it with relish, but neither my mother nor Tungi, the Prince Consort, could get anywhere near it.

Dicky and I repeated the formula of which we had made such a mess a few days before: squash at the Villa Hügel followed by dinner at the Dort-mund Officers' Club, this time taking with us the incoming and retiring colonels, both of whom played a fair game. Peter and I played several times in the next few months. He tended to 'play his rank', trying to dominate the centre of the court without having won it, and on one occasion I drove the ball into the small of his back. 'By God, Michael, that's the last time you do that!' he exclaimed, but he allowed me more room in future. This time at least we knew the way to the Officers' Club; it wouldn't have done to drive the two colonels around for a couple of hours looking for it. The vomitoires were not needed.

Lt. M. H. S. Howard R.B., H.Q. No. 1 T-Force, B.A.O.R.
23rd April 1946

Darling Mama,

Notice the new address, it is what we have eventually decided to call ourselves. Today we have issued our first orders as such, and are working completely unaided by the Bucks battalion. Luckily there is not much to do as people are just getting over Easter, so our first testing is not to be too severe.

On Saturday I spent a more or less normal day as Jim Quick the G.2 was away and I had to be in the office on and off to sign the odd scrap of paper which presented itself. On Sunday I went to church in the morning and for a drive in the afternoon; we had tea at Neheim and went on from there through Arnsberg through the Buchwald, which is a wooded area of about 500 square miles, quite unequalled by anything I have seen in England— we just haven't the room for that sort of thing. Then we came out of the wooded part into a sort of bowl-shaped valley with not a single tree; and in the middle of the bowl there was a small steep-sided hill, with a tiny village on top. We ground up into the village in bottom gear, where there was the most lovely view. Then as it was getting dark we drove on along the north side of Möhne, up to Soest, where we had a first-class dinner and wine to gladden the heart of man, and so the odd thirty miles to bed.

Then yesterday I played hockey as part of the Battalion 6-a-side team. In the first round we won by 3–0 of which I scored all three; in the next round we won by 2–1, and I scored both; then we won 5–1, of which I scored four; then in the semi-final we came up against the final winners H.Q. 1 Corps, who beat us by 1–0. So really we did pretty well, especially as we were one of the smallest units in for the show; I may say that the fact that I scored so many goals was not entirely disconnected with the fact that the half behind me was an international who had a vague idea as to how to play the game, but you can see that I did at least pay my way. It was the best exercise that I have had for some time, and proved to me that I am fitter than I thought I was, which is some comfort. Then Dicky and I finished up a good day by bidding and making two small slams against the Colonel and the 'Q'.

The most heavenly weather continues—there have been only two dull days since I have been in Kamen, although this is a spot where one is least able to appreciate fine weather, one can merely say that it would be worse if it were raining; as a matter of fact I rather malign it—it isn't a bad spot at all, and all the cherry and plum blossom in everybody's back garden makes it look quite cheerful.

The work continues much as before with the few odd perks thrown in that brighten things up, not that most of it isn't interesting in itself, and one really comes across quite a few refreshing types in the course of one's duties. One of my evacuation officers on detachment is an ex-Guards type with an MC and an enormous moustache and a whacking great 'Oxford accent'. So far our only contact has been by phone, but we are already quite good friends and are going to meet at a cocktail party on Saturday—I must say, he sounds delightful. Today the Colonel has gone up to H.Q. Rhine Army to arrange for the posting of my buddies, viz Messrs Corbett, Murray, Smyth, Marshall, and Smith. This may amuse Papa—he will appreciate a certain lack of hesitation to use what little influence I can lay my hands on; it is quite a different thing doing it for one's self, as this is only that I gain by having the pleasure of their company if the scheme comes off. If they do get posted here they will be arriving very shortly as T-Force can't really wait for them, they are wanted at once. Most of them are at least as bored as I was at Ogbourne and would pay quids for a posting, especially as they will catch the summer out here. And although I like a lot of the fellows here, I have got much more in common with them than with any of the others here, and

speak more of the same language on all subjects—I can now but pray for
their posting to receive the official blessing of the authorities.
Must close now.
All my love,
Michael

There was a good deal of dithering over what the name of the new unit rising from the ashes of 1 Bucks was to be. First mooted had been No 1 RR&R (T) Force Unit, at which we jibbed. It would have obliged us to spend our time explaining to anybody who had not heard of us—and that was everybody—what the various Rs stood for (Reparations, Restitution and, I think, Research), and even the revelation that the T signified 'Target' would still have left them in ignorance of what we actually did. Being designated No 1 (of two) accorded us no real precedence. The reader will recall that it was 5 Kings, who became No 2 T-Force, who had been in the lead in the glory days of the race across the North German Plain to the Baltic. Perhaps now that our territory encompassed the vast majority of German industrial targets in the British Zone, it was our turn to assume the lead.

Tuesday 23rd April was the final handover date, and the issue of the first Unit Orders. 1 Bucks marched out. The entire staff of the Intelligence Section, along with their two interpreters, stayed with me. A handful of the key Orderly Room staff—a staff-sergeant and two corporals—stayed with Dicky Muir, now Adjutant to Peter Brush. Some of the 810 Company Pioneer Corps CSMs and CQMSs were made up to Regimental status, all retaining their previous badging. We had no badge of our own except the shoulder-flashes we devised: a white 'T' in a black square and another with thin parallel bars of black, green and red—traditional Green Jacket colours.

Covering the desk, I had missed my proposed day out on the Saturday but went to church on Easter Sunday. I wonder where? Perhaps there was a garrison church at I Corps Headquarters at Iserlohn, eighteen miles to the south, but I can't be sure. An afternoon drive including tea at the Officers' Club at Neheim makes it all sound very much the English Sunday afternoon in the countryside, except that there will have been no scones, no clotted cream and no strawberry jam. And no honey.

The River Ruhr near Arnsberg

Neheim was the headquarters of 49 Division, and also of the Belgian Brigade which formed part of that division. Driving out of the town, we noted with some satisfaction the high water mark visible half-way up the ground floor on the fronts of many of the buildings, a legacy of the breeching of the Möhne Dam by the legendary 'Dambusters'. We stopped to pick up a Belgian *poilu* thumbing a lift in our direction. We asked him in French where he was

going, without reaction or response. We tried English: nothing. Then German: still nothing. Then he twigged that he was being questioned. *'Vlaamse'*, he announced proudly—Flemish. Between the three of us we had not a word of Flemish, so by signs we agreed that we would continue on our road until he indicated with hand-signals that we should stop and let him off. The Belgians were detested by the local citizenry to the point of provoking hostility, which was very rare in Germany. The Belgians' reputation was for gratuitous cruelty, and perhaps this viciousness was a response to the way their own population had been treated during the German occupation. Retaliation took the form, in that heavily wooded country of the Arnsberger Wald, of stretching steel wire across the road between the trees at a height calculated to decapitate any despatch-rider on a motor-cycle. I took care never to ride my motor-bike in that area.

The tiny village on the steep hill was Hirschberg. Its situation remained as charming fifty years later, quite unspoiled. Standing on its conical hill, it looked smaller than it actually was because from the higher land around you could not see all of it at once. It was devoted to saw-milling and the working of wood.

In the hockey on the Bank Holiday Monday, we gave a good account of ourselves against several regular battalions—we who were decidedly irregulars. In our team as centre-half was a civilian employed as an interpreter by B Detachment. Having been a Belgian international before the war, he knew his way round the pitch and had recovered most of his form. I had played for Rugby School on the left wing, and was at my best over short distances—a boon in the six-a-side game. So he fed me skilful passes which enabled me to outpace the defence and score. We became better at the eleven-a-side game when some of my Rifleman friends joined us.

The ex-Guards evacuation officer whom I was so looking forward to meeting was Lieutenant F A E (Fred) Bonney at B Detachment at Heisingen near Essen. He had had 'a good war', earning an MC with the Coldstream Guards, later transferring to the East Surreys, and subsequently finding himself attached to 1 Bucks. He stayed when 1 Bucks went, possibly because his experience in the evacuation function was valuable, and possibly at his own request, for he had formed a close relationship with a German lady living in that neighbourhood. At that time, such an open relationship with a German woman, while nominally within the limits laid down by Montgomery, was tolerated in T-Force at the outlying detachment at Heisingen in a way which I believe it would not have been at headquarters in Kamen. Fred spoke fluent German, and harboured an abiding detestation of Germans in general, with presumably that one particular exception. He eventually married the lady when it became possible, and he was one of the first individuals to buy a Volkswagen out of his own pocket on a commercial basis, so that he could drive her around without infringing the regulation forbidding the carriage of German civilians in War Department transport. Actually, T-Force had a dispensation from this regulation, but only on duty. Fred's loathing of the Germans was evidenced by his referring to them all as 'Mofs', a derogatory term new to me at the time, and by his harsh treatment of any that crossed him. One dangerous driver who did so had all the air let out of his tyres as a lesson: summary justice. Mof was a word which he and others had picked up on their way through Holland; it was peculiar to the Dutch, but had no direct equivalent translation. It was intended to be abusive and was reserved by them exclusively for the Germans, the product of their hot resentment of the vile treatment they had received at German hands during the occupation. As an evacuation officer Fred's conduct was exemplary and totally professional.

Our shortage of junior officers to carry out the intelligence function in the detachments was such as to take Peter Brush on a mission up to Rhine Army Headquarters at Bad Oeynhausen to try to get a small handful of personnel of our (my) choosing, with their names and army numbers which I had fed to him, posted to us urgently. In the end, the only one we got was Robin Smyth, who was to become my Assistant Intelligence Officer. Two of the others went to the 2nd Battalion, one to the 1st, and one to Greece. Suspicious of our unorthodox and unexplained role, Army HQ were not going easily to let us have just what we wanted, even in the face of Peter's powerful pleading. But other Riflemen were to join us fairly soon. We were fortunate; they were all to prove no less acceptable as colleagues.

T-Force as a whole was described as an 'industrial and technical intelligence' unit, operating under the aegis of the British Intelligence Objectives Subcommittee. Perhaps it seems perverse to draw a distinction between those who were engaged in the intelligence function and those who were not. Our mission was to secure and deliver both to British industry and to the civil trade and industry ministries and service ministries the fruits of German technology in whatever form. This manifested itself in the physical evacuation of plant and equipment, documents and blueprints, and scientists and technicians. I suppose that any activity failing to contribute directly toward that evacuation was, to my way of thinking, ancillary, and simply a service to the intelligence function. One such service was that of providing accommodation, sustenance and transport to the thousands of investigators and assessors who came out to identify targets, and who were entrusted to our care. That function was rather that of hotelier, quartermaster and travel agent, and I have never quite been able to rid myself of the sense that it was a lower-grade activity which could perfectly well be performed by troops of inferior rank and calibre.

Within No 1 T-Force the intelligence function was the direct responsibility of the Intelligence Officer, who worked directly to the staff officers at HQ T-Force. At a time of peak activity, he had the support of another officer as his assistant, and at all times an intelligence section of eight clerks and interpreters, all NCOs except for two riflemen. The Intelligence Office was a part of the headquarters of No 1 T-Force Unit, and had control of the Evacuation Office at each of the three remote detachments, and the fourth at Kamen. Each was run by a lieutenant, or in one case a captain, who would have one or more lieutenants to assist him, and a smaller group of NCO clerks.

This was the role performed by the young officers, for the most part of my own regiment, who were to spend the remainder of their service with us until their release at some time before the end of 1947. I knew that those from the Rifle Brigade or KRRC had been selected for a commission in the first place for their leadership qualities, their capacity for independent thought and action and decision-making.

The detachment commanders were majors who, while they nominally had the ultimate responsibility for ensuring the good performance of the Evacuation Office of their detachment as well as its administration, actually played no direct part in the evacuation function.

This reflected precisely the situation at unit headquarters, where the Colonel, his second-in-command, the Adjutant and the Quartermaster played no part in the evacuation process run by the Intelligence Officer, supported as he was in the field by a small cadre of officers in their early twenties. None of the older and more senior officers showed any inclination to interest themselves in duties for which they may also have lacked the flexibility and imagination. Nevertheless the exercise of good sense saw to it that there was almost never any friction between the two sides of the house. The whole thing worked, and even a later sequence of poor colonels failed to wreck it.

Lt. M. H. S. Howard R.B., H.Q. No. 1 T-Force, B.A.O.R.

30th April 1946

Darling Mama,

I always feel rather overawed when I sit down to type on a piece of paper this size, but I think that I shall be able to plough through this one—there are quite a number of things I ought to talk about if I only remember. I shall wade through your last two letters point by point.

My squash racquet—could you please send it now. Two members of the Mess have already had theirs sent, and both arrived quite intact; I suggest that a combination of short bamboo poles and my khaki socks, which I want also, judiciously arranged, should do the trick. Also my other pair of underpants, please, and that pair of boots which I left behind to be repaired, and say an odd half dozen of Daddy's handkerchiefs if he can spare them. I saw the results of the Lingfield meeting, and wondered how many of you lost your shirts on it. You can't have gone far wrong if you backed Gordon Richards for a place each time—he was placed four times, and not at really short odds—anyway I hope you were thoroughly entertained whatever the result.

I should like to see the two dogs together—they should be rather a pretty sight. Battle should not cause much trouble, he has the most delightful manners; if you can teach your hound to take her food as prettily you won't be doing badly.

David seems to have managed his jaundice in as timely a fashion as he managed most of his leaves in the last year—it all seems to have panned out very nicely. I can see no good reason for holding back the news of their engagement much longer—it won't make any difference in the long run when they announce it.

The chances of getting leave early in June are rapidly diminishing, owing to the fact that all our leave has been held up by the change-over to T-Force. It is much more likely now to be nearer the middle of July. Anyway I shan't mention the subject again until I have something more definite about it all. As I have said, if the opportunity offers, I shall fly over to England on escort duty about the end of May. It all depends on training somebody else up to be able to take my place, as I cannot afford to let the paper pile up while I am away. Luckily Tony Chance arrived yesterday, and although he is officially attached to one of the detachments, I have got a priority on his services, and I am getting him to understudy me so that he can take over my chair at a moment's notice.

A rather amusing thing happened to me the other day; Jim Quick wrote a stiff letter to H.Q. T-Force telling them off for some mistake they had made, using therein the phrase 'It is not understood at this H.Q. by what series of typographical errors this conclusion was reached...' The letter was brought in for me to sign in due course, and I made my mark on it as requested. The next thing I know is a stinger from the G.S.O.1 at H.Q. Rhine Army wanting to know since when it has been the custom of lieutenants to address rebukes to H.Q. Luckily he is a friend of Jim's, and it was all smoothed over—but now I read most of what I sign, and anything I leave to Jim to sign if it is at all dubious.

I would at the moment be on a three-day trip to Berlin were it not for the fact that Jim is away, and we cannot both be away together, so unfortunately I had to delegate the job to one of the others; I am hoping for another chance when I have got Tony trained. In ten days from now I am swanning off to Frankfurt for 48 hours on a job, which should be quite good fun.

My list of friends whom I am trying to get out here has one or two additions, and now reads: Murray, Smyth, Smith, Corbett, Marshall, Waddell and Lascelles—but I'll slay him if he gets out here, or send him to the Russian Zone or something; there is as yet no indication as to what success the scheme is meeting with.

Brush arrived here wearing no medal ribbons, and then suddenly put up a '39–'45 Star, to which he later surreptitiously added a D.S.O. and today he blossomed forth into an O.B.E. Everyone was a little shattered by it, and no one has dared to ask him about it, but it is presumed that he got it for services while a prisoner of war.

No more news for the moment.

With all my love,

Michael

I wonder whose squash racquets we had been playing with thus far, that only now was I sending for my own. Perhaps the sports officer of 1 Bucks had accumulated a stock. A cunning arrangement of socks and bamboo canes was recommended to keep them from damage in transit through the parcel post, weight no object. Now that at last my father had persuaded the army to let him go, I was assuming that he would be sick of the sight of his khaki handkerchiefs and could spare me some.

Upon his return from France in June 1940, my father and his comrades were billeted in the horse-boxes at Newbury racecourse, and this was where he acquired Battle, a white crossbreed with a bit of Jack Russell in him, and perhaps some Scottish terrier. Perfectly mannered at all times and without vice, he was the ideal escort for my mother's standard black poodle bitch. Because 'Vulcan Rosamund' was clearly too much of a handle for everyday use, the poodle had been dubbed 'Mou-Mou' at the WVS canteen in Forest Row. My

'Battle' - Moumou's 'guard of honour'.

mother told her colleagues there that in Fijian all animals were called 'manu-manu', and only subtle variations in the inflection of the voice could convey more precisely the nature of the animal in question. Mou-Mou was as near as they could get to the Fijian original, and Mou-Mou she remained, despite the availability of the other name which was evidence of a more aristocratic lineage. She did indeed learn to take her food most delicately, she had a very soft and sensitive mouth; one day, after a hunting expedition with Battle, she came back and while not appearing to be carrying anything in her mouth, dropped in my mother's lap a baby rabbit, quite unharmed. Walking beside my mother, she would gently grasp the hem of her mistress's skirt in her mouth as they went along together. Once when the Old Surrey and Burstow hunt met in

Vulcan Rosamund - 'Moumou', keeping within safe distance of Mama's skirt.

our neighbourhood, the two dogs joined the pack, and had to be whipped out. At no time did Battle have any designs upon Mou-Mou, and would not permit any other dog even to entertain such impure thoughts. Mou-Mou's honour was quite safe.

The arrival of Tony Chance from 1RB some six weeks after I had last seen him at 54RHU at Osnabrück was a predictable consequence of their discovering that as a military man he was not built in his father's image. Quite unsoldierly, in fact, Tony was cautious and fastidious, perhaps to a fault. He never ventured abroad without a haversack slung over his shoulder containing a sweater, a bottle of water, a toilet roll, a comb, a spare handkerchief and some aspirin—and probably an identity tag stating: 'If found, please return to…' He was the only means at that time by which I might be able to excuse taking an early leave. Formally he became one of the evacuation officers at A Detachment which, like Unit Headquarters, was based in Kamen, so he became a welcome member of our Mess, the first of our eventual tally of three Old Etonians. He was quite without any feel for treating the civil population, including our own domestic staff, as if they might actually be human; for him they were there to receive orders, preferably delivered by means of a sharp bark. He had a place waiting for him at Corpus Christi College Oxford.

My having signed Jim Quick's letter of none-too-subtle if justifiable criticism of HQ T-Force could have been deemed bordering on insubordination. Fortunately for me, the matter fell into the hands of our very tolerant GSO1 David Edwardes who, through Peter Brush, gave me a mild slap on the wrist. It taught me to read, even if only cursorily, everything which came before me for signature, of which there was later to be sometimes a great deal.

We didn't ask why, when he arrived, Peter Brush's battledress was innocent of the medals which he later put up, except for the 1939/45 Star. Very shortly this was joined by the DSO, which we learned (but not from him) had been awarded for his part in the Defence of Calais at the end of May 1940, which held up two German Panzer Divisions for three days and made possible the evacuation of the Allied armies at Dunkirk. The citation was finally gazetted in September 1945, by which time all accounts of the action had at last been collated, but it was quite bare of details of any sort, even the fact of his having been taken prisoner there at the end of three notably bloody days. In fact he had fought like a lion, was thrice wounded (including being shot in the throat from behind by a French fifth-columnist), each time rising from his stretcher at the Regimental Aid Post—on the last occasion wrongly believing himself to be the most senior officer left alive, and therefore ready to assume command of the battalion in a hopeless situation.

We knew that Peter had come to us from commanding the disbanded 8th Battalion in Germany, but the period between that and the battle in Calais was a blank. His OBE (Military) had been gazetted in London on Thursday 18th April and he came down to breakfast on the 30th wearing the ribbon. We were all too well-bred to comment on it, as if assuming that it was the most natural thing in the world. Again, there was no explanatory citation, a sure sign that it was for something that the War Office would rather not talk about, and he volunteered nothing.

Later we learned that the OBE was at least in part awarded for a rather good escape attempt which got him out of Oflag V-B at Biberach and nearly into Switzerland near Schaffhausen. (His companion in this adventure was Terence Prittie, a resourceful and inveterate escaper, who got over, under or through the wire on no fewer than six occasions.) The remaining grounds for Peter's OBE were left more shadowy. By repute he had run the intelligence network in the camps, getting news and information from one camp to another, and it was said that this was done partly in concert with Dick Heard, who had been the Chaplain of the Queen Victoria Rifles at Calais, where he was awarded an MC. Heard also earned an MBE for services while a prisoner, and the rumour was that rather more than just wafers passed between this particular minister and his flock during communion. Receiving and disseminating information did much to maintain morale.[12]

Lt. M. Howard R.B., H.Q. No. 1 T-Force, B.A.O.R.
7th May 1946

Darling Mama,
Yours of 7 pm, 3/5/46 got here 11 am 5/5/46—pretty good! Also one other. Glad Anne and David are so happy, I saw the announcement and acknowledged by wire. God bless them both.

---

12 After the war Dick returned to Cambridge as Dean of Peterhouse, and we first met there face to face in 1948, both wearing a Rifle Brigade tie. I never dared ask him to verify the story of the communion wafers. In 1990, at my instigation, his widow and daughters joined us in Calais at the fiftieth anniversary celebration of the Defence.

That reminds me—I feel like the Deity on the 7th Day after Genesis, Ian and Barry are being posted here at once, and as many as six others may follow if I pull hard enough.

Lovely drive on business today via Soest, Gesecke, Brilon, Winterberg, Arnsberg and home—more lovely scenery I have never seen. I have driven 300 miles in two days and am going another 140 to lunch with 2 R.B. tomorrow. Robin, whom I dote on, is on a beastly course at Hythe. I said if he wants to get away one weekend, let you know and you could pick him up at Tun. Wells on Saturday and deposit him there Sunday evening. He is happy just to sit in a chair and prattle on, look at flowers or views, and far from needing entertainment provides that commodity for others. Anne could talk ballet or history, his specialities I think.

Something more coherent later when I am less tired. I work like a nigger but am well up in calories so don't worry.

Yours ever,

Michael

In those unenlightened days the term for working extremely hard was to work 'like a nigger' or 'like a black', and no-one thought anything of it. The 'N-word' is of course now taboo, and one would have to explain its use away, though 'black' is now used in preference to 'coloured'. For my own part, I grew up as a child with Fijians both in our employ and as welcome guests in our house, with a firm conviction born of close observation that the Fijians, and not least the Melanesians who are by definition black,[13] were in most respects superior to the white race, a prejudice I have never entirely overcome.

Despite the Navy's dissuasive attitude towards junior officers marrying, my sister Anne and her fiancé David Scott had decided not only to announce their engagement in the *Times*—which we received in the Mess—but to go

13 As opposed to the Polynesians or Micronesians – the prefix 'mela-', of course, deriving from the Greek word for 'black'.

full-steam ahead and marry in September, thus allowing my mother just four months to complete the preparations. Bearing in mind that she had only just moved into a new house, this would be something of a challenge in those days of scarcity and austerity.

My round trip that day took me about 160 miles through lovely country but unlikely terrain for industrial targets. I think it must have been something to do with securing timber supplies for crating up the machinery and equipment we were taking out of our main target area, the Ruhr basin to the west. We maintained for the purpose a depot in Kamen itself, supplying all four detachments and under the control of my section. Timber was in great demand for the repair and reconstruction of bombed houses, so the depot was kept under armed guard. Black market prices were sky high, though we would have paid the official controlled rate through the requisitioning process by which we had absolute priority. While the civil population might risk arrest and prosecution for theft, they would hesitate before risking being shot. A twenty-four-hour armed guard was found by A Detachment.

I was cock-a-hoop when we learned that the posting-in for Ian Murray (another for the hockey team) and Barry Smith had been approved. But this was the point at which Rifle Brigade regimental resistance to T-Force's perceived poaching of young officers effectively swung into action. The two never arrived, and in the event Ian went to 1RB and Barrie to 2RB. Robin Smyth was still tied up on the mines course at Hythe, a fate I had earlier escaped. Nasty things, mines. They tend to explode incontinently, and are best avoided.

Lt. M. Howard R.B., H.Q. No. 1 T-Force, B.A.O.R.
10th May 1946

Darling Mama,
I apologise for the incoherent effort of the night before last, but I hadn't written for
so long that I had to pen something before going to bed. Today my boots, racquet,
hankies, pants and socks arrived, thank you, and also a letter from Anne.

I am very busy really, enjoyably so. I usually manage to get away to do a job in the jeep, which means a pleasant day's outing, but usually necessitates working from 6–7.30 on my return. Two days ago I had lunch with 'B' Company of 2 R.B. up near Münster. I knew all the officers there, and had quite a good time. Michael Power has got a platoon on detachment about 80 minutes run from here—I am going to pop in on him one day soon. Today my journey was Kamen, Werl, Neheim, Arnsberg, Meschede, Brilon, and back—I don't know if you have a map you can follow it on, but it is the most beautiful scenery you could imagine. The road runs either along flat valleys or halfway up the hillside. From the valley to halfway up you have the odd cottage and orchard with cows grazing, and on the hilltops pine, fir, and larch. In the last four days I have driven 590 miles, so you can see that I'm not really so chairborne.

I have managed to get Ian and Barry posted. Michael and John can't be spared. I have yet to hear about Robert, Brian, Robin and Roddy.

I am very comfortable here, and in no way bored. There is a friendly atmosphere in the unit and I have a good staff; I shall be glad to stay as long as I can until the Varsity gets me released. This is the only unit in Germany which is not a liability to the taxpayer in that the consequences of the work have a considerable and direct bearing on our economic recovery. This does help one feel that one is doing a good job of work. Yesterday I had Shinwell's son into the office, a pleasant and amusing fellow, a Lt. Colonel, and rated as a V.I.P. You should have seen Dicky Muir trying to be diplomatic and talking about coal and Labour Ministers etc. Shinwell must have thought him an awful fool—but he does try so hard.

I had a statement from the Bank. I am £68 to the good and now drawing £17/17/0 as a Lieut. plus about £5 per month field allowance.

No more news.

I am in the process of 'acquiring' a camera and will send you some snaps back.

Please send envelopes any quality.
If nobody is reading that Reprint book The Outnumbered *I would be glad*
to read it again.
With all my love,
Michael

Separated for so long from her children between 1935 and 1939, when she had written to us weekly, my mother now also expected a letter per week. In fact, since I had been in Germany, my strike rate had been considerably higher. This was due in part to the need to acknowledge safe receipt of a succession of parcels and packets of various sorts, sent through a not always reliable postal service. But also, for me, almost every experience was a new one, and was occurring against a constantly changing background for which there was little precedent.

Having at that point sat in the IO's chair for just over a month, it was quite premature for me to say that I 'usually' managed to get out of the office to do a job for myself—the price being having to work at my desk for an hour or two in the evening before, and sometimes after, dinner.

An invitation to lunch with B Company 2RB was not to be passed up. The Battalion had been up at Flensburg on the Danish border, and in mid-April had moved down to the vicinity of Münster only forty miles north of Kamen, but with companies dispersed between smaller towns round about. Battalion HQ was in the Wasserchloss at Burgsteinfurt, where the sanitation was unimproved since the twelfth century. B Company and HQ Company were at Greven, twelve miles north of Münster.

Michael Power had been the prefect in charge of my dormitory at Rugby when I arrived there in the summer of 1940. It had been a worrying time for him; his father (later Admiral of the Fleet Sir Arthur Power) was captain commanding the aircraft carrier Ark Royal, always a prime target for the Luftwaffe and survivor of many near-misses. Michael himself had been with the battalion on its way up through Italy, where he had been wounded in the shoulder. Now at Coesfeld, his platoon's previous billet had briefly been eleven miles away at Dülmen, where they had for a few days occupied the only three undamaged houses that remained.[14]

I owed my invitation as a guest for lunch not to any particularly close friendship with any of the officers, but probably to their curiosity about the apparent attempt to build a Greenjacket enclave in T-Force under Peter Brush. Commanding B Company and my host at lunch was Tony Rolt. He had an MC from Calais and another for persistent audacious attempts to escape, which he regarded as an officer's duty. His now legendary scheme to depart by glider from Colditz Castle was frustrated only by the end of hostilities. Not entirely surprisingly, this daredevil had a post-war career as a racing driver, and won the Le Mans 24-hour race in 1953. He once gave me a lift in his jeep from the station at Bentheim on the Dutch border when returning from leave. It was a virtuoso performance and it frightened me to death. I cannot imagine why I had only 'quite a good time' in such agreeable company.

Roddy Bennett's was the new name added to the list of requested postings. He had been in my platoon at OCTU and later with me at Ogbourne, and he was in due course to make it into T-Force, when he would be stationed at Leichlingen with D Detachment—another plus for the hockey team since he had played at Downside.

We took some satisfaction from the knowledge that, quite apart from the duties of occupation which we fulfilled within our sphere of influence, there was a tangible benefit to be derived for the economic state of the nation from the main and unique role of T-Force: the evacuation of machinery, documents and scientists from the German military-industrial complex.

---

14 A target for the RAF and later for the USAAF because of the presence there of an oil storage depot, the town had been well-nigh obliterated to the point where there was a serious debate as to whether it should be rebuilt on the existing plan, or simply bulldozed and a new town built on a site nearer the river.

Such a program may be looked upon somewhat askance today as extracting the 'spoils of victory' and has been described as 'looting'. But this is to misunderstand the feeling of the time after six years of destruction and death had followed so soon on the four years of unimaginable bloodshed of the First World War. Germany, so the theory went, should be deprived once and for all of the means of making war, and must be made to pay for the damage done to the Allies' industrial infrastructure. So when our hours of work became really quite onerous, the knowledge of our potential contribution to economic recovery back at home brought an unfailingly generous response from the NCOs and other ranks in the Intelligence Section who otherwise might have felt entitled to complain. They never did. Perhaps at the very least, the T-Force project illustrates that, if tempted to start a war, one should be very, very sure of winning.

In 1946, Emmanuel Shinwell was Minister of Fuel and Power in Clement Attlee's Labour government, and in Germany coal was king. It was the key to the industrial recovery of the country, and to the ability of Germany to support itself and to cease to be a drain on the Exchequer. Shinwell's son Ernest was a lieutenant-colonel in the Black Watch and, while posing as just another BIOS investigator (an expert *ad hoc* in cigarette-lighters, as it happens), he had been given a brief by the minister to test morale among the miners in the German coalfields, seats of a suspected communist tendency. He had been flagged as a VIP, and after he had been to visit me in my office I gave him an invitation to dine with us in our Mess. His itinerary had been devised by the North German Coal Control. Dicky Muir was perhaps over-effusive in buttering him up; later Ernest Shinwell became an associate of the notorious Kray twins and was sentenced to three years' imprisonment for deception. His father's entry in *Who Was Who* makes no mention of his ever having had a son.

The somewhat dubious-sounding acquisition of the camera is an affair that I don't recall at all, probably conveniently because I may well have paid for it in cigarettes. However, I do remember that it was a very ordinary camera.

Film was available from the NAAFI, and developing and printing services were provided in Kamen by Fotohaus H P Thiel, who also offered enlargements on request. They had no interest in being paid in Rentenmarks, and asked for three cigarettes per roll of a dozen exposures for developing and printing, which I was glad to give them. I must have used about a roll every other week, at least in summer. It didn't feel like a black-market operation, even though it was probably illegal.

My mother subscribed to a book club, the Reprint Society, which sent members a book per month, a reprint in a uniform edition. One which particularly impressed me at the time was *The Outnumbered*, a novel by Catherine Hutter set in the Austria of the thirties. We have it on our shelves at home today.

Lt. M. Howard R.B., No. 1 T-Force Unit, B.A.O.R.
12th May 1946

Dear Mama and Papa,

Note the plural, but I am pretty hazy as to Daddy's whereabouts; and also note the address, it seems the only satisfactory one; anything with anything else on it seems to tour Germany before getting here. Thank Daddy for some more fags, which have just arrived safely, but via 8 Corps and 30 Corps.

Today I am playing squash again, this time with Brush and Dicky and the four is made up by Oliver Fiennes' brother Nat, who is a Company Cmdr in 2 R.B. and who lives about 30 miles away at Haltern. I would play Oliver if he weren't up by the Dutch frontier—he is just that little bit better than I, so that it gives me satisfaction if I manage to beat him; we used to play up at Ranby. Also Mike Power up at Coesfeld might be glad of a game from time to time as he probably gets pretty lonely being on platoon detachment.

I have now been in this country for two months and ten days. For the first ten days it snowed; since then it has rained twice, been windy twice, and for the rest we have had the most beautiful weather—going around in shirt-sleeves the whole time. It is literally a 50-1 chance against it being a bad day.

Would it be a bore for you to start sending me the Sunday Times when you have finished with it? We see it very seldom, and if you don't get much opportunity of hearing the news or news commentaries, it is the best thing I know for keeping one abreast of the news in every sphere. I like to know what is happening in the theatre and cinema.

My leave will almost certainly be in the beginning of July now. I am really rather glad, as I didn't fancy England much during the Victory celebrations. Nevertheless you can start thinking up ruses for getting me bags of petrol to blue while on leave. I would rather like to be there for the Lords match this year if I am to miss the O.R. reunion on June 6th.

Sussex look like being a bright cricketing side this year, which is good for Daddy—Hove is really no distance away, and Horsham not all that far. No more news really; the big news will be when Ian and Barry come. I should also like to have Robin, Michael and Robert, but don't look like being too successful. It was nice of Robert to send a card to Anne—I always thought he was nice as well as being funny.

[Held up through lack of envelopes. Now arrived.]

[Letter follows.]

[Write off my birthday this year—it makes it all rather a farce with me out here—we can have a party later.]

With all my love,

Michael

Writing on Sunday morning, I was looking forward to a game of squash in the afternoon, when we were to play doubles, always a hazardous enterprise in so small a court. Nat Fiennes would make up the four. He was commanding A Company 2RB, and had installed them in mid-April at Haltern, south of Münster and not far north of us. He was very much a friend of Peter Brush's from their time together in 8RB after VE day. By the time that battalion had been disbanded, Nat was the only officer surviving who had landed with them on D-Day, a statistic he must have found rather unnerving to live with. He had been Adjutant, one of whose duties was to see to the notification of next-of-kin, and many of the casualties had been young subalterns, as tended to be the pattern in the vanguard of any armoured advance.

To me, Nat was most easily identified as the elder brother of my friend Oliver Fiennes whose company was too far away for the court at the Villa Hügel to be as easily accessible for him as it was for Nat. The brothers were the surviving sons of the 20th Baron Saye and Sele, a very old creation, with their seat at Broughton Castle near Banbury. Their older brother Ivo, incidentally not a Rifleman like his brothers, had been killed in action in 1941, leaving Nat as heir to the barony which he now holds. The family name is, properly, Twisleton-Wykeham-Fiennes. Oliver and I had joined together at York and been commissioned together at Winchester in 1945, after which we were briefly together as we continued our training that autumn in Vic Turner's 9th Battalion at Ranby. There we played squash on a private court in the neighbourhood which had been put at our disposal. An athlete, Oliver was fast and nimble, and mostly he beat me.

When we were first at Ranby in the freezing winter of 1944, he managed to persuade half a dozen of us at pre-OCTU to join him on Sunday and walk two or three miles to evensong—a habit we had acquired at school—at the church of St Bartholomew at Sutton cum Lound near Barnby Moor. By contrast, I once went to Broughton with Oliver on a fine summer Sunday to fetch his (even then) vintage cabriolet Lanchester, with the Dickey seat behind, down to Winchester while we were at OCTU. We got terribly sunburned. After New College Oxford, and still with that strong Christian faith, Oliver discovered a vocation. He was ordained and went on eventually to become Dean of Lincoln.

In the Mess we got no Sunday paper, and our daily *Times* did not give as good coverage of the arts as the *Sunday Times*, with the reviews led by the great James Agate as theatre critic until his death the following year. It was a better paper in those days.

I hoped that in retirement my father would interest himself in Sussex county cricket. In those years just after the war, Sussex acquired the reputation of playing entertaining cricket, win or lose, and Hove was a fine place to watch them. He himself had played for Trinity College Dublin in 1913 before going out to Fiji, where he was a great supporter of the game which had been introduced into the colony much earlier by the Royal Navy. He had a reputation for spotting and coaching raw talent in remote districts where he served. The great ambition of Fijian cricketers was simply to be the fastest bowler and to hit the greatest number of sixes. My father sought to introduce an element of refinement into their game, but Fiji never attained at cricket the distinction they were to achieve at rugby football (which my father, with the help of a couple of others, introduced into the islands, having himself played for Trinity in 1912/13). In 1934, I sat at the feet of Queen Salote watching Fiji winning a series of three rugby Tests against Tonga.

> *Lt. M. Howard R.B., H.Q. No. 1 T-Force, B.A.O.R.*
> *21st May 1946*

Darling Mama,

My birthday will have to be more or less a write-off this year, the difficulties involved by time and space are too great to be all that festive—I shall probably be Duty Officer anyway. I think that the dinner jacket is a good idea, and we can fix all that when I come on leave.

The pressure of work is unparalleled—on Sunday morning alone I got off 12 letters before lunch! At the moment I am in the throes of evacuating some 150 tons of mining machinery from all over the shop, having evacuated 250 tons of miscellaneous stuff this last fortnight. Not to mention the fact that we are removing to the U.K. on an average 5 Germans per week.

Also there is the odd Nazi to be rounded up, and from time to time a café to be raided. And you couldn't count the number who come and weep at me daily, on the toes of both feet. Some of that is most entertaining. I never turn anybody away as it is always a chance to improve my German. Of course there are always the pathetic cases who have had a raw deal and about whom one can do nothing. A scruffy looking miner came along the other day and explained how some Yanks had commandeered his radio, could I give it back to him. When I explained that I had no control over the Yanks and thought it unlikely that he would get it back he said, 'And it was a recent purchase too.' And as he had probably been saving up for years to buy it, that almost finished me.

The German police here are pleasant fellows, but from time to time the old Gestapo habits break through: they persistently terrorise a sheep-like population by petty acts of tyranny. The other night we ran in a girl who was reputed to be outspokenly pro-Nazi, and I have never seen anything so Gestapo-like as the police chief interrogating her. All this is far too deep-rooted in the German character for my liking.

Before I forget—Gillette razor blades please, if you can get them: also a bottle of Thawpit Dabitoff—or something similar would be welcome.

Rumours prevalent here that petrol comes off the ration in England in a month: any foundation in fact?

Ian and Barry told by the Warhouse[15] that they are too young at a year older than myself. The application is going up again with a few odd comments.

Rain here for the last few days, and the crops need it too. The soil in this district is pathetically poor—too much taken out of it in the last 10 years, and their agricultural methods are centuries out of date.

I sailed on the Möhne See with Tony Chance on Sunday for 3 hours. Not enough wind to be exciting, but enough to be interesting—16-footers with a

---

15 The War Office.

jib and mainsail—quite fun. Tea at Möhne where we met Gerald Lascelles,
and dinner at Soest—a pleasant day.

Reference £1 from Uncle Ben—if Anne cares to buy a record or two with
it there is no reason why that should not be done now and you have the plea-
sure of it before I return. It will be the ultimate fate of it anyway. I must
stipulate that one item is Litolf's (or Litoff's) Concerto Symphonique, No 4
I think, played by Irene Scharrer—a short thing, just the two sides, I recall.
The remainder is at Anne's or your discretion.

Urgent plea—a decent pair of braces—mine have bust, and my shoulders
aren't broad enough for the army pattern, or something. Do you have elastic
in England yet?

With all my love,

Michael

I see that a trend was already becoming evident, in my expression of a wish
to avoid extravagant celebrations of birthdays, particularly my own, which has
remained with me to this day. Was it a manifestation of a sense of inferiority,
a wish to avoid being made a focus of attention, a recipient of congratulation
of which I did not feel worthy? I was searching for pretexts for discouraging
any attempt to make too much of it in the form of a party at home while I
was on my leave which was due shortly. Such a function could only involve
people whom I hardly knew—my real friends would all be elsewhere.

I revealed more of what we were up to in the way of evacuating machinery than
I probably should have done. And here was a first mention of Germans, scientists
or technicians removed to the UK, which my parents already knew formed a
part of the activities for which I was responsible. Their names came down from
BIOS in London to HQ T-Force, to the one of the three staff captains who was
responsible for 'personalities'. They would be passed on to me for allocation to
the evacuation office in one of the four outlying detachments, almost always
whichever was geographically best placed. The 'personality' would be delivered

to an escorting officer who might be one of my people, but most frequently was nominated and drawn by HQ T-Force from a pool of conducting officers who were not members of T-Force. Conducting officers accompanied the teams of BIOS investigators and assessors to see that they stuck to their brief and didn't get into trouble. Escorting officers would deliver the personality to the BIOS detention centre, formerly the Beltane School at Wimbledon ('Inkpot'), which had until 1941 been an expensive independent boarding school offering a progressive and unconventional education with a whiff of Druidic ritual and Celtic theology about it. While it will not have been uncomfortable, it was ringed by barbed wire, by that time more for the detainees' protection than to enforce their incarceration. The burghers of Wimbledon may not have been ready for the sight of Germans wandering the streets at liberty. Here the BIOS investigators and members of the Services' research establishments who had requested their evacuation came to see them. Whether they were 'interviewed' or 'interrogated' is a moot point, but either way they were fed questions which they were obliged to answer, and they generally came quietly. Reports of these meetings were published at the time and are still available to be seen.

Among the duties which fell to me as Intelligence Officer, perhaps a throwback to the days when the job was being done in an infantry battalion, was the responsibility for internal security in Kamen. This involved maintaining relations with the Civil Police in the town. They were across the cobbled market square from our headquarters, keeping an eye out for anything which might pose a threat to the safety and security of T-Force as the occupying power in that place. It was their job to check any activity running counter to the terms of the Control Council's Proclamations Numbers 1 and 2, the Terms of Surrender, which had become the law of the land. The police seemed to feel little or no obligation to intervene in situations where there was a likelihood of violence or injury, particularly where an incident was of a domestic nature. There would be occasions when I deemed it necessary to oblige them to act.

The role also involved hearing any grievances or complaints made against the occupying power, and seeking to suggest a means of redress if redress was possible and justified. Usually, it was not. If there had been some abuse by one of our men, then something might be done; finding the American GI who many months earlier had purloined the new radio of a poor miner was not on the cards. Some cases were sad, of course, tales of rotten luck for which there was no remedy. But people were mostly just suffering the consequences of the folly of their masters or of themselves, and getting their just desserts. If at times I found this function entertaining then it was because some of the requests we received were unrealistic to the point of being ludicrous, not because it satisfied an as yet undisclosed *Schadenfreude* on my part. However, acting as a vestigial Ombudsman, albeit with very limited powers, I felt it was important that plaintiffs should be heard. I think this did not after all take so much of my time as my letter suggests. I was to a degree protected from the frivolous by the *ad hoc* filter system consisting of my sergeant, Wigg, and Sergeant Wallace the interpreter, plus my two corporals.

From time to time, along with Sergeant Stevens the Provost Sergeant, I would accompany the civil police in a sweep of the small number of late-night cafés and bars. This might involve the detention for questioning of anyone suspected of contravening any of the terms of the proclamations governing the relations of the German population with the occupying power. And, in order to protect the health of our troops, we were required also to order the medical inspection for venereal disease of any unknown, lone female found in such places. These sweeps could cause much distress to those entirely respectable women, young and old, who had not been warned to steer clear of such places, and thus avoid exposing themselves to the risk of considerable indignity. I gained little pleasure from this aspect of our duties, but it had to be done. The good health of the soldiery is always a high priority. A running register was kept, in the possession of the Quartermaster, of women known to have contracted one or more venereal diseases, and any of our troops could refer to this list if they were in doubt about the wisdom of going with a particular woman. I had a copy in the drawer of my desk. The existence of the list did not in itself invariably act as a protective for our troops. Our first regimental sergeant-major, who came to us from one of the Pioneer companies under command 1 Bucks, was repeatedly off duty due to infection, treatment, and then reinfection, on account of his evident inability to resist the charms of a particular lady who figured prominently in the Quartermaster's register. We had to let him go. Those who were diagnosed as infected were obliged to seek treatment; prophylaxis was not always successful. However, the list did have its uses. One of our Army Catering Corps cooks, newly posted to us aged 17, came to see me to request permission to marry. I asked for the fortunate lady's name and privily checked the list. There she was, with what was vulgarly known as a 'full house', clap and pox. I asked how old the lady was. 'Thirty-six, sir.' Did she have any family? 'Yes, sir, one son.' And how old was he? 'Nineteen, sir.' I told him I would think about it and let him know. Within twenty-four hours he had been posted and physically removed to Berlin, with instructions that he should be given an 'FFI'—free from infection inspection—before being allowed anywhere near an army cookhouse. Highhanded? Or did I do him a favour?

Ian and Barry, whom I had been told had been posted to us and who were both marginally older than myself, were informed that they were too young! They were at once posted elsewhere, Ian to the 1st Battalion, Barry to the 2nd. T-Force was not being allowed to snaffle the regiment's better subalterns.

I entrusted myself to the skills of Tony Chance as a dinghy sailor for three whole hours on that Sunday. If he seemed a little apprehensive at first, I was surprised to find with what confidence he ordered me about—mainly on the jib. It was confidence that he did not always exhibit in other directions, but was born of experience and practice in similar boats in similar conditions. As I have already suggested, the Möhne See was not easy; shifts of wind were frequent, sudden and unpredictable. We met the much-maligned

Brian's cousin Gerald Lascelles at the club. The last time I had seen him was in about November 1945 when we both were at Ranby in the 9th Battalion. I did not remind him that on the last occasion I had poured both him and Geordie Leslie-Melville (younger twin of the Earl of Leven) into the back of my MG at closing time at the Chequers at Ranby, where they used to do their serious drinking, and drove them down the Straight Mile to the camp. They appeared unlikely to make it unassisted. This was the third time I had provided such a service, and I think they had rather come to count on it. The Officers' Club at Soest where we had dinner became our preferred spot for a meal out. On dark winter nights, when we were reluctant to inflict upon a civilian driver the misery of waiting for hours in the cold, the club had the advantage that the road home was straight and little frequented at night when we might have had a drink or two. On one such night, when I was driving, as I usually was ('Michael is our best drunk-driver'), we had a rear wheel puncture. We managed to jack the Volkswagen up, but could not seem to get the spare back in its place. Then we realised that Jack Griffiths was trying to put the wheel nuts back the wrong way round. We sorted that out and got them nice and tight, but when I started up and let in the clutch, nothing happened. I tried again; same result, so I got out to see what the trouble might be. We were still jacked up. Relative immunity induced in us an attitude to drinking and driving which later took some little time to get out of our systems.

One pound was the sort of sum an uncle could expect his nephew to be jolly grateful for in those days—such a handsome sum would buy quite a number of gramophone records in 1946. Untutored as I was, a Concerto Symphonique for piano and orchestra by Henri Litolff had caught my fancy. I was right, it was No 4 (out of five), Opus 102. I had heard it played by Irene Scharrer. It was just the Scherzo she recorded, the most famous disc she ever made (and the only thing for which Litolff is now remembered).

Elastic braces and sock-suspenders had disappeared from the market with the fall of Malaya in 1942, and the rubber plantations had not yet got back into production in the few months since the defeat of Japan. The British still had much to learn about producing synthetic rubber, from IG Farben's factories in the Ruhr, to which T-Force was conducting our investigators.

CHAPTER 3

A brave sergeant – A suicidal scientist – A murder – A cultured family – Some disappearing uranium

Lt. M. H. S. Howard R.B., H.Q. No. 1 T-Force, B.A.O.R.
26th May 1946

Darling Mama,

It is hard to write to the three of you under the same roof without repeating myself, but I will try. Firstly thank you for the letter and parcel (not coals to N). When I return victorious from the continent we can have a party and label it my birthday. As for festivities here, I am (a) Orderly Officer, and (b) recovering from a bad cold and sore throat, so the possibilities are few, beside the odd bottle of fizz in the evening.

Yesterday after lunch Tony Chance and I took the G.2's Mercedes over to the Möhne See, where we sailed for 90 minutes in what is known as a 'spanking breeze'—we had tea there and then returned to the Mess to entertain an R.B. colonel staying with Brush. After dinner we had a few rubbers of amusing, slightly inebriated, and not very profitable bridge (only 1500 down).

My cold I caught, I think, from four or five violent changes of weather in the last few days. My sergeant is in a similar state, and we have managed to keep working by a good deal of commiseration, aspirin, and whisky. We are now both well over the crisis. By way of a recuperative holiday I really am going down to Frankfurt this week.

I hit the headlines the other day in an indirect sort of way—please find my press cuttings enclosed. We evacuate about eight of these guys per week. Luckily my responsibility for them ends when they leave this country. I pulled all these fellows out last week from I.G. Farben at Leverkusen: a Dr Wingler should have been with them, but he tried to commit suicide and defaulted. I may say that the lieutenant mentioned was not from this unit, which accounts for his cluelessness.

Jim Quick, the G.2, is going on leave on the 15th June, returning the 29th, and he is being demobilised on the 15th July, so that I have got to get my leave in between those two dates—these seem fairly firm dates, and you can more or less bank on them.

I have with me 23 coupons which cannot be used out here, and should last me until the end of August. I shall send them to you to use in case I need anything from England or if any of you want anything. I have a dressing gown in mind, also some more white flannel shirts and pants—mine have rather had their day.

Also enclosed find cutting of some interest: it indicates more or less definitely that I shall not be up this October—the subject of a rather snappy letter to Col. R. S. Clarke M.P.

No more news for the moment.

All my love,

Michael

I was writing on Sunday 26th May, my twentieth birthday, and I was Duty Officer. Evidently I had received confirmation that both my father and my sister had managed to disengage themselves from their respective Services, and were at home. I was still unsure when I would return on leave to join them, and sleep in our new home for the first time. It was also my parents' first home in England for twenty-three years. I conceded that we might have a birthday party after all.

Quite a number of those who remained from the early days in Germany had 'acquired' German cars which had been taken on strength by the unit by

1. Cat Street House, Upper Hartfield

2. The author's parents, September 1946

3. The author's sister, Anne, by Georgie Lyon

4. Mess Dinner, farewell for Col. Brush. L/R: Ronnie Coe, Col. Nason, Cpl Weatherall (standing), Freddie Turnham, the author, Ken Wilson, Tony Chance

5. Peter Brush

6. Ronnie Coe, Col. Nason

7. Fred Bonney

8. Tony Lucas, John Bayley

9. Mess Dinner. L/R: Don Cropper, Roy Smith, Robbie Cooper, Bill Adams

10. *The Intelligence Section: L/R: Cpl Fox, L/Cpl Stern, Sgt Wallace, Rfn Holt, Rfn Barran, Sgt Wigg, the author, (front) L/Cpl Abbott, Cpl Clarkson*

11. *The author, summer 1947*

12. *Robin Smyth, summer 1947*

13. *Anne's wedding with David Scott*

14. *John Bayley*

15. *Watching an early football match against a German team: Richard Simpkin, Roddy Bennett, John Bendit, Tony Scolding*

16. The Kunsemüller's garden. The Planschbecken, right, the vegetable patch, left

17. The author, at ease in the garden

*18. Christa, Ina-Maria ('Fränzchen'), the author,
Dr Kunsemüller*

19. *Margret (smiling) and Fränzchen (frowning) in the Planschbecken*

20. *Hanns-Gerhard Kunsemüller, recuperating at a hospital near Prague, with Margret, 1944*

21. *Officers v. Other Ranks, football in fancy dress, Christmas Day 1946. L/R: Rfn Ashcroft, two unnamed, Sgt Hodgson, Dgt Defriend, Col. Nason, RSM Ambrose, Dicky Muir, Robin Smyth, Don Cropper, the author, Charlie Lambert*

22. Romanesque towers of a ruined church near Dortmund: a useful landmark – 'turn left at the church'

23. Christa

24. Margret, by the pergola

inclusion on the inventory (Army Form G1198), and thus became official. Jim Quick kindly gave us the use of his 1.4 litre Mercedes saloon—nice enough—for Tony and me to go down to Möhne See for another sail. Another car was that which Fred Bonney, Evacuation Officer at B Detachment and now a captain, had liberated as his platoon felt their way tentatively along the road north into Bremen in the first days of May 1945. Seeing a shining example of German automotive engineering in front of him, rather dawdling as if the war were miles away, Bonney whistled up his platoon sergeant in his Humber scout car who promptly overtook the prey and slewed smartly across the road to stop him. Fred's target was a splendid machine, a straight twelve-cylinder with an enormously long bonnet, the driver's seat in a cockpit at the rear. The owner asked for a written receipt and got one signed by Fred, thus: 'This Mof once had a damned fine car, now he has nothing at all.' Actually he did have something—the now abandoned 3.6 litre Mercedes which Fred had 'won' earlier; they did a swap. However, within a week Fred had lost his prize to a more senior officer, and it ended up in the hands of Brigadier Barraclough who became Deputy Regional Commissioner Land NordRhein/Westfalen. The car could be seen parked outside the offices of the Military Government in Düsseldorf, and so could Fred who would go there to gaze longingly at it. I didn't get close enough to see who built it, but there is no record of Mercedes ever having produced a straight twelve. There were said to be three of these monsters built in Germany, including one for Goering. Fred did not think to establish the identity of the 'Mof' in question; given the scarcity and prestige of the car in question, he must have been a big-wig of sorts, one who got away—at any rate for the time being.

In those days we still didn't know that a proper cold such as the one Sergeant Wigg and I had evidently passed on to each other was transmitted by a virus, and not by changes in the weather. Aspirin, whisky and commiseration could nevertheless make one feel better about having a rotten cold—as they still do. Wigg was never easily forthcoming about his past. I didn't like to press him, and what I did learn came out in little bits over a relatively long period. He was a younger son of quite a big family who lived in a sizeable house in Teignmouth. They ran a large car and at one time even had two cars, unusual for the folk in a country town in those days. The faintest Devon burr was detectable in his speech. In 1938, when he left school—which I took, from various signs, to have been the local grammar school—he was content to join the army as a private soldier. He joined the Black Watch, and by the outbreak of war he was an officer's batman, a personal servant and runner. An officer would choose for this job the man he would most like to have with him in a tight corner, and Wigg was certainly of the type. By D-Day he had become a corporal/sniper, and landed with the 3rd (Assault) Division, but before long he had been mortared and blown up, and slightly wounded. When he rejoined his unit it was as an intelligence clerk/corporal at 3rd Division HQ. He was blown up again, which did his nerves no good at all, and he was medically down-graded. On return, he was posted to 1 Bucks which had been a beach-landing group consisting of medically graded men, and they were employed in Line of Communications duties. In fighting near Nijmegen he earned a good 'Mention in Despatches' for his conduct in action. On reaching Brussels at the end of March 1945, 1 Bucks was assigned to the T-Force role, and Wigg was awarded his third stripe as sergeant chief clerk in the Intelligence Section. He was right at the heart of things from the very beginning of the operation.

Hitting the headlines over the IG Farben operation was overstating the case. I had been directed to evacuate eight scientists to the Beltane School in Wimbledon, and this task I assigned to D Detachment in Leichlingen which was only five miles away from Leverkusen. This operation, which involved a greater number of human targets than usual at one time, came to the notice of the general public because in the course of the party's journey—in England, I think—some débâcle over transport arrangements occurred due to the inexperience or stupidity of the lieutenant who was acting as escorting officer. The incident (which has proved resistant to my attempts to rediscover its precise nature) was reported in the newspaper, and I sent the cutting to my mother, quickly denying responsibility for the occurrence, and pointing out that the lieutenant in question was not one of my people.

My choice of the word 'defaulted' in relation to the eighth scientist was no careless one. The word has a particular meaning: one defaults on an obligation. The seven scientists who did present themselves[16] were evacuated during the fourth week of May 1946. They were interviewed at Wimbledon during June, July and August, and the interview reports can still be read at the Imperial War Museum at Duxford. The eighth man, Dr August Wingler, who was also supposed to join the party travelling under escort to Wimbledon, failed to do so because he had attempted suicide and was deemed unfit to travel. His reasons for avoiding the trip to England were evidently so strong that either he tried to kill himself, or presented the appearance of having done so, in order to avoid what he may have supposed would be an intolerable ordeal. Why? None of the other seven felt threatened by the impending trip, at least to the same extent.

Wingler was a chemist of some distinction who had with two others been awarded the Emil Fischer Memorial Medal of the German Chemical Society in 1928 while employed by IG Farben at Leverkusen, then known as Farbenfabriken Bayer AG. The award was made in recognition of the discovery and patenting of two dye-based pharmaceutical chemicals in 1926, firstly Acridine, and then, by combining it with arsenic, Rutenol. Both of these were put forward as cures for typhus, and fifteen years later experiments were carried out at Auschwitz by the notorious Dr Mengele, as well as one Dr Vetter of IG Farben, on inmates who first had been criminally injected with blood infected with the typhus virus. These large-scale 'experiments' were invariably fatal. When told that he was required for interview in London, Wingler, who perhaps benefited as co-owner of the patent from the use of these chemicals in this vile application, may have concluded that he could hardly escape interrogation on the question of complicity, even at one remove, in the fatal procedures at Auschwitz. For that reason he may well have

---

16 Professor Otto Bayer and Doctors H Roelig, P Stoecklin, W Becker, R Stroh, Caspar and Baechle.

had what the lawyers call *mens rea*—a guilty mind—and felt unable to face what he assumed was going to be a searching interrogation into these matters.

His suicide attempt failed, but the consequences to his health were serious enough to prevent his intended evacuation to London, and he was never sent for again. It is possible that those who had asked for him had learned all they needed to know from the others. With the co-operation of Michael Pohlenz, personnel director at Bayer at Leverkusen at the time of writing, I have obtained copies of August Wingler's service record at Leverkusen, and it is mysteriously innocent of any mention of a suicide attempt, or of hospitalisation, or—stranger still— the award to him of the Emil Fischer Memorial Medal, the highest award in his profession, and surely a feather in the cap of Bayer. Two inexplicable omissions—until, that is, we learn that when Wingler retired at the age of 70 and took his pension in 1958, he spent the next nine months working as a volunteer in Bayer's archive. Here he would have had the opportunity to wipe the record clean both of the suicide attempt, and the medal for the discovery of particular chemicals later put to such lethal use, a combination which might have laid a trail toward implication in mass murder. I see no reason to suppose that he may not have been a decent and honourable man. Fortunes of war.

I would be very sorry to lose Jim Quick on 15th July; he had been so kind to me and such good company. About this time he took me up to T-Force HQ to meet face-to-face the staff officers whom I was already getting to know well over the telephone and through our written correspondence. I worked on a day-to-day basis with three particular staff captains (GSO3s) each of whom handled one of the three portfolios: machinery and equipment, documents and blueprints, and personalities. They were Reggie Fox, Bernard Sarson, and Arthur Hammond and, though their names may not appear again within these pages, they were instrumental in all the projects mentioned here, and therefore an account of my time with T-Force would not be complete without proper introductions.

They all answered to the GSO2 who was at that time Pat Hughes, a major in the Norfolks, a big man with a curiously high-pitched voice. Hughes had been involved in the very beginnings of T-Force before it was officially embodied on 1st April 1945. Arthur Hammond (also of the Norfolks) had been best man at his wedding, and Pat's understudy and successor Denis Gilson was his brother-in-law. It was the sort of nepotism which ensured that you could get on with the people you had to work with—vital when you are working under pressure. They were all to be gone before too long, having done their stint.

Reggie had a chest full of campaign medals. His Africa Star marked the fact that he had fought there for a few days before being put in the bag by the Italians during one of the periods of retreat, and sent to a prison camp in Italy. From there he was released when Italy declared war on Germany, and he rejoined his regiment and fought with them in Italy for another three or four days before being taken by the Germans, and sent to a prisoner-of-war camp in Germany—another medal. From there he was released by the advancing British in time to put in another three days' hard slog before the surrender—medal number three. One gong for each of the three campaigns, plus the 1939/45 Star and hey presto, as Reggie himself would cheerfully point out, he had four medals for a dozen days' fighting. Maybe he exaggerated!

Reggie was replaced by a cavalryman, Major W Pilkington, whom we called simply 'Pilks'. Dropped by parachute behind what passed for the lines during the invasion of southern France from North Africa, Pilks had severely sprained his ankle on landing. He was nursed back to a complete recovery by the reputedly beautiful daughter of the farmer on whose property he had landed, and whose ministrations he did nothing to resist. In fact, there was even a suspicion that he had allowed his recuperation to continue for some time beyond strict medical necessity. At any rate, the tide of war swept past him for a while, and he caught up with it a little later. Perhaps that was why there was no place for him when his regiment reformed in Germany in the postwar period. He was a genial eccentric who did not regard himself as primarily a military man.

Bernard was a Sarson of the Sarson's Vinegar family, and was therefore known to us, perhaps predictably, as 'Vinegar'. In those days and for many years after, the hoarding signalling the location of the family vinegar factory stood by the railway just to the south of London Bridge station. Vinegar was replaced by Roger Underhill, who had come into the picture by chance as a conducting officer escorting a BIOS team. A lieutenant in the Gloucesters, he had shrewdly identified an opportunity to make himself first agreeable and then indispensable to the people at HQ T-Force. He was a bright, amusing and intelligent man, handsome and charming, always with a certain panache. When he took over the documents portfolio, he was younger than I, and a captaincy went with the job. I think he was to put up his third pip before I did, although my promotion was to be published earlier in the *London Gazette* and therefore ranked before his. We thought that at any rate one of us was briefly the youngest captain in the Army of the Rhine. Roger and I became good friends and close colleagues. After T-Force closed down he obtained a regular commission in the King's Royal Rifle Corps and achieved a majority, serving in the Regiment at one time with two company commanders who were to become Field Marshals, Sir Roland Gibbs and Lord ('Dwin') Bramall. Later Roger became the Director of the Institute of Advertising. He died, too young, in 1990.

Arthur Hammond, handsome and very fair, was succeeded in charge of the personalities portfolio by a young woman entering her middle twenties, Mrs Jean J Hughes-Gibb. She was a civilian, appointed by Brigadier W E H (Ted) Grylls, who had known her socially and rescued her from a less demanding job into which she had found her way at Army HQ, Bad Oeynhausen. She had been seeking a change of scenery and an escape from the United Kingdom in the aftermath of a failed marriage which had followed perhaps too soon upon devastating widowhood. Her first husband was Brigadier Frank Vogel whom she adored, and to whom she had been introduced by Ted Grylls. She was petite and young and pretty, and for us radiated an aura of mystery which attracted not a few who danced attendance upon her. Her male colleagues, unused to female competition at work, referred to her affectionately, if dismissively, as 'the Frippet'. During her time in Germany she met Gerald Draper, who was then a lieutenant-colonel in the Irish Guards, attached to the Judge Advocate General's Department and a member of the Nuremberg prosecuting team. Retiring later as Colonel, Draper achieved distinction as a jurist and became Professor of Law at the University of Sussex. They married in 1951.[17] Upon this third marriage, Jean decided to use her other given name, Julia, so it is as Julia Draper that, now for some twenty years widowed again, she has made her memories available to those concerned with writing the story of those days.

We used to enjoy the opportunities created by the need for the occasional meeting with these colleagues of ours over lunch at the 21 Club at Bad Oeynhausen, the best food in the Zone other than that offered at the Excelsior Hotel Ernst in Cologne.

Lt. M. Howard R.B., H.Q. No. 1 T-Force, B.A.O.R.
8th June 1946

Darling Mama,

[1. See that TOSCA is on form]

I feel that I have not written for some days, so herewith an effort to redress the balance.

My sore throat is now almost entirely cured, but I still have the odd dry tickle in the throat, so I hope to be on the top of my form when I return. I am trying to work out how to apportion my precious time. I should arrive home early on the 14th, but the night before if possible. On the 14th I shall yawn and stretch and sit in the sun, if any, and say well it's good to be back. Then on the 15th I shall go up to Lords, with as many of the family as can bear the strain of watching a Test match, and hope there to meet Robert and Robin: leave in time to do a show and if possible catch the 9.20. Could you be prepared to put up Robert for Saturday night? Sunday spent showing my part of Sussex to Robert, and generally nattering to him. Monday,

---

17 Draper was quite disabled by ankylosing spondylitis, and Jean devoted herself to his care and support during a long and happy marriage.

perhaps a round of golf and a good potter. Tuesday Lords again, to an evening concert perhaps—and stay the night in town. Wednesday morning up to Rugby—stay the night—Thursday morning, shopping in town, return by 12.30 to E[ast].G[rinstead]. At disposal of family until Friday night. Cricket at Hove or Horsham on Saturday.

That leaves Sunday and Monday spare for anything else that may crop up, before reporting at Harwich on Tuesday. I don't think I will risk flying. One is so likely to be held up for 2 or 3 days if the weather is bad, and I don't really want to emulate the young man whose press cutting I sent you. For goodness' sake don't lose this program, it looks feasible, and I have not an earthly of keeping it in my head: so put it in a drawer to remind me when I arrive. And one thing more—the 14th must start with a milk and rum, and absolute silence to follow. From the 6th to 12th I shall be without my sergeant, one of the worst things that can befall any man. As I work like 2 men already, and he like three, I shall therefore have to work like 5 to keep above water. The intervening sea journey won't refresh me much, not if it's anything like the last.

I hope you liked the photographs of my 'I' section, a pretty gaga-looking lot—nevertheless, all equipment and machinery removed from a chunk of Germany the size of Wales passes through their hands, so they can't be all that stupid.

I shall try to bring home a whisky and a couple of gin, and some liqueurs if I can. Most of the wine here isn't worth while, and the champagne we get isn't worth lugging over.

For various reasons I shall not return laden with loot. I arrived here too late for anything in the real looting line, and I am just not prepared to haggle with greasy Black Market Boche. The only thing I have done in that line is to sell enough fags to stop me drawing too much on my bank balance, which is just as well, as one lives out here at the rate of what would be at least £10 a week in England: it costs us nearer £2, and that is the sale of 25 fags. Still, I can put you in the picture when the warrior returns triumphant.

Most people back from leave say that England is hell, with everything in short supply and everybody trying to make money out of you, but most of them weren't there for as long as I and not so recently, so I know what to expect. I couldn't be more glad that bread is being put on the ration. My general attitude toward the Boche has in no way softened, but you see some things that shake you a bit.

You may have read in Thursday or Friday's paper a report, highly inaccurate, of an officer 'of a special force' shot up by Polish D.P.s—it was one of my Evacuation Officers, and it has made life even more difficult. Everybody is so blooming overworked and nervy in general that we take offence at anything—luckily most of us are due for leave any day now.

To add to our difficulties, two of the Company Commanders are up for carrying German women in W[ar].D[epartment]. vehicles, and another for misuse of petrol. Another has been removed for a combination of both offences. You have to be awfully careful, it is so easy to go wrong. Luckily the one or two individuals I know never even ask for so much as a single cigarette—though they accept if offered. There are still some good people in Germany, not many, even if the nation as a whole are a flop. More on these later and not by letter. This particular part of Germany is pretty strongly Catholic, and was not actively very Nazi, though they had their fair share of party members.

It has been raining intermittently for 10 days, a bit of a bore. Luckily it is just what the crops want. Some of the wheat round here is a good 5ft tall—all they want now is 6 weeks' sun. In this area they grow no spuds at all, apart from the odd row in the garden, and every day you see a train with people swarming all over, even on the roof, off to Münster and Osnabrück in search of potatoes. It seems plain to me that next winter in Germany is going to be harder for food than any preceding one. In this area they grow a lot of fruit, so that should help them out, but further north they are in a bad way. Very few families here get only the 1053 calories from the rations.

The 'Russian menace' is an interesting question. In the Russian Zone those who are anti-communist leave the Zone, which means that (a) there are fewer people in the Zone, (b) the remainder are better fed, and this raises Russian prestige. This district, being industrial, has a tendency toward communism, which is combated by the Catholic element. The other day I stopped a truck which was ostensibly bringing goods in from the Russian Zone, just outside the communist H.Q. for the Ruhr, and found it to contain communist propaganda pamphlets. Action was taken—when Shinwell's son came out here ostensibly to examine the production of German cigarette lighters, his real mission was to study Anglo-Russian feeling in the British Zone. He got a basin-full here.

Order for priorities of shows if possible (a) PORTRAIT IN BLACK, *(b)* THE WINSLOW BOY, *(c)* THE SACRED FLAME, *also interested in* THE GUINEA PIG *and* THE KINGMAKER. *Films,* SPELLBOUND, THE YEARS BETWEEN, JOUR SE LEVE, MILDRED PIERCE. *Consult the others for opinions on these.*

No more news for the moment.

All my love,

Michael

I seemed to think that most important for my enjoyment of my leave was that every nook and cranny of my time should be both planned and filled once I had had a day's recuperation from a week's work without my Sergeant Wigg. Wigg was as remarkable for the hours he put in as for his mastery of the procedures and insistence upon the quality of his section's performance. As a consequence of the damage to his nerves in Normandy, he was never so happy as when he was fully and constantly occupied, and the nature of his duties saw to this. He had the extraordinary capacity, without any apparent special effort, to call to mind instantly the names and reference numbers running into some thousands, of machines and pieces of equipment, and document serials, and the factory names and dates associated with them. In periods later when our work might temporarily have slackened off briefly, he was no less reliable, but he became moody—without ever losing his delightful sense of humour. Infrequently, he would release tension by getting blind drunk, lapsing more and more extravagantly into his amusing and inventive dog-German, which he dreamed up with his girlfriend Margarete. He was the sort of person to whom things always happened. I think this was due to his always sympathetic appearance and demeanour. Before I knew him, at the end of 1945 he was approached out of the blue by a strange, distracted German woman who told him that her husband had just been taken by a horde of enraged Russian DPs—Displaced Persons—into the woods above Menden, ostensibly to be lynched. Wigg told the Colonel, who replied, 'Wigg, you speak German, why don't you go along and see what you can do?' Unarmed, he got on a motor-bike, and reached the forest clearing just as the DPs were throwing a rope over a stout branch. Heaven knows how he did it, but he reappeared shortly thereafter with the intended victim on the pillion. His nerves may have been a bit vulnerable, but there was nothing wrong with his nerve.

It became clear that the contretemps involving the unfortunate lieutenant escorting the seven IG Farben scientists, on which I had earlier sent home a newspaper cutting, had something to do with their travel and perhaps lodging arrangements, due to the weather and the consequent disruption of flights. By implication they must have been flying rather than crossing by ferry, which was sometimes the case.

The photograph I sent home of the Intelligence Section had been ordered by Jim Quick. There were two, one which was taken by him of all the rest of us, and one taken by Corporal Fox of the rest including Jim—who wanted it as a memento of times he had really enjoyed attached to 1 Bucks and latterly to ourselves under the name of No 1 T-Force, at Kamen.

After all these years, I am really quite shocked to discover that I must myself have sold cigarettes for Rentenmarks to pay for some of my personal expenses, Mess bills, and so forth. While trading cigarettes was acceptable in return for services performed by German civilians who didn't want and couldn't use Rentenmarks, paying for my consumption of Steinhäger or my losses at bridge with cash obtained by selling cigarettes to civilians was another matter. (Though pride prompts me to point out that my bridge losses were few: nett I won money.) I have no recollection of so doing, and am quite sure that I myself had no direct dealings with any German involved in such a trade, though that hardly excuses it. Most likely one of my NCOs, even perhaps the Mess corporal, did it for himself and for a number of us, and I think it was a practice which was taken for granted and condoned. Nevertheless, in retrospect my pride and conscience are wounded, since I subsequently adopted a rather censorious attitude toward it. This was all to come to an end anyway when BAFSVs (British Armed Forces Special Vouchers, or 'Baffs') were introduced as the currency for the transactions of the Armed Forces on 1st August 1946.

Readers today may be disconcerted by an apparently casual attitude to 'loot'. My only looted possession was a large and very good Telefunken radio which I actually inherited from one of my friends in 1 Bucks when they left. I kept it by my bed, and was able to capture a whole range of European transmitters, many of whom played classical music at night. My camera, which was a fairly ordinary German one, I obtained legitimately from the NAAFI. Anyway, acquiring loot was only really possible during the period of 'hot pursuit' and immediately after, but not when law and order had been reintroduced, by which time it would have been recognised as theft.

DPs were for all of us an occupational hazard, part of the landscape in the Germany of the immediate post-war period. As the Allies penetrated into Germany they discovered 5.79 million people, natives of other countries, living there mostly under conditions of forced labour. The largest single national group was the Russians at just over two million. Over two million also, as a group, were the Belgians, Dutch and French, of which the latter formed 1.5 million. Work under tolerable conditions had become an acceptable option for which the French might volunteer. The next largest was the three-quarters of a million Poles. After the end of hostilities several national repatriation schemes swung into action, and the numbers of Belgians, Dutch and French quickly dwindled almost to nothing, as did the number of Russians, who would be very far from regarded as returning heroes. Those who had been captured in the fighting would be seen as cowards, collaborators and traitors, and all would be suspected of having been contaminated by undesirable influences. Many would be eliminated on return. By the end of 1946 the total number was down to 295,000, of which eighty-nine percent were Poles; the DP problem had effectively become a Polish DP problem. Most of these were regarded as 'unrepatriable'. The homes from which they came now lay mostly in what had become Russian territory, and all of what remained was to be subjugated to a Stalinist regime for decades. For some, suicide was preferable to repatriation—the easier way out. The Polish DPs were herded into what were effectively concentration camps, for they could not be allowed to roam free. Their situation was hopeless, there was no visible end to their misery, their rations were short, their freedom curtailed. Many would suffer from 'wire fever', and there were breakouts from time to time in the course of which, driven beyond endurance, a complete lack of discipline or self-control led to criminal violence, robbery, slaughter of animals, arson, rape and murder. Eventually a number of countries, including Germany, established resettlement programmes under quotas for the Poles, and the problem dwindled to nothing, but in 1946 and 1947 it posed a rumbling threat to the public order, with eruptions from whose consequences we were not exempt.

The 'officer of a special force' reported in the British press of 6/7th June as having been shot by Polish DPs was Captain Max Patterson, 26, of the Royal West Kents, who had been attached to 1 Bucks but stayed with us in April, and was my evacuation officer at D Detachment at Leichlingen. The murder, for such it was, took place during the night of 28th May when he was taking his German girlfriend home in one of the unit's cars (which, of course, he should not have been). They were flagged down by an obviously distressed woman who told him that drunken Polish DPs were ransacking the farm where she lived, shooting the pigs, and raping and terrorising the family and others living there. Max and the girl set off in the car down the track leading to the farm buildings. Suddenly shots rang out, and Max was dead. With great presence of mind in a chillingly frightening situation, the young lady at once turned off the engine and headlights, and lay doggo. Nobody came near, so after a while she managed to ease Max's body into the passenger seat so that she could get into the driving seat. She started the engine, quickly turned the car, and drove off back to the detachment at Leichlingen. They turned out a platoon which went after the Poles, and the Poles ran for it. One of them was shot by Rifleman Bland, firing his rifle from the hip in the dark. The rest escaped, but were later identified by being missing from their camp. They had made their way over to the eastern border of the British Zone where they were caught and arrested, tried, and condemned to death by firing squad. The sentence was carried out by a squad found by a battalion of the Welch Regiment which was stationed in those parts.[18]

The brave Max was buried in the Cologne Southern Cemetery, and there his body remains. I hardly knew him personally, but his loss added to our shortage of officers in the intelligence function of the unit. Tidying up this affair was an administrative matter which did not concern me, though I would myself run into the dangers endemic in the situation of the Polish DPs. Max should not, of course, have been carrying a German civilian in WD transport. Two of our company commanders, at C and D Detachments, were charged with that same offence, and concomitantly and almost inevitably with misuse of petrol. I think they must have got away with a reprimand—anything worse than that would surely have caused the sort of disruption upon which I would have remarked in my letters home. Dealing with such a matter would have fallen to Peter Brush, and he was not looking for any publicity. Discipline in a widely dispersed unit, among officers from a range of corps and regiments,

---

18 Subsequently, when the battalion was disbanded, several of the senior NCOs including RSM Richards who had been involved in the firing squad, were by chance posted to No 1 T-Force and joined us at Kamen.

was always going to be difficult. It would have to be largely self-imposed in a situation where temptation needed no searching out.

In wartime a platoon commander's duties included the censorship of his men's letters home, and his own were liable to be censored too, but by now this was no longer the case. However, I was uncertain at that point whether our letters home, which went by Army Field Post Office, might ever be subject to covert random censorship. I must also have been uncertain as to what, in the context of fraternisation, was deemed appropriate behaviour for an officer—for the men, I knew what was tolerated—and whether there was intended to be any distinction. To put the question would only focus attention on oneself. I hadn't thought it through, and more likely I was not yet ready to put anything on this delicate subject in black and white. I had anyway the immediate prospect of airing the matter with anxious parents face-to-face.

The trains which we took from the Hook of Holland when going and returning from leave passed on a line running within three hundred yards of the Mess at Kamen, and ran on up through Hamm, some to HQ Rhine Army at Bad Oeynhausen, and some to Münster and Osnabrück. The line was not just for Army trains; there were also a number for the civilian population. The area round Münster, the Münsterland, was where potatoes and other root crops were grown. From the Mess and the houses nearby where we slept we could see the trains as they came by, so crowded that they were crawling with humanity, on the roof and hanging on to the sides by their fingernails. These 'passengers' were desperate to get up to the Münsterland to scrounge something edible to take back to their families in Essen and Bochum and other towns of the Ruhr where nothing grew. The central Ruhr was one of the areas where, due to the breakdown of distribution channels, the minimum ration for the civil population was not being met in full. Driving through Essen on Route 1, I saw people staggering in the street whom at first I thought drunk. They were quite simply starving. One day, contemplating the view of the railway from my room, I saw a man fall off the train; he was conveniently far away, there was nothing I could do. Ten minutes later there was a ring on the door-bell. I went down and opened the door, and there he was—very tall, thin, and hollow-cheeked. He could not speak, but grunted and pointed to his open mouth. I led him to the kitchen in the Mess, and told them to give him a plate of hot food, then direct him back to the station at Kamen where he could cling to a train going in either direction, toward Essen or the Münsterland.

My mother, who was a better correspondent than myself, had identified for herself the 'Red menace'. We were well aware that part of our function was that of 'interdiction', that is to say denying the Russians targets that we would either want for ourselves, or merely not want them to have. The anti-commu-nist Catholic influence in the Rhineland, which encompassed to a degree the Ruhr, was countered by the tendency among the industrial workers at the low-est level, and in particular the miners, towards communist sympathies. The balance between these two influences was one which the British government was anxious to get the measure of. At the same time, the situation, as far as we knew at that point, was still fluid. As an occupying force, we could not afford to give any impression of weakness, hence my reaction to one particular visitor of a rather distinguished appearance. I spotted him coming across the square one day. He caught my eye because he seemed to be striding with a purpose rather than just ambling as so many others, lacking or seeking to conserve energy, appeared to be. For want of a better option, the guard on the door brought the man in to me.

'What can I do for you?' I asked.

'I have come to volunteer my services, Sir,' he replied promptly.

'For what?'

'For the Air Force.'

He had been a pilot trained on the Messerschmitt 262, the most advanced and most successful of the Luftwaffe's jet aircraft. I had no remedy but to tell him that there was absolutely no possibility of that.

'But you are going to need me against the Russians,' he reasoned.

Tacitly, I too had come to the conclusion that the Russians were now our main threat, but it was something that we could not yet openly acknowledge. Nor could I ask him to leave his name and address; to have done so would have implied an admission that we might indeed be glad of him after all.

'*Sei nicht so frech,*' I said. ('Don't be so impudent.') I ordered the guard to show the man out.

But the ambivalent nature of our relationship with our one-time allies was impossible to hide from the occupied population. During the first round of local elections later that autumn, there were incidents involving Russians appearing in uniform at the polling stations in Essen and elsewhere in the Ruhr, attempting to intimidate voters and influence their voting intentions. The Military Government let it be known that they deplored such tactics, and we were asked to make it difficult for the Russians to get near the polling stations during the second round of voting which was due to take place the following Sunday. In our care at that time was a Russian team of about two dozen, housed by B Detachment at Heisingen while they were overseeing the dismantling of the Krupp steelworks at Borbeck. We were not in a position to give them orders and we knew that a polite request would be politely ignored. What we needed was a *deus ex machina,* and the machine in question would have to be the transport which moved them round. The day before the election was a Saturday, a suitable day for recreation and jollification, and so we proposed a party—an invitation no Russian had ever been known to refuse. The plan was executed to perfection. Fairly late on Saturday night, by which time neither Tony Lucas nor I was entirely sober, we crept out of the party accompanied by Tony's Airedale 'Alastair' and approached the Russians' cars which were within the detachment compound, and thus not under immediate guard. The filler caps being at a convenient height, we relieved ourselves into the petrol tanks and, just in case this might not be enough to do the trick, we also introduced shredded orange segments into the tanks too. Alastair, who had perhaps hitherto marvelled at the human ability to resist the urge to pee on any available target, found our sudden conversion most intriguing—especially with the embellishment of the orange segments. The puzzled Russians were obliged to spend most of the following day cleaning out not only their petrol tanks but also the fuel lines leading to the carburettors, and the carburettors too. Apparently they were far too busy to loiter about menacingly at polling stations.

In these somewhat unpredictable times, Tony had acquired Alastair, in part, as a guard dog. He was a dog of high intelligence whom Tony quickly trained to harbour a deep distrust of all Germans, and infallibly to identify them as such. If, perchance, Alastair took it upon himself to harry a German, Tony would feign displeasure, all the while calling out in English, 'Good dog, Alastair! Well done, Alastair!' The locals thought Alastair an 'untier'—a monster. With Brits, he was fine. Did Germans smell different to him too?

I expected my family, especially my sister whose principal passions were the ballet and the opera, to remain *au courant* with the London theatre. I was able to get tickets for us to see *The Winslow Boy*, Terence Rattigan's dramatic recreation of the true-life Archer-Shee case involving a boy at Osborne Naval College wrongly accused of stealing a five-shilling postal order. Dramatic it was, with a good court scene, and it has weathered well, having been produced again in London to considerable acclaim fifty-three years later. It was soon made into a film, which I discovered in August 1949 showing in the Dutch port of Vlissingen (Flushing) under the title of *'Op dat Recht geschiedt'*—'Whether the Right Thing Happened'—a modest oversimplification of the issue, and hardly crowd-pulling.

Lt. M. Howard R.B., H.Q. No. 1 T-Force, B.A.O.R.

10th June 1946

Darling Mama,

The fact is that after (a) a party on Tuesday night (b) Wednesday night in the train, (c) Thursday night on the boat, I shall be in no fit condition for anything but bed on Friday night, so I think that it would be better to write off the idea of the 14th in town.

I have now got a rendezvous at Lords on the 22nd with our Q.M., one of the corporals, maybe Sgt. Wigg, Robert Waddell, and maybe Dicky Muir if he can fly over. There should be some brisk trade at the tavern.

I have used the golf clubs on several occasions since being at Winchester. They must be in the club somewhere.

As leave approaches I get an even greater revulsion for bright lights and loud noises. London seems less and less attractive. One day's shopping, the odd day's cricket and show will suffice I think.

I intend to arrive in London at 9.30 on Friday morning, do one or two small shopping items, visit the bank and catch the first train down. I'll ring you from Victoria if I have time.

All my love,

Michael

Given how busy we purported to be, and that Jim Quick was due for demobilisation on the 15th (in fact he held the fort for a little longer), any idea that Sergeant Wigg and one of my corporals and I could possibly all have made a rendezvous in England, at Lords, on Saturday 22nd June, was fantasy. In the end I met up with the QM and Robert Waddell who, contrary to the hope expressed in my letter of 30th April, was still stationed at Ogbourne. It was England's first postwar cricket test match, and was against India. The opposition was captained by the Nawab of Pataudi (senior) who had earlier played for England as well as Oxford and Worcestershire in the decade before the war. On that first day of the test there was uninterrupted sunshine, and Alec Bedser took seven Indian wickets.

The QM was Captain Quartermaster John G (Jack) Griffiths of the Royal Welch Fusiliers, and he had been with us since 1 Bucks had marched out in April. A regular soldier pre-war, he had been a company quartermaster-sergeant, commissioned during the war, and had seen his share of action in Italy. Well over six feet, he had played good first-class rugby football at centre three-quarter in his day. That day was probably now past, something of which he convinced himself after accepting an invitation to play again while he was with us; he was run to a standstill. He played a decent hand of bridge though, and was entirely comfortable in a Mess with younger officers from other, perhaps 'smarter' regiments.

Jack was a very good quartermaster, knew all the tricks of the trade and did not hesitate to deploy them to ensure that it would be easier for us to do our jobs. Always concerned that the younger officers should enjoy a full sex life, if we had been out late at night he would invariably meet us at the breakfast table with the somewhat less-than-subtle: 'Did you have her, boy?' Keeper of the aforementioned list of ladies of the town, it was to his office that the men repaired, either when in need of prophylactic measures or when those measures had failed. It was said that he favoured a potent remedy involving a pint of hot gin and parsley, a known diuretic. His relationship with his secretary Frau Rademacher, a war widow, was manifestly less than equivocal. Later he married Dawn, a provost sergeant in the ATS, who kept a firm eye on him and marvellously enhanced his prospects of enjoying a ripe old age. He was still with us when I had my 'demob' party, and in August 1949 I went to see him and Dawn at Minden when I visited the rump of T-Force who had been given the task of setting a valuation on our evacuation operations.

Lt. M. Howard R.B., as from H.Q. No. 1 T-Force, B.A.O.R.
26th June 1946
(actually at The Hook)

Darling Mama,

Nothing much to relate, but nothing to do but write. I arrived at Victoria in good time and left my luggage at the Grosvenor, and toddled onto a bus going down Piccadilly.

From there I posted you the petrol coupons, and got through to Ian Murray on the phone. For four days he has been waiting to come over and should be in Germany any day now, and should be in T-Force soon after: also Barry Smith.

We fed at Harwich, and embarked about 6.00 and sailed at about 8.00. It became roughish quite soon, and after playing poker dice with some congenial members of the Household Cavalry, retired wobbling to bed at midnight. When I awoke we were alongside here, and the horizon restored to normal.

Breakfast at 8.00, and a good shave in hot water to follow—and now hang around until about ten I suspect, waiting for our train. I am tickled by the prospect of stopping the train outside the Mess door!

See what the Socialist Government has done for us. I am not allowed to change a £5 note into Marks, in spite of it being signed by the Chief Cashier of the Bank of England: instead I am given a dirty piece of paper by way of receipt, signed by a Lieut. in the Pay Corps. Once you could buy a train ticket from Kirkutsk to Budapest with a £5 note!

No more news.

All my love,

Michael

The Grosvenor where I left my left my luggage was not a hotel I would have used for any other purpose. It was the station hotel at Victoria where I had arrived from Forest Row, and therefore not to be confused with the

Grosvenor House in Park Lane, a hotel in a quite different category. Rather, the Grosvenor was one of a handful of establishments which included the Strand Palace and Regent Palace, hotels known during the war as 'temporary quarters for temporary officers with temporary wives'. While the Regent Palace closed its doors in 2006, the other two still survive, and doubtless these days enjoy spotless reputations.

At last it seemed that my efforts to get Ian Murray and Barry Smith to join us were going to bear fruit. Like everyone else, they would have to pass through 54 Reinforcement Holding Unit at Osnabrück, and the danger was that they might be misdirected from there. And indeed they were, Ian to 1RB and Barry to 2RB. The general assumption by the Board at 54RHU was that any young rifleman coming before them ought—and would want—to go to a battalion of their own regiment. Four months earlier they had been truly shocked when I had the audacity specifically to request posting to an irregular unit. 'What on earth do you *mean*?' they had asked, incredulous.

The ships used as troop ferries had no facilities for serving a main meal to a large number during the crossing, so our evening meal was served at the transit camp at Harwich at a most unfashionable hour, leaving a distressing gap until breakfast. If to pass the time one was obliged to play a common game of chance like poker dice ('pokey die'), it was I suppose preferable to do so with members of the Household Cavalry, in the absence of anyone from one's own regiment. Whether retiring unsteadily to bed at midnight was due to one too many nightcaps, or merely to the movement of the boat, I do not recall.

The train from the Hook, known with misplaced optimism as the 'Rhine Army Express', actually took a circuitous route. If you had not arranged for a unit vehicle to pick you up at Bentheim or Rheine near the Dutch border, the train would bring you through the Ruhr, rattle through the station at Kamen without stopping, and thence right past our Mess and on to Hamm and Rhine Army HQ. However, it had been discovered that, if you pulled the communication cord while passing through Kamen station, the train would helpfully grind to a halt at a point about three hundred yards from the Mess. We also discovered that it was possible to negotiate beforehand with the engine-driver by advising him that if he did not pull up at that point of his own accord, you would pull the cord anyway and oblige him so to do. If at the same time you offered him a couple of the little Dutch cigars, available singly at the Hook, he would take them, honour would be satisfied, and he would do as requested. The short three-hundred-yard trek across the fields carrying my suitcase saved me an hour or so on more than one occasion.

On this trip I must have been without Rentenmarks in my wallet to take care of immediate needs *en route*, hence my unsuccessful attempt to change a five-pound note (one of those lovely crinkly white ones with the legend written and signed in black). I cannot now imagine what I might have received in exchange that could have been negotiable. It was surely fanciful to suppose that at any time in the past the booking office clerk at the railway station at 'Kirkutsk' (I must have meant Irkutsk, lying a little north of the Mongolian border) would have been able to verify the signature of the Chief Cashier of the Bank of England to his satisfaction, to the point of issuing a ticket for anywhere at all, never mind Budapest. A gold sovereign might have done the trick. However, as is the usual custom, after two years in power the Labour government had become whipping-boy enough for me to blame it for my not being allowed to buy the Rentenmarks I needed. The introduction of 'Baffs' was still a few weeks off.

Lt. M. Howard R.B., H.Q. No. 1 T-Force, B.A.O.R.
30th June 1946

Darling Mama,

Writing this sunbathing in the garden, so anything from a squashed ant to a clod of earth may appear on the paper. Summer has really come again out here—it is heavenly.

I took over just where I left off—apart from the fact that I returned like a giant refreshed to run the course, I might never have been away. All my files only took about 12 hours to straighten up.

T-Force played cricket yesterday against the North German Coal Control— I dropped two catches, but we got them out for 71. I went in first, and was still batting when we passed their total, with two wickets fallen, for a pretty breezy 48. Dicky Muir scored the other 24 required to beat them—quite an R.B. affair. A good party at the Coal Control after.

Really no other news.

All my love,

Michael

My billet at the doctor's house had an open southern aspect on the garden side, and I would lie out in the sun on a li-lo on the terrace. My fair skin obliged me to be careful not to over-indulge, and anyway I would not have time for it during the heat of the day, except perhaps on a Sunday. So we kept the pleasures of the garden for the evening. In the garden there was the *Planschbecken*, a plunge pool, about five metres square and a metre deep, with clematis and roses growing on to a pergola. It was not suitable for swimming, but a pleasant place to cool off, and after a warm June day during a run of fine weather the sun brought the water up to a tolerable temperature. It provided a focus for social intercourse.

The fact that I had been able to slip so easily back into the office routine was thanks to the conscientiousness of my section, led of course by Bob Wigg. (Except in formal situations, I called him by his first name.) Having caught up during Thursday and Friday, I permitted myself the luxury of a day off to play cricket on the Saturday. Our opponents, the North German Coal Control had created a ground between the Villa Hügel and the lake, the Baldeney See, through which the River Ruhr flowed westward toward the Rhine. The horseshoe-shaped ground was almost encircled by a narrow and little-frequented private road with large horse-chestnut trees along the perimeter. With access to pretty well unlimited means, and employing Krupp's gardeners, the Coal Control had lavished a good deal of care upon the pitch, and it was in remarkably good condition. Our team was captained by Dicky Muir who, learning on enquiry that I had captained my house at Rugby—hardly a qualification at all—decided that I must play. A handful of others remained from the 1 Bucks team of the previous summer. As Adjutant, Dicky exuded the air of authority required of a captain, and put himself on to bowl at once. He justified his self-confidence by bowling terribly fast and taking a number of wickets. Determined to observe what he believed to be etiquette in these matters, Dicky felt that as Intelligence Officer I should open the batting. My lack of opener's technique was compensated for by a good eye and a strong wrist. The Coal Control bowling almost at once depended heavily upon Parkinson, who had played for Lancashire before the war, bowling left-handed 'Chinamen' out of the back of his hand. I knew nothing of his reputation until later, and in the course of a short innings persisted in hitting him four or five times into the chestnut trees. By the time that we had gone in to bat, a long religious procession composed entirely of women clad in black was making its way along the road circling the ground, in the shade of those same trees, carrying banners and chanting something very like a dirge as they processed, and presumably celebrating the Feast of Saints Peter and Paul (29th June). I was determined not to let them distract me from the job in hand, and these ladies were equally determined not to let me distract them from their devotional ritual. They were nevertheless keeping an eye on the farouche proceedings taking place in the middle, and when I hit the ball into the trees above them, from where it inevitably fell down onto their heads, their chanting was punctuated by cries of distress and indignation. Never had their veneration of Saint Peter and Saint Paul been so rudely disturbed. Thankfully, the situation was brought to a reasonably speedy conclusion by our reaching the score of 72 for 2.

On these occasions a party was the conventional end to the activities, and the NGCC hospitality was notorious. Both innings were short, and so the champagne was out by around tea-time. I played one other game for T-Force, against No 2 T-Force, again at the Villa Hügel ground. I had forgotten about it until reminded fifty years later by a member of No 2 T-Force Old Comrades Association, armed with a score-card. We had lost. I never wrote home about it.

Lt. M. H. S. Howard R.B., H.Q. No. 1 T-Force, B.A.O.R.
9th July 1946

Darling Mama,

At a conference at Rhine Army a few days ago the following facts were revealed. That in our equivalent unit in the other Corps District they handle roughly a third of the amount of equipment. Also that in the other T-Force my job is done by a Staff Captain and two ordinary Captains—it made me feel faintly aggrieved, I must confess. I wouldn't mind drawing pay for three Captains! But this story has I hope a happy ending—true virtue is to be rewarded: before lunch on Saturday the Colonel came in and said, 'Congratulations on your promotion.' The recommendation has of course to be submitted to the Brigadier for his O.K., and of course I have to wait for it to be published in unit orders before I can blossom forth into three pips. I think I shall be the first of my vintage to achieve a Captaincy. I can't help thinking that the element of luck has entered into it when I think of all my former platoon commanders who are still lieutenants—such as Mike Power, John Vint, Alex Bateson and the rest. It really makes no difference to the job, but I do get an extra 3/6 per day out of it, and it may enlarge my gratuity. Don't address me as such until I let you know that it has been published in orders.

We have had the most lovely weather recently. I have only played cricket the once, but there have been the most lovely warm days when it was much too hot to work, and we just lay about and slept in the sun. One of the Mess gardens has been most beautifully kept and you can lie there and forget the rest of Germany. The family who used to live in the house have kept it up to scratch: it is the doctor's house—he is a nice fellow and interesting to talk to. His wife is a doctor, his son age 21 was an Officer Cadet at the end of the war, and is also going to be a doctor: his elder daughter, aged 23, is married to a doctor who is a prisoner of war in Karkov. She has a 10 month old infant, but she is going to be a doctor too. The younger daughter aged 19 also would like to be a doctor, she doesn't think she will ever qualify as she is not good enough at the subjects that matter. I quite often meet them in the garden and natter to them, and I have been asked round to feed with them: that I had to refuse. The younger one, Margret is good looking in a rather Wendy Hiller sort of way, and intelligent and entertaining—she makes a bit of a change to the ordinary run of conversation in the Mess, and as a product of the Nazi régime she makes quite an interesting study subject—not that my interest is entirely academic. But soft, or I shall be misunderstood. They are the sort of people I would have liked to know in happier times, and I have been so rash as to say that if ever any of the three children find themselves in England, I would ask them to stay. So prepare for a visitor in 1950. The son is Hans-Gerhard, and the elder sister Christa. They seem to have occupied quite a slice of my letter, but as you will appreciate, such a 'hardworking individual' only gets chances to make contact with the Boche out of school, and they are the handiest and pleasantest contact that I can find.

My visit in September should be easy enough. I am arranging to escort some documents over on the 11th, and should arrive in England late on the 12th. I will have Brush's permission to take a 72-hour pass starting on the morning of the 13th, and leave England by plane on the 16th, and return to my unit that night. Only 5 days away, so nobody will mind even if they find out…

No more news at the moment. (Dicky said that it would take about a week for my promotion to come through from Rhine Army—so I must be patient.)
All my love,
Michael

The conference at 'Rhine Army' was held at HQ T-Force at Bad Oeynhausen, which also housed the headquarters of the British Army of the Rhine. It was attended for our part by the CO, Lieutenant-Colonel Peter Brush, and what he discovered there about the organisation of our opposite numbers, No 2 T-Force in XXX Corps District in the eastern half of the British Zone, deeply offended him. The intelligence work which in our set-up was being run by a junior lieutenant (myself) was being handled in theirs by three captains. Furthermore, I think that by then Roger Underhill at HQ T-Force, younger than myself, had just put up his third pip, and Peter was quite determined to redress the balance. It is also just possible that he thought I was worth it. The remedy lay in his hands. He came into my office to congratulate me, perhaps a little prematurely because there were one or two formalities to be observed, such as the approval of the Army Commander and publication in Unit Orders.

I had not had the courage to talk to my parents while on leave about the subject of personal relations with German civilians, with all its potential for misunderstanding or embarrassment—not that I had anything to regret or apologize for. Doctor Kunsemüller and his family had been allowed the use of their garden since the turn of the year when 1 Bucks moved in, primarily to enable them to grow vegetables in the kitchen garden for their own consumption. But they kept all the rest of it in good order as well, chiefly because the doctor's wife, whose first name Ina remained a mystery since she was properly styled *'Doktor Frau Doktor'*, was a keen and expert gardener. But her husband was denied the use of the rooms which he had previously used for his medical practice, and which lay unused. Within a fortnight of the new colonel Peter

Sesekedamm No 8, the Kunsemüller house, from the pergola.

Brush arriving, and on my advice, Doctor Kunsemüller made a formal request for an interview, and Peter, ever reasonable, conceded the professional use of the waiting and consulting rooms and surgery. These rooms had a dedicated external entrance, and could be kept entirely separate within. Two had large plate-glass picture windows, eight feet wide, giving onto the terrace on the garden side. In warmer weather and out of surgery hours the open window provided a means of communication with the garden, where the family might be tending the vegetable beds and flowers, and we might be relaxing.

Their son, Hanns-Gerhard Kunsemüller was occasionally in the garden. Released early at the discretion of the US Army commandant in Kamen following his service in the infantry (rather than being held as a prisoner of war), he had informally returned to his medical studies and like all the rest of them became a doctor, married a doctor: he still lives in that same house. We have visited him there in recent years. I said, 'You smoke too much.' He replied, 'Well, you gave me my first cigarette.' *Touché.* More frequently in the garden was Christa Haller

Ina-Maria — 'Fränzchen', aged one.

with her baby daughter Ina-Maria, known as 'Fränzchen', who was allowed the run of the place in such a safe environment. Christa, tall, willowy, and serene, carried with her an aura of *noli-me-tangere*, perhaps engendered by her unhappy situation, of which we were aware. Robin and John confessed that they found her quite enchanting. Perceptive Christa, who missed nothing, told me she thought they were a little bewitched by her. She was quite right. None of us had any ideas about her, beautiful, warm and charming though she was. In that quiet garden she was an island of calm, beyond our reach. And then there was Margret. She had been nineteen in February, nine months younger than myself. Pretty, not formally beautiful, animated, open, and shy but confident, she used to come to her father's consulting room to work when he

was not using it. Her parents, properly protective of their younger daughter, allowed her at first only to engage in conversation through the open picture window to the terrace, a limitation they later relaxed when they got to know us all better, and trust us.

The Hotel Stadt Kamen, ca. 1995, formerly HQ No 1 T-Force Unit: the picture window of my office on the right.

As time went by, the group in the garden representing the forces of occupation included, as well as myself, Robin Smyth, John Bayley, Johnny Pepys Cockerell, and on occasion Jack Griffiths the Quartermaster, in whose hands the management of our accommodation and quarters lay. My letters didn't mention the arrival of John Bayley in the late spring. He was decanted from a truck precisely in front of the picture window of my office which was raised above ground level, and from where I surveyed the comings and goings in Kamen's main square, Am Markt. He wandered somewhat hesitantly into my office and saluted lamely (all his salutes were lame).

'And who the hell are you?' I snapped, which only increased his nervousness.

View across Am Markt from the Hotel, today: the Rathaus, the Evangelical and Catholic churches.

'I'm J-John B-Bayley,' he replied.

A lieutenant in the Grenadier Guards, he did not at first seem to me to be a valid substitute for the Riflemen I had been hoping for. The son and brother of Guardsmen, he had been detailed off to work with Nigel Nicolson and collaborate with him in the writing of the history of the Grenadier Guards in the Second World War—which Nicolson later completed in two volumes, along with Patrick Forbes. Nicolson couldn't get on with John, the least soldierly of

John Bayley and Margret Kunsemull|ler.

creatures (or was it the other way round?) and asked for him to be removed. Much later I asked John how it was he came to T-Force from the Guards.

'Well,' he said, 'I was k-kind of p-pushed out.'

If the Guards were unable to recognise it as their loss, it was certainly our gain. John would have exercised a civilising influence on any Mess, particularly the Guards. He stayed with us in Kamen, in the Evacuation Office of A Detachment, until the time came for him to be demobilised to go up to New College Oxford at the beginning of October 1947. John had a room in the house, and was often with us in the garden in the evening. He had a great rapport with Margret; they talked and talked while at the same time John nursed his admiration for Christa.

What was becoming evident to me about the Kunsemüller family was that they enjoyed a good conscience. Their relations with us showed no trace of deference, their sense of self-worth was entirely valid, and they accepted the limitations imposed by their people's recent unhappy history—but not the illegal requisition of their property. And here they had legitimate cause for their sense of grievance. The first troops lodged in that area had been Americans, and the US Army had requisitioned the group of four houses of which the Nazi Burgomaster's was almost of necessity one, and the doctor's another. By rights the doctor's should have been exempt, but it happened anyway, and getting it undone was stupidly allowed to become a matter of the authority and prestige of the occupying power. But although right was theoretically on the Kunsemüller's side, they had nevertheless been fortunate even to recover the use of the practice rooms and of the garden, and they would have been well-advised to let the matter rest there for a while.

They invited me to an evening meal with them, perhaps because they felt I had been helpful in getting the doctor back the use of his rooms (I had merely put the case on its merits to Peter Brush, no special pleading), or perhaps in the hope of future favours. However, given the level at which the civilian food ration then stood, it was impossible for me to accept, even though I was able to observe that a number of his patients, many of whom were from the stricken mining community, brought him little gifts of food or coal. They had no other way of compensating him for his services. Had I accepted their invitation to share a meal with them, I would no doubt have been questioned upon the requisitioning of their home, or at least my advice would have been sought. I would have had to tell them to leave things be just for now. But no such inhibition prevented either me or Jack Griffiths agreeing to have a drink with them all after dinner at their rather cramped and inadequate quarters in the hospital. The evening helped us to understand very well their wish to get back into their own house—although the subject was not raised directly with us on that occasion. That was just as well, billeting and requisitioning being one of the Quartermaster's areas of responsibility; anyway, Jack would always tend to take his tone from the Colonel at the time, even though the original requisition had been irregular.

I admired the readiness of the younger daughter, Margret, to stand her ground in any discussion. Although never aggressive, she also failed to display any hint of deference to our position as members of the occupying power in that place.

Margret with Fränzchen in the garden.

It was this that introduced a refreshing element of directness and honesty into our dealings. Our chance evening meetings, never prearranged, in the shade of the garden in the cool of the evening, became more frequent and more sought after on both sides. We spoke in a mixture of English and German, always finding a *mot juste* in whichever language seemed right for the point in question.

The proposed September visit, a long weekend pass, was to be for my sister's wedding on Saturday 14th, and my colonel and colleagues at HQ T-Force were happy to provide me with a pretext: the delivery to London of secret documents, a cover story which was always available if required. Given the hours I was putting in, I was not going to feel too bad about it.

Lt. M. H. S. Howard R.B., H.Q. No. 1 T-Force, B.A.O.R.
20th July 1946

Darling Mama,

I have a nasty feeling that my last letter to you is still languishing somewhere in a pocket. The latest about my captaincy is not promising. We are having too many majors and captains posted in, and some of them are having to drop one, and it is hardly the time to make a junior lieutenant up to captain in their stead. Nevertheless it has been approved at H.Q. B.A.O.R., and the approval is on its way down to us: it rests for the Colonel to say.

I am writing this from the Atlantic Hotel, Hamburg. I left Kamen at 8.30 this morning, and by two p.m. I was in 2nd Echelon G.H.Q. here—239 miles in 5 hours on the road—mostly Autobahn. I am trying to arrange some rather tricky postings for the Colonel, with only mediocre success. I

return via Celle, Hanover, Bad Oeynhausen, etc. tomorrow, arriving Kamen
6 p.m.

Roddy Bennett and Rowley Prideaux-Brune have arrived, I hope the first of
a long string of R.B. reinforcements. We have hooks on Ian and Barry too!
The beautiful architecture and cultural atmosphere of Celle makes a grim
comparison with Belsen 5 miles up on the same road.

No more news.

All my love,

Michael

My promotion to captain still appeared to be on a knife-edge,[19] but Peter
Brush had set his heart upon it, and by then I had little doubt that he
would have his way. We were still short of officers, which placed a heavy
workload on those already in the field, but Roddy Bennett arrived at some
time between the 10th and 20th July, just about in time for his twentieth birthday, and went straight down to fill one slot at D Detachment at
Leichlingen. He later recalled how young we had all been in relation to the
weight of responsibility we carried—not that any of us felt over-faced by
it at the time, one just got on with it. Another rifleman, Rowley Prideaux-
Brune, who was unknown to me but known to Peter Brush, arrived at the
same time. An Old Etonian, Rowley was commissioned some six months
before me, and was the son of David Prideaux-Brune, a retired lieutenant-
colonel of the Rifle Brigade whom Peter also knew. Peter would certainly
have wished to find a better job for Rowley not only on that account, but
also because he was very bright. However, both positions were already
occupied, that of Adjutant by Dicky Muir and that of Intelligence Officer

---

19 Promotion even to captain had to go up to Army Commander for approval. There were said to
be two hundred lieutenant-colonels and three hundred majors supernumerary to establishment in
Rhine Army, many of whom would be obliged to drop one or two pips in the peacetime army in
the period in question.

by myself. So he stayed with us at Kamen in A Detachment for a number of weeks before moving on to a slot which opened up for him elsewhere and for which he had been angling.

By now Dicky Muir's newly-acquired confidence in his own authority was on show elsewhere than just the cricket field. The commanding officer over at C Detachment at Ratingen had found his own particular solution to the problem of a lack of entertainment. Major Powell had been foisted upon us by a desperate 2nd Echelon Postings because he had signed on for a further term, though his previous unit had apparently been keen to be rid of him. Perhaps on a hunch one day, Dicky dropped in on the Officers' Mess at Ratingen a bit before one o'clock. The place was deserted. He asked a waitress where the officers were.

'They're at the other Mess,' he was informed.

'*Other* Mess?' he said. 'Where is that?'

The waitress gave him a street address, to which he drove at once. It was an undamaged house—a great rarity—with its blinds drawn and the lights on inside. Dicky walked in through the unlocked front door and there, in the best front room, was Powell, naked and far from sober, and accompanied by two or three ladies also in a state of undress. To be drunk on duty and absent from one's post was bad enough. And while a degree of commerce between soldiers and the local ladies of the night was not unusual, the really shocking aspect of the affair was that, in a country where so many people were living in terribly cramped and insanitary conditions, the local Housing Office would have had to be persuaded (bribed?) that the house be certified as unfit for human habitation in order for the ladies to be installed. Presumably, also, food and utilities were provided from the proceeds of sale of cigarettes, liquor, and the company's rations. Powell's feet hardly touched the ground. As Adjutant, Dicky managed to summon the influence from somewhere to have the major out of Germany in thirty-six hours, and out of the army in forty-eight. And it was just as well. Within days the Special Investigation Branch was on the trail and sniffing round Ratingen. But the bird had flown, and the other chicks had been despatched to their several nests, wherever those may have been. The SIB was persuaded that the matter had been cleared up, and chose not to pursue it.

I had been sent up to Hamburg because it was the seat of 2nd Echelon GHQ Rhine Army who had control of officer postings. My mission was to argue the case for us to be sent more young officers, and I was chosen for this job because I had a more direct knowledge of the intelligence job for which the officers were needed and because, as evacuation officers at the detachments, they would be working to me. However, as a mere lieutenant, I probably lacked the seniority to make much impression on the majors and colonels with whom I dealt, and I felt that I was meeting with only limited success. Nevertheless, postings-in of Rifle Brigade officers (and one from the 60th) did continue as a consequence, until finally we had a full complement.

Hamburg was a hard drive in an open jeep, even in fine weather, and the stretch which passed through the beautifully preserved and largely undamaged town of Celle, had not then been made up to autobahn. The close proximity of the site of the concentration camp at Belsen, the horrors of which were by now well-known, made a chilling contrast with the cultural gem of the city. It is a contrast which was, and still is repeated at Weimar, that historical and cultural treasure-house in Saxony, again undamaged by war and beautifully preserved, standing only five miles from the concentration camp at Buchenwald.

Capt. M. Howard R.B., H.Q. No. 1 T-Force, B.A.O.R.
24th July 1946

Darling Mama,

The Colonel whipped me in today and said that the Gods had given their blessing, and I might put up my third pip. He told me to go and get properly dressed so as from lunch time I shall blossom forth in all my glory. Just a trifle pleased at being the first of our bunch—although Denis Kelly with the 6th Airborne is also up for promotion.

The trip to Hamburg was most enjoyable. The journey up was 239 miles in 5 hours flat, via Bad Oeynhausen, Hanover, and Celle. Celle is a lovely old town, a bit bigger than East G.—all 17th and 18th century and very well preserved. I had a good look at Hamburg, of which 60 per cent is still in quite good shape. The other 40 per cent is burnt to a cinder, acre upon acre with not a room habitable: a dismal sight as it must have been a beautiful town. On the way back we were diverted from our route as they were blowing things up near Soltau, and I came through Verden, Nienburg, Minden. In Verden, a smallish town, I saw a Y.M.C.A. with officers' tea room attached and went in. It was run by 2 English girls who were charming—they made it all quite like home. They don't get many English officers in and they seemed thrilled to get a chance to feed somebody.

If any of you are in London in the near future, could you drop in at Pulford's, 19 Albemarle St., and get me some black metal pips—tell them the 'patrols' size, the smallest 2 pairs of them, and one pair of the service dress size. Could you also send my patrols. I left them behind as I thought I wouldn't need them, but I now find that I would be glad of them.

I was invited out to the doctor's house a few evenings ago. The Q.M. and I went along after dinner and stayed chatting until midnight, sipping some German liqueur. They are nice people, and very entertaining. The son was 21 at midnight, so we all drank his health. The younger daughter is v. intelligent and prepared to argue on any subject—very good entertainment value: also very attractive—I must look out for myself!

No more news for the moment.

All my love,

Michael

In the tacit competition for who was going to be first to achieve his captaincy from our company at the OCTU, I was keeping a weather eye on those whom I rated as likely contenders. None of those who went to either of the two regular battalions in Germany, or indeed elsewhere in the Regiment, was in the running, as a strict order of precedence and seniority was maintained there. It was among those otherwise occupied that this modest eminence—the third pip—was more likely to be earned, or at least bestowed. Rumour had it that Denis Kelly, who had gone to join a battalion of the Air Landing Brigade of the 6th Airborne Division in Palestine, was a leading prospect—a spell as assistant Adjutant was thought likely to turn into the real thing. But then fate struck. Late one night there was a full emergency, and at the very moment that the battalion had to be turned out, Denis was found to be paralytically drunk and incapable. Ignoring the advice of comrades to have himself reported sick and lie doggo in bed, he insisted on being carried legless into action, thereby significantly blotting his copybook, at least for the time being. On another night he might have got away with it, and even though this one episode didn't betray a tendency or a trend, it was enough to pose a question mark over his suitability. His threat to my own hope of precedence receded, for long enough anyway. A third pip was something that only a few achieved in the course of their twenty-seven months of commissioned service, and to be the first of that élite few to attain it felt like a real achievement. It came eight weeks after my twentieth birthday.

Candidates for a commission in our age-group, originally thirty each in the Rifle Brigade and KRRC, had already been through a selection process. In our case this was conducted by Colonel Vic Turner in 1943 during his round of the schools. Of the thirty selected, twelve had been weeded out during the first five months of preliminary training, so by the time they had received seven months' officer training and been commissioned, the remaining eighteen were beginning to look like the élite that the Regiment, without apology, was seeking.

I was wrong about the extent of the bomb damage to Hamburg. My jeep didn't take me through the worst stricken areas on my way to the comforts of the Atlantic Hotel, close by the waters of the Alster. The worst of the damage was done by 'Operation Gomorrah' during the nights of 27/28th and 29/30th July 1943 in the largely residential areas lying directly to the east of the Binnenalster, where sixteen thousand multi-storey apartment blocks were left gutted. Eight square miles of buildings were incinerated but left as shells, with their walls mostly still standing. Even the tarred roads caught fire. Fifty thousand perished in the firestorm, mostly from lack of oxygen and carbon monoxide poisoning, a million were left homeless, and one and a quarter million fled the city, some to the open country. Hitler was reported by his entourage as fearing that further attacks of similar weight might force Germany out of the war—the people's will to resist destroyed. The more rational Albert Speer harboured the same fear. Air Marshal 'Bomber' Harris was only slightly wide of the mark; another couple of nights like that might have saved us all a lot of bother. A later survey of bomb damage showed fifty-three per cent of Hamburg suffering moderate, heavy or total damage. Even then the tonnage of rubble per head of population in Hamburg came only to 20.9 cubic metres, as against Cologne's 32.1, an even more shocking intensity. But everyone had their own candidate for 'worst damaged', depending often on the circumstances in which they came to see it.

Segregation between officers and other ranks was usually maintained within canteen facilities. In Verden there was a YMCA for the troops, while officers had a tea-room attached, run by the two English girls. There was a handful of organisations, some with a religious flavour, some with a bias against alcohol, or both, some working together, some operating independently, to bring tea and sympathy to 'our brave boys'. They aimed to offer a pleasant alternative to the NAAFI, but where beer was not an option. Most of the staff dedicated to providing these services were maiden ladies or at least single women (like Patricia Meehan, author of *A Strange Enemy People*) who might be there for entirely altruistic or charitable reasons, and with a real vocation for service. Others were simply there to chase men. My two, both clearly somebody's sister, were, I am sure, as pure as the driven snow. Verden was the HQ of the 1st Armoured Division, which contained the 7th Armoured Brigade, but the girls' delight at our arrival suggested that they may not have been having much luck in luring the officers away from the Mess bars and the clubs, even if their scones were a real treat and their chatter charming.

'Pips' can be sewn on battledress, even in time for lunch. For service dress or patrols they had to be of metal, enamelled black, and I had not been sufficiently confident of my promotion to order them in advance from Pulford's of Albemarle Street, who had made my uniform. Perhaps I would now have confidence enough to draw attention to my enhanced status by wearing my green patrols for Mess occasions or going out to dine, as did Peter Brush and Dicky Muir.

Capt. M. H. S. Howard R.B., H.Q. No. 1 T-Force, B.A.O.R.
6th August 1946

Darling Mama,

It wasn't until I got your letter today that I realised that it is quite a few days since I had written to you; hence this in a hurry. I am not too busy today, as yesterday was a holiday in the army, and nobody wrote me any letters, official or otherwise.

On Saturday I had to go for the Colonel to see the Commander of North Rhine Region Mil. Gov. in Düsseldorf, and had lunch with one of our detachments there. Then I went to Heisingen near Essen and picked up Tony Lucas. Then we made our way hot foot, or rather, hot jeep, to Osnabrück, and arrived in time for tea with 1 R.B., where I saw Dicky Partridge and various others, and also spent rather a hectic evening. The next morning we returned for lunch at Kamen, and then went to the Möhne See, and drove round in the evening. Yesterday being a holiday, I thought it would do Sgt. Wigg good to get out, so I packed him into my jeep, and we went for about a 150 mile drive through the most lovely country on a beautiful afternoon. So that was three days away from the office, and I feel all the better for it. Also tomorrow I am managing to get away on official business right down south to Siegen, near the American Zone.

My slight overemphasis on my German friends was perhaps a reaction against no comment in that direction by my family. I think that it was also perhaps an effort to make you aware that a problem does exist. It is all part of the general feeling of the soldier out here that that side of British policy is very short-sighted, as I am sure it is.

As for the personal side of it, I do take care not to offend anybody in the unit, either subordinate or superior, both for obvious reasons. But I do find that to sit in the Mess evening after evening, discussing the three inch mortar, or the war strength of the armoured division, or re-fighting this or that battle, is infinitely tedious. I would rather spend my time talking to a pleasant and intelligent German than a stupid and uncongenial Englishman; as I have said, I take care not to stress this in public. And if you come to think of it, apart from such subjects as art, literature, etc., there must be a certain number of things that I believe in which I ought to feel that Germans should believe in too. And I want to get to know the people here, and I can assure you that I wouldn't learn much if all I did was to listen to the rot that is talked in the Mess. The doctor's family is the only 'luxury' I allow myself in this respect, and they are sane and pleasant people, whatever language they speak.

As I said, I shall not make a fool of myself over rations, petrol, legal quibbles, or in any other respect, so don't worry.

This in a hurry—more later.

All my love,

Michael

During wartime bank holidays had necessarily been rather glossed over, but in 1946 the peacetime army was able to celebrate with a day's holiday on Monday 5th August. Evidently I took advantage of the long weekend.

Peter Brush sent me in his stead for a meeting with the Regional Commissioner, Land NordRhein/Westfalen at Düsseldorf, who at that time was J P Asbury, whose claim to fame was that he was a JP. He was less in the public eye than his deputy, Brigadier Barraclough, who owed his notoriety to his declining to permit future Chancellor Konrad Adenauer to sit down at interview, and then sacking him as Mayor of Cologne on 6th October 1945—in retrospect an error of judgement for which he was pilloried. I was asked what we were up to in the field of evacuation of equipment, documents and personalities.

Saturday night, which Tony and I spent with the 1st Battalion the Rifle Brigade at Osnabrück, was evidently 'hectic' to the point of oblivion, since it has left no lasting impression on my memory. Dicky Partridge had been another member of our intake at the Greenjacket OCTU, and a school-friend of Ian Murray and Brian Lascelles at Wellington. For those of us who were detached, visits like this served to maintain an umbilical connection with the Regiment, and as a way of keeping track of one's friends.

Once I had persuaded Bob Wigg to take a rare day away from his desk, we went for a long drive in the area known as the Sauerland, to have a first look at what had been the German Army Ski School at Winterberg. They had retained all their prototypically Aryan ski instructors for our benefit, and we had an eye to making a subsequent visit, which we did in January and December of the following year. Bob was a man with a delightful sense of humour and his very own brand of dog-German, which was laced with the army's Hindi and Arabic. He was good company at any time and a keen, if sceptical, observer of the German scene. He had an informal attachment—an engagement was not yet possible—with Margarete Sievert, a refugee from Pomerania who was a waitress in the Sergeants' Mess. I was later to discover that the *Wohnungsamt* (the municipal housing department) had registered an address in Kamen for them both, dating from the first days of 1 Bucks. He had added his name in order to afford her some protection. It was quite irregular, and the army didn't know about it.

It was some anomaly over the evacuation of an enormous, heavy-duty lathe from the factory of Waldrich which took me seventy miles down through beautiful forested country, broken by high hills and rivers, to Siegen, most of two hours' drive at that time. Discreet enquiry revealed that Waldrich, the proprietor, had been a lieutenant-colonel in the SS, and as such mandatorily liable to an investigation, but none had ever taken place. On the information laid by me an investigation was carried out, and he was found to have no record of anything which might render him liable to a charge.

My letter of 24th July must have rung alarm bells in my mother's mind; the very idea that I might have social rather than, say, master/slave relations with German civilians must have set them off, not to mention the suspicion that social might easily develop into sexual relations, as indeed they might. She would have regarded me as an innocent abroad in the matter of dealings with women, for I had never introduced her to anyone who could have been called a girlfriend. No doubt she saw me as someone who could easily be taken advantage of by a rapacious Gretchen. The British press, even the *Times*, which they read at home, had its fair share of stories of officers who had disgraced themselves by taking advantage of some of the many delights to which access was so easy. Almost all involved women, many involved alcohol or transport, and quite a few a heady brew of all three. My mother did not know that by then, by order of the Army Commander himself, only the billeting of soldiers upon German families, and marriage to a German were forbidden. Social contacts of all other kinds were permitted provided that they were conducted 'with dignity'. This was a word which could certainly have been used to describe my relations with the Kunsemüller family. The same was also true of Marianne and the Grevel family, to whom I had been introduced in March, the only others where the question might have been posed.

It was a difficult subject. Despite appearing to carry the consent of the Army Commander, there were always those who were not yet reconciled to the idea of 'kissing and making up' with Germans of any stripe. This included members of my parents' generation, as well as those soldiers who had been engaged in and survived bloody action when some of their mates had not, and of course the bereaved families. These were sensibilities which could not be ignored and certainly not trodden on, and I had to bear this very much in mind. All my meetings with the Kunsemüller family, and particularly with Margret and Christa, were open to view and indeed to participation by my brother officers with whom I shared my billet. Peter Brush knew this, and would not have hesitated to say had he thought that relations went beyond what he, as Commanding Officer, was comfortable with. He had met and rather liked the doctor.

Even though conversation in the Mess appears to have given us grounds for thinking from time to time that we might as soon be elsewhere, at least there was still bridge. Occasionally, especially as the evenings lengthened, we would make up a four between Peter Brush, Dicky Muir, Jack Griffiths and myself, and sometimes the Second in Command, Ronnie Coe, who also played a fair hand.

Ronnie was a Major in the Cheshires, a good county regiment (the 22nd, founded in 1689). He had fought with them all the way up Italy, and had been awarded an MBE, though we never found out what for. He preferred it like that. He never divulged his exact age, but we placed him in his late thirties, perhaps forty. Proud of his Majority to the point of revelling in it, he was always looking for the deference and respect he thought due to his rank as a 'field officer'. Indeed he had stayed on in the army when demobilisation had fallen due for him, at least in part to continue to enjoy his status. He didn't care to tell us much about his personal circumstances, but we knew he was married and had a couple of daughters of school age. We wondered whether a reluctance to disrupt their lives accounted for his not bringing his family out, or whether after a long war and much separation he no longer got on with his wife. Ronnie rather hinted at the latter. He was a farmer, I would say of yeoman stock, but he harboured a nagging suspicion that he was not quite out of the top drawer, and this resulted in a chip on his shoulder larger than his major's crown. He indulged in a sort of reverse ageism which held that the young—that is, the subalterns—were not as good or as tough or as strong as he was, and his attitude to all was tacitly challenging. Accustomed in the Mess from which he came to being addressed as 'Major' or 'Sir', he was uncomfortable in a Mess where the subalterns addressed his own colonel by his first name, and only saluted in the morning on the first encounter, unless on parade. Peter would quite often retire upstairs after dinner to write letters, or on equestrian matters, and then Ronnie appeared perhaps subconsciously to seek to dominate the Mess, at table or in the ante-room. The combination of the public-school ethos, the effortless assumption of superiority by these young men, and the relaxed Greenjacket interpersonal relations, all conspired to rile him.

He had arrived, posted in from the Cheshires in Berlin, a day or two before Peter Brush. He came in his own 3.6 litre Mercedes convertible which he had 'won' in Berlin, and which we took on strength. He was driven by a German civilian of Estonian origin, Max Leihburg, who acted also as his interpreter, personal servant and batman. Max was a pleasant, mild, educated and cultivated man, a chemist by profession, and said to have been found peddling aphrodisiacs on the streets of Berlin until Ronnie rescued him. We discovered him to be married to a German lady, with whom he no longer enjoyed marital relations. We did not at first know of her existence, or that she was still a part of the ménage, or that she had extra-marital relations with Ronnie, and that he had installed her in accommodation (to which she was certainly not entitled) in the southern part of Essen. It was said to be a villa, with a view to the Baldeney See, but none of us ever went there. Ronnie's other sport was rowing, single sculls, which he practised on the lake under her watchful eye. His duties within T-Force did not form part of the intelligence function, and therefore occupied him from Mondays to Fridays only. So he went to the villa most weekends, spending Saturday night there, and if he did not exhaust himself rowing then she would attend to that later. Ronnie would be at the breakfast table in Kamen on Monday morning, and we would ask, 'Nice weekend, Ronnie?' 'Yes, thank you,' he would reply, 'nice weekend.' While he had no idea that we all knew perfectly well how and where he spent his weekend, we were allowed to know that he went sculling and later, when he competed in a German rowing regatta at Duisburg/Wedau, we were even permitted to go and cheer him on. Sometimes at the weekend, perhaps if it was raining, Ronnie would arrange to play squash with Tony Lucas at the Villa Hügel, just round the corner from Tony's Mess at Heisingen. Afterwards he would say, 'Must be off home now,' and Tony had no idea that Ronnie was not going to be spending the night at Kamen.

Over the course of nearly two years Ronnie never ceased to show contempt for everything that he was not. He would pick an argument with the younger officers in the Mess, those he could identify as having been educated at Eton and Rugby, Uppingham and Ampleforth, and would often say, 'Of course, I haven't had the expensive education that you chaps have, but my opinion is that...' Then we would interrupt and say, 'Yes, Ronnie, we know, but if you didn't draw attention to it, no-one would notice.' He was also PMC—President of the Mess Committee—which did not actually exist as a committee, so its president acted alone. He was responsible for our rations and for the menus, and he saw to it that we were fed imaginatively and well, meals often starting with a varied mixed hors d'oeuvre. Such variety was very welcome in an otherwise limited diet. But he dealt arbitrarily with the Mess staff; man-management was a skill unknown to him. They hated him and it showed. One morning Robin Smyth, shaving at one of the twin basins in the Mess bathroom, found himself standing next to Ronnie who was shaving at the other with his cut-throat razor. Ronnie stood motionless for a moment, staring at his image in the mirror, then hurled his razor at it, shouting, 'You ugly bastard!' Poor Ronnie. He was not a handsome man, and his presence had a depressing effect upon the life of the Mess.

Ten years later, in Guatemala City, as I was closing the office one Saturday at midday, I looked diagonally across the intersection of the avenue and the street, and there in the sunshine stood Ronnie Coe with the very lady. He introduced her as his wife, but he did not vouchsafe her first name; to me she was to be 'Mrs Coe'. Early in 1950 John Bayley, who kept in contact with Erich Braatz our interpreter in Kamen, who in turn remained in touch with Max Leihburg, had written to me that 'Herr Coe weds Frau Leihburg.' Refraining from revealing that I knew exactly who she was, I took them to the Palace Hotel and bought them a drink. They were on their way to New Zealand where he was going to farm—a new start in a country where they would have no history except that which they chose to reveal.

Capt. M. Howard R.B., H.Q. No. 1 T-Force, B.A.O.R.
10th September 1946

Darling Mama,
I may arrive before this, but just in case it gets to you on Friday morning, I am writing to say that I shall be coming. The last few days have been not without incident. I have had my passage cancelled twice, but now I am on an assignment which seems foolproof. I also nearly had my trip put off by the Colonel, as I am prosecuting officer in a court martial case which has been adjourned. Until today I have not been able to write with any optimism about being able to make it. I shall telegram to you tomorrow morning, and again if possible before I leave on Thursday morning from Bad Oeynhausen. We should arrive in London about 10 on Friday morning and then I have to deliver the 'cargo' to Wimbledon, for which the Board of Trade provide a large car. I shall try to persuade the driver to drive me home—she may, you never know. Otherwise I shall travel down in the 12.03 with June Harvey.
I have been working like about 3 men for the past 10 days. 2 or 3 high

level flaps to cope with, and all the G.2's work to do in addition to my own.
And then I have had to prosecute in this court martial. I have been up until
midnight at my desk four nights this week.

Ian Murray came down for a very pleasant 24 hours—we went to the Möhne
See, and had a good dinner at the Soest club: he envied my 'set-up' enormously.
I have taken the liberty of asking somebody quite unknown to any of you
down to the wedding—a certain Sam Pringle, who I met here, and has just
been demobbed. He is most extraordinarily pleasant, and is going back to
London University after three years in Africa, and one in India! His papa
was a Liberal M.P. in the twenties, quite well-known I believe, but I have
never heard of him.[20]

I hope to bring about 5 bottles of champagne and three of probably cognac,
but something better if I can get it. The fizz could do for Anne and David
alone or perhaps just the family and bridesmaids.
I must close now.
Expect me on Friday.
God how relieved I am!
All my love,
Michael

I think there must be at least one letter missing because the previous letter
in my mother's cache had been dated 6th August, and anything more than
a week or ten days between letters ranked as a black mark which had to
be explained away. Exigencies of the service would usually do. Although
there were lulls during which I could take time away from my desk to enjoy
myself, the demands of the service had indeed begun to weigh heavy. Matters had to be dealt with as they arose, and every letter *in* meant at least two
letters *out*. Some matters had to be handled out on site and thus involved a
sortie and personal intervention. The concept of 'nine to five' had no place

---

20 William Pringle, MP for Penistone 1922–24.

in arranging our timetable. Start time in the office was fairly immutable at around eight o'clock, lunch absorbed forty or fifty minutes, coffee and tea came to us at our desks, and if we cleared whatever lay before us there would be a drift back to our billets or the Mess by about six. The timetable was determined by the workload, and all matters were treated as urgent. It was a *modus operandi* which gained us a reputation for efficiency, and if that meant that I had to be at my desk until midnight for four nights running, then so be it.

The Colonel had arranged through HQ T-Force that I should be excused duty as a member of the court on external courts martial, but I was asked to prosecute one of our own corporals who had struck and injured a civilian. The case was, after all, adjourned in time for me to make my trip home on the Thursday.

This was just as well, because my sister was due to be married at Colemans Hatch on the Saturday afternoon, and HQ T-Force had assiduously assembled a package of secret documents which in their view simply had to be delivered to 'Inkpot' at Wimbledon under officer escort. By coincidence, I was designated for the not-very-onerous task, and it was arranged that I would be driven from Fenchurch Street to Wimbledon on Friday morning by a lady driver. In the event, she could not take me on to Cat Street House, so I travelled down on the train to Forest Row along with one of Anne's bridesmaids.

I am not sure what contribution I expected three bottles of cognac to make to the wedding feast. Perhaps when raking over the embers afterwards we could get down to some serious champagne cocktails—Angostura bitters and sugar-lumps were always available. The wedding reception took place in persistent rain, the sides of the marquee on the lawn had to be rolled down, and we were denied the glorious view across to the Ashdown Forest and up to The Camel, the clump of trees at the top. But everything else was perfect; the bride and groom left the church under the crossed-swords of David's brother officers, as tradition demanded.

Two or three high-level flaps seems a bit excessive now, so I wonder what qualified them as such in my mind. One in particular I do remember at that time. The Foreign Office, under whose responsibility the Control Commission operated, was by now reasonably persuaded that a prostrate and defeated Germany was no longer the enemy, despite a state of war still obtaining technically. No, the *enemy* had become the Soviet Union, and an increasing part of our function was interdiction, that is, the denial to the Russians of targets of intelligence interest, whether military or civil.

One night I was called in the early hours on one of the two telephones by my bed, and a codeword was muttered conspiratorially in my ear. It meant absolutely nothing to me; I had simply not been briefed in advance. It was the GSO2 at HQ T-Force, and he had no option but to identify himself, and to explain to me 'in clear' what the operation consisted of. There were said to be eleven thousand kilos of highly refined uranium ore lying in a loose pile in the cellars of Krupp's Widia Works at Essen (whose main business was in carbide steels). A quadripartite team including four Russians was due to be visiting the site in a couple of days and it was vitally important that there should be no trace of the uranium remaining by the time they arrived, or they would be entitled to make a bid for it. How on earth had it been left sitting there for so long?

Nothing for it but to get straight on the phone to Fred Bonney at B Detachment at Heisingen, not five miles from Krupp's Widia Works, and tell him the story in clear. He set to work immediately, and they rustled up from somewhere enough empty steel three-inch mortar bomb boxes, with a handle at each end, which limited the contents to a weight of this dense material that required no more than two men to lift. The entire heap, every scrap, was boxed and loaded onto a ten-ton Mack truck and delivered to me by early afternoon at Kamen. The springs of the truck bore the gross weight of the uranium plus the mortar-bomb boxes surprisingly well. I collared the Mess corporal, Corporal Weatherall, and told him to draw a Sten gun and a couple of magazines, sit on the load, take it up to the RAF at Bückeburg, '…and if any bastard tries to take it away from you, shoot him. And get a receipt.' Which he did, from a squadron leader, for 11,000 kilos.

The material was almost certainly 'yellowcake', a form of triuranium octoxide which is, contrarily, greenish-black, and puts its possessor one of the steps on the way to producing fissile material for the uranium bomb. There had been a production of this material at the Auergesellschaft at Oranienburg some twenty miles to the north of Berlin, in total about a hundred and eighty tons. Of this, sixty tons was captured by the US Army in Frankfurt at the end of March 1945, and it is said that some of that was subsequently used in the manufacture of the atomic bombs dropped on Hiroshima and Nagasaki in August. All the rest is presumed to have remained at Oranienburg, and when it became clear that the Russian army would get there before anyone else (indeed, by agreement) the US Air Force raided the Auerwerk with a force of six hundred and seventy-five B17 bombers (not by agreement), causing very heavy destruction, and rendering the factory non-viable. A proportion of the high explosive bombs dropped had chemical delay fuses with varying length of delay, from days to weeks or even years.

About six months later a captain in the Special Investigation Branch (SIB) asked to come and see me. The RAF had weighed the bomb boxes for their own purposes before flying them over to England, but the nett weight of the contents was never established until the boxes reached their final destination, when it was found to be 6,000 kilos. It was meant to have been 11,000. Where were the missing 5,000 kilos? 'Search me,' I said. The SIB spent quite a while nosing round, and the only conclusion they could reach was that there had never been 11,000 kilos at Krupp's Widia Works in the first place. As there was no weighing equipment accessible to where the material had been dumped, it had been an estimate, and an inaccurate one. Or had someone in Krupp's been squirrelling away a couple of kilos at a time for sixteen months, and had it since crossed the border at Magdeburg in quantities which would go in a haversack? It was a conclusion they shied away from. The pile had appeared undisturbed.

Ian Murray, who I had hoped would be posted to us, reached T-Force at Kamen at last, but only as a guest, envious of the flexible structure within which we plied our trade. But there was no way back. A couple of years later I saw him from time to time at Cambridge; he was up at King's (as was Dicky Muir) and he played hockey for them against the Peterhouse side which I captained. In a Greenjacket OCTU athletics team which I had taken from York to compete with the great Roman Catholic school at Ampleforth in early 1945, he and I had represented the OCTU at 100 yards. They were fitter than us, but not faster.

CHAPTER 4

The benefits of gnomes' blood – Tuppence and her violets –
A cruel winter – An unnerving break-in – A Christmas
break-out

Capt. M. H. S. Howard R.B., from the Transit Camp at Harwich
15th September 1946

Darling Mama,

We got up to Victoria and straight into a taxi, but Prunier's was closed. We
looked at Hatchetts and turned up Swallow Street, and eventually finished
up at Martinez, where we had a good lunch—I dashed off at 1.45 and
jumped into a taxi, said, 'Drive like hell' and caught the 2.00 train with
three minutes to spare. I thoroughly enjoyed every minute of a rushed 48
hours, and I don't see how it could have gone better—I wish I could have
been there longer to take some of the work off your hands.

I'm sure Anne and David think they couldn't have had a better send-off. I
thought the bridesmaids were sweet, a really charming pair, and June very
attractive.

I forgot my pyjamas—the only thing, I think. I am in no particular hurry
for them. The film I shall have developed, and send you all copies—with one
for June of herself, if it turns out nicely. I ordered some of the wedding from
the 'official photographer', and gave my address as 'Cat Street House'—
could you forward them when they arrive please.

Now seems a good moment as I am all square after paying for the wedding presents with my last allowance—with my rise in pay as Captain up to 23/- a day, I can manage quite well without my allowance. My last statement of account was £118, and I am owed £25 as two months' back pay as Capt. If I have to drop the third pip at any time, I might be glad to ask you to help out, but I anticipate holding the captaincy until Christmas at any rate.

My birthday present to you Mama will have to wait until I come home on leave—I just can't combat the difficulty of trying to do it at this range.

On the train I met Harry Huntsman, an O.R. and 2i/c of 'B' Coy 2 R.B., so we immediately formed a clique of two. I usually manage to find one rifleman by way of congenial company.

I can think of nothing else for the moment—I will be better about writing.

All my love,

Michael

P.S. If I write to Mrs. David Scott, what would the address be?

June Harvey, one of my sister Anne's bridesmaids, had spent two nights with us at Cat Street House. I had invited her to lunch at Prunier in St James', not realising that they would be closed on Sundays. It was a favourite family haunt, partly because the restaurant reached well back from the street and round a corner, so that during the period of the assault from the air by V-1s and V-2s, danger from flying window glass during one's meal was much reduced. Madame Prunier had abandoned her two establishments in Paris to the Germans and spent the war in London where hers was the best fish restaurant, which suited our taste. My mother first took us there, and I also once went as the guest of the Baron Marochetti who briefly graced the modern language teaching staff at Rugby. He took a small handful of his best pupils to lunch there after the end of term as a reward for their efforts. He was personally friendly with Simone Prunier, and we were very well looked after. I had, to the disadvantage of my pocket, come to the conclusion that when going on leave or returning to unit, the most civilising thing a young officer could do was to have lunch at Prunier or tea at Gunter's of Curzon Street. The taste of the cucumber sandwiches or the chocolate ice-cream at Gunter's was much enhanced by having it served by a lady whose swept-up hair and aristocratic mien gave her a close resemblance to the forty-year-old Diana Wynyard, playing in London in *Portrait in Black* at that time.

But Prunier was closed,[21] so we took the taxi on, first to see if Hatchett's was open in Piccadilly, and then to Swallow Street which ran through to Regent Street, where there was the chance of getting a table at one of three good restaurants in a row, Kempinski, Veeraswamy and Martinez. We succeeded at the last. Had that failed, there was still the possibility of Bentley's a few doors down on the same side, perhaps the second best fish restaurant in London.

The pair of bridesmaids was completed by Nik Humphreys, but in fact there were also two children, the daughters of my brother-in-law David Scott's cousin Richard Murdoch. Known to the radio public as 'Stinker', Richard had progressed from dramatics at Charterhouse and the 'Footlights' at Cambridge to become an accomplished light comedy actor on the stage, but in particular as the counterpart to Kenneth Horne in the popular radio series *Much-Binding-in-the-Marsh*. Earlier in the war, Nik had shared a set of rooms with Anne at St Hugh's College Oxford.

Since leaving school and joining up I had been lucky enough to receive a small allowance from my parents, which it was agreed should continue only until I was earning my keep. That point seemed to have been reached with my actually being due pay as captain, plus the field allowance which went with it. When I had first joined the army, on three bob a day, the parental allowance had been more than welcome, even though we used regularly to double our income by betting at the greyhound track at Worksop, benefiting from the advice of our platoon sergeant 'Dodgy' Bill Asling that, at Worksop, number

21 It closed its doors for the last time in 1976.

two trap opened first, number five trap second, and then the rest together. When I was newly-commissioned, my allowance from home enabled me to live beyond my means, but as a captain there was no further excuse for it and it was something of a relief to feel able to leave it behind.

I had met Harry Huntsman when lunching earlier with B Company 2RB. I had not known him at Rugby; he was two years my senior and in another house. But where two or three are gathered together wearing black buttons, there shall they form a clique.

Capt. M. Howard R.B., H.Q. No. 1 T-Force, B.A.O.R.
18th September 1946

Darling Mama,

Back again in harness with a vengeance. On Tuesday the whole unit went to a weapon training meeting at which Roddy Bennett was 3rd, the Colonel 4th and I 5th—and won 10/-. Today I was prosecuting on a court martial which continues tomorrow. A tedious affair, as half the witnesses are Ger-man and persist in committing perjury, for which they in due course will be prosecuted. My desk is in disorder anyway, and I shall be working late for some nights to straighten it out. Then on the 23rd Bill Adams goes on leave for three weeks, and I shall have to cover his job during his absence. Then before he returns my sergeant leaves and so I shall literally be doing three people's work. I shall try to keep writing! T-Force is likely to become more and more run by Control Commission officers, but I was glad to be assured that if the situation were to arise, I would be among the last three to go as I am regarded now as one of the 'old hands' and know most of the 'T-Force answers'.

It feels horribly as if winter had started—wind and rain without cease. Hard winters usually set in at the beginning of November in this country— I can only pray for some fine weather first. The people already look miserable and hungry, and if they now start looking cold as well, it would make the

winter intolerably long. Did you read that article in the Times *by Beveridge?*
I left it behind for you somewhere.

That film I took will be ready tomorrow—any worthwhile snaps I will let
you have a copy of.

19 Sep 46. The photos give a good idea of the house, but are hardly works
of art—the marquee got in the light. One of the two of June was quite
good.

No more for the moment.

All my love,

Michael

P.S. Margret thought the house lovely—they don't have anything of the
same style at all in Germany.

I had returned to find nothing that I didn't expect, a backlog that would take
several days—and nights—to clear.

For the first time in five months Peter Brush decided that it would do no
harm to discipline and morale to institute a session of weapons training—
especially bearing in mind that the Regiment owed its reputation since its
earliest days to skill at arms, and particularly the rifle. Naturally, we felt that
he was absolutely entitled to remind us of the profession in which we were
temporarily engaged, even though we were primarily occupied in something quite different—as long as he didn't do it too often. However, for
me it was yet another day away from my desk, a desk which badly needed
my attention after nearly a week of neglect. And my absence would be prolonged by my having to prosecute at another local court martial which ran
into a second day. The defending officer was Bill White (of the Rifle Brigade) who had joined us recently at Kamen. He was making a mess of the
defence, and I came to the conclusion that he was not, even at eleven o'clock
in the morning, entirely sober. I was almost moved to ask for an adjourn-
ment on those grounds, and had to balance the prospect of getting him into

trouble against having the accused, whom I was prosecuting, inadequately defended. I took the easy way out.

Plentiful cheap liquor was a potential snare for everyone, and it was a trap into which Bill, who was excellent company when sober, or even only half-cut, had allowed himself too easily to fall. He came down to breakfast one morning when he had been with us a couple of months.

'They're all in there, in the bathroom,' he announced.

'Who are, Bill?'

'Why, the gnomes, of course. They're digging up the tiles with pick-helves. I've been burning their buttocks with blow-lamps.'

We were not quite sure how real the gnomes were to him. Were they his little green men? Was this the first sign of *delirium tremens*? That lunchtime, because someone had something to celebrate, we mixed a cocktail of rum, port and orange juice. In came Bill and ladled himself a full glass.

'Ah,' he declared, looking at the reddish mixture, 'gnomes' blood.' It endowed him, he explained, with 'gnomic energy'.

Soon afterwards we were asked whether we could spare someone to move across to No 2 T-Force as Assistant Adjutant, and we sent Bill. It turned out that virtually his only duty was to be with Colonel Percy Winterton over the lunch hour and try to prevent him from falling backwards off his bar-stool— but at all events to catch him if he did. Reports were that the performance of his duties was exemplary; we had no detail.

Since Jim Quick had been demobbed, Bill Adams had been attached as GSO2 Liaison, and he, like Jim, had his desk in the corner of my office. Also like Jim, he was wonderfully easy to get on with. His absence on leave did not give me a great deal extra to do, because his was more in the nature of a watching brief so as to assist the Intelligence Officer (me) with any difficulty over matters of policy, particularly in dealing with senior officers externally and liaison with Military Government at the higher level. If things proceeded in their usual even way, his absence would hardly be noticed, except that I would miss his company. Sergeant Wigg going on leave was altogether a more serious affair, not least on account of the detail which he kept in his head, and his familiarity with precedent and with particular cases which went back a long way. My two excellent corporals would be obliged to carry a greater burden and to refer to me more often. We would continue to function as before, but it would mean harder work over longer hours. Never mind, we were young and keen.

The fact that T-Force was increasingly run by civilian officers did not bring with it any visible change at command level for some time, and there was no change at HQ T-Force in the personnel with whom I dealt. Jean Hughes-Gibb, already installed, was the only civilian, and we had all become accustomed to dealing with a non-military lady. At our level, in the field, we had one civilian—though ex-service—posted in. Don Cropper was employed as one of the evacuation officers at A Detachment in Kamen, where he became a member of our Mess. This created no difficulties, nor any change in the flavour of life in the Mess. He had previously held rank as a major and knew the form; he very seldom ventured an opinion other than on matters of fact. He wore his service medals on a dark blue battledress, and he had done time as a prisoner of war, so his new situation didn't represent an appreciable change.

Several months later he was followed by another civilian, Rufus Harris, whose war service record was in the London Fire Service. In due course, Rufus took over the A Detachment Evacuation Office. Short, dynamic, highly intelligent, humorous, educated and civilised, he learned the job quickly, and when my own job began to run down in the second half of 1947, I was entirely happy to hand over what was left to him. But intelligence work in the field was to remain in military hands at all levels certainly for the next fifteen months, and until after I had left. I was assured by HQ T-Force that I had become one of the few indispensables, and would undoubtedly be the last to go in No 1 T-Force—other than Sergeant Wigg, who was still in harness in 1949.

The cold fingers of an unseasonably early winter were beginning to grip the civil population. The supply and distribution of food and of fuel for heating were, if anything, worse than a year previously. It was the cold which would kill the old and hungry, those who had been able to hold on during the warm summer. Skins became yellower, the gait unsteady. The rhythm of the passage of horse-drawn hearses through the town square in front of my office would become ever more regular and insistent.

The photos I had taken at my sister's wedding reception were developed and printed by the next day and were much like all wedding photographs, mementoes of an occasion. Perhaps I should have been more tactful than to tell my mother that I had already shown them to Margret in the intervening twenty-four hours. Cat Street House, which Margret thought lovely, was really only an elongated cottage, charming but hardly imposing.

Capt. M. Howard R.B., H.Q. No. 1 T-Force, B.A.O.R.
20th September 1946

Darling Mama,

I hope this letter is timed right, as it is to wish you many happy returns of the day. I shall have to wait until I come on leave to get your present; as circumstances were against it last weekend, and the only thing one can get out here is cheap scent!

Today was my busiest day ever. Apart from being acting Adjutant for Dicky, my own office turned out 96 letters, all of which I signed, and about half of which I wrote. Clearances are coming through fast. To pack all the machinery for this quarter we will need a pile of wood of nearly 9,000 cubic feet!

The most terrible weather—hurricanes, tempests, tornadoes are all a commonplace occurrence.

No news that I haven't told you already. Take a good rest after things have returned to normal.
God bless, and again many happy returns.
All my love,
Michael

My mother's birthday qualified for a separate letter, rather than one in the normal series. I was counting on it not taking more than three days, the usual time required.

Busy-ness in the office was coarsely measured by the number of letters processed during the day, but one should not be misled into thinking that each of these represented anything in the nature of a full page of foolscap of closely-argued reasoning; they did not. They dealt with matters of fact: determining the movement of machines, documents and men from A to B, their authorisation, their timing, packing, transportation; occasionally how objections or other difficulties should be dealt with; very occasionally statements of principle or policy. And, once in a while, a threat, for instance for failure to comply. Addressees would be any of my four Evacuation Offices in our detachments in the Ruhr; HQ T-Force, the BIOS Secretariat at 32 Bryanston Square, The Ministry of Supply, the Board of Trade, or branches of the Control Commission at Regional HQ in Düsseldorf. However straightforward most of these may have been, ninety-six letters in one day is still a lot. We were very busy. Communication with our targets of whatever sort were usually by means of a visit from an officer or NCO, when orders would be given.

'Clearances' to proceed with the evacuation of equipment were obtained from the RDR Division of the Control Commission/Military Government at Düsseldorf. When we received a request, whether for a single machine or a whole section of a plant, we sent an application for approval to RDR Division. They would consult with their appropriate branch, and permission would be granted by means of return of a signed Form 80G, without which we could not proceed. In the earlier days refusals were rare. Later, as the policy of enabling Germany to achieve a positive balance of trade began to bite, there were refusals—but not many, and anyway the company requesting a machine could always contest a refusal. The German owners deprived of their equipment received in lieu a copy of the Form 80G, on which they might later make application to their government for compensation. Thus the loss would fall upon the German government rather than upon the owner of the equipment. In some cases the equipment would not be in current use because of the shortage of the raw material required to operate it, or perhaps a shortage of power, and its absence would have little immediate impact. If the equipment was directly linked to war production, we would classify it as 'warlike stores or booty' and it would be subject to confiscation without the need for a Form 80G, although the classification itself could be contested by application to Military Government. Once a machine had been cleared for evacuation, the first step was to quantify the amount of timber needed to crate it up for shipment, first by truck to the depot at Geesthacht, and thence to a UK port and on to its ultimate destination. We always kept enough timber in stock to meet the foreseeable requirements. Nine thousand cubic feet of wood could broadly be taken as two and a half thousand tons—the load of five hundred five-ton Mack trucks. That means we were deploying more than five such trucks every day, another measure of our level of activity.

Documents—blueprints and other instruments of intellectual property—were copied rather than removed. So while their owners lost their exclusivity, the originals did at least remain *in situ*. T-Force had control of the supply of the scarce 'Ozalid' paper for making copies. As for so many things, there was a thriving black market for Ozalid, and we had to keep it under armed guard as well as lock and key.

'Personalities' could be evacuated without reference to the Control Commission for interview or interrogation—both terms were used, and the dividing line was fine and quite arbitrary. However, if their removal was deemed likely to cause disruption in the production of supplies vital to the operation of the economy in the Zone, an objection might be raised, which might or might not be heeded. Most of the scientists evacuated were people engaged in research and development rather than in the process of current production. This was not so of people who were properly 'technicians' rather than scientists, but most of these could nevertheless be spared for a period of a few weeks without production being grossly disrupted.

> *Capt. M. Howard R.B., H.Q. No. 1 T-Force, B.A.O.R.*
> *6th October 1946*
>
> *Dear Daddy,*
>
> *This to wish you many happy returns of the day; as with the other members of the family, I'm afraid I haven't got the ingenuity to cope with the problem of a birthday present at this range—it will have to wait until somebody sees fit to send me on leave, which they are likely to do early in November.*
>
> *The snaps I sent Mama a day or two ago should give you quite an idea as to the immediate surroundings of my billet, but give no inkling of how depressing Kamen is.*
>
> *As I am at the moment not only doing I.O. and G2, but 'I' Sergeant as well, I have been driven back to employing a German typist, but to nip all pernicious rumours in the bud, I have chosen the 'I' Corporal's girlfriend!*
>
> *Thanks for the snippet about economics and the Foreign Service. I feel that economics in the same way that history does, forms a good background for any job nowadays.*
>
> *No more particular news—once again many happy returns and all my love,*
>
> *Michael*

The simultaneous absence of Bill Adams and Sergeant Wigg created a difficult situation as we were coming up to a period of maximum activity, and probably not for the last time. More secretarial help became essential, and my request was approved by Peter Brush. However, I thought it wise not to choose a secretary following anything in the nature of a beauty contest in case there were any suspicions about my motives, so when Corporal Fox put forward the name of his girlfriend it seemed an easy way out. A mild, mouse-like creature, by no means pretty, widowed with a boy and a girl who were as skinny as their mother, she clearly needed the extra meal at midday which went with the job. She left so little impression on me in a personal way that I cannot now even remember her name; as things turned out later, she may well have remembered mine. All my section had girlfriends from within Kamen, but Sergeant Wigg's had come from the East. I don't think it crossed the minds of any of us that she could have been the target of pressures from either Russian or pro-Communist sources to divulge information about our activities, and in this we were probably remiss.

Capt. M. Howard R.B., H.Q. No. 1 T-Force, B.A.O.R.
9th October 1946

Darling Mama,

Winter is here—our central heating goes on in the morning tomorrow for the first time. The strange thing is that there is a bitterly cold wind in the morning, which drops at about three in the afternoon, and in the evening it is really quite mild.

Marianne was 20 on Sunday—several of us went along to the party, and danced until three. Luckily that was the night we had the extra hour. There was a very nice surgeon from Leipzig there, and the dentist who we go to if anybody has toothache. Most of the conversation was in German: I now understand everything I hear except for the odd word or two, and they all assure me that my spoken German is 'ausgezeichnet'—excellent, and although I personally don't notice all that much improvement, I have no doubt that I really have done so.

A few things I would like sent if possible, please (a) 2 bottles of some repu-

table black leather dye, (b) Some thick black socks (if Britain can make them)—I think you have some coupons of mine, (c) A book called either The Outnumbered or The Persecuted; it appeared in the World Books as a reprint in about February.

Today was rather wearying, training my typist, but nevertheless we got off about 35 letters.

I thought violets grew only in the spring, but they are still blooming like anything here—I have had a small vase of them in my room for some three months now.

The work here is one long succession of coping with problems or people or both, and is rather fun, and must I'm sure be of value. There is reputed to be one officer at H.Q. T-Force whose sole employment is to smooth over rows I have with Mil. Gov., but they don't seem to mind much as we have established a reputation for getting the stuff out fast.

On my leave in November I think I shall have to anticipate my release by ordering a suit—it should be ready by May!

The photographs of the wedding really turned out awfully well, and the close up of Anne and David was radiant. The ones of them 'under the arch' and the bridesmaids were all good too. My girlfriends say she is lovely and that David looks charming.

No more news for the moment.

All my love,

Michael

Seven months into my first year on the Continent, I was not yet conversant with the vagaries of the onset of winter in a continental climate. The walk from the Mess to the office in the morning was enough to get one off to a cold and wintry start, and the central heating was very welcome, although the afternoons and evening were calm and more like autumn at home.

Marianne, to whom I had been so summarily introduced during my first week in Kamen, had her 20th birthday dance at the Grevel's home; the house was not large, and there was just about room to shuffle on the 'dance floor'. We all took a bottle to help things along and keep it going until three, and nobody was much bothered as to whether we were within the 'frat' laws or not. It was the Grevels we had turned to for advice when we needed a dentist, and their friend was very good. Grinding my teeth in my sleep I ruined one. He expertly reconstructed it in a couple of sessions, about an hour in all. I asked how I could pay him, knowing that money was of no use to him. A few cigarettes, he suggested. I gave him a carton of 200, and he seemed to think he had been more than adequately compensated. Small and dark, he seemed to me slightly sinister in appearance, with the air of a theatrical villain.

Relations with Marianne, though friendly enough, showed no signs of becoming anything more. I never knew, I did not ask, how she ordinarily occupied her days. Mere survival was then the order of the day, and it some-times called for quite demeaning expedients. She was a bright and attractive young woman and, with her pretty figure, dark good looks and flashing eyes, she might well have dared to hope that someone might come and lift her out of the unpromising situation in which she found herself. But it was not a role in which I saw myself. I could not afford even to think about it; I was not to be her White Knight. Would an arm's length relationship satisfy her? There was no overt show of reticence on my part because there was no call for it. Neither was there any show of impatience on her part—not yet at any rate.

Such affairs as the party were, as a matter of good manners, almost entirely German-speaking, and I was quite ready to lap up any compliments which might come my way, even if feeling a measure of scepticism. But having a certain facility with languages is not quite the same thing as being a linguist, and I have never really thought of myself as the latter—I have met too many people who really are. But I did have the ear and an imitative faculty accurate enough to give the impression that I was more fluent than I actually was. This brought with it the disadvantage that native speakers would at once assume it safe to let loose a barrage which tested me to the limit. This, combined with intellectual laziness, has left me with not much beyond the certainty of being fed and watered, fuelled and guided. When faced with a torrent of incomprehensible German, I learned to wait until it had dried up, and then nod sagely and say, *'Ja, das kann ich mir sehr wohl einbilden!'* ('Yes, I can very well imagine it!') Surprising how often it is appropriate.

The violets by my bed hardly got there under their own steam. I knew that some grew in a little copse in the field between us and the railway line, which in the spring had been full of lilies of the valley; there may have been another source of supply I knew not of. My 'washerwoman' Elli Kumperlink was a girl of seventeen, who also made my bed and dusted and cleaned the room. She suddenly took it upon herself unbidden to put an egg-cup full of violets on my bedside table and, seemingly at all times of the year, magically to renew and refresh them—into October at any rate, and possibly beyond. A local girl of peasant stock, modestly behaved to the point of shyness, she was known to the soldiery around the Mess as 'Tuppence' as it was unkindly supposed that she could be had for that sum. But I never saw her engage even in idle conversation with any of the men. She would never look me in the eye, and if at any time I returned to my room when she was working there she would blush to the neckline and scuttle from the room. Were the violets something of the language of love? When I was leaving she delivered to me, unsolicited, a photograph of herself which I have never found it in me to throw away. It stood for a lot of violets and a lot of modesty.

To my father, the term 'girlfriends' would have meant any females with whom I had even the slightest acquaintance, nothing heavier than that. In this case it meant Margret and Christa Künsemuller, and Marianne Grevel and her two sisters who, upon seeing the wedding photographs, declared my sister lovely and her husband charming. Well, they were.

Convinced that what mattered most was to get the targets out, and to leave matters of policy where they belonged, for the most part I did not enter into any controversy with officers of the Control Commission who might have their own reasons for contesting the evacuation of particular equipment. If the target had been classified as 'warlike stores or booty', then no clearance was required. But if any CCG officer wished to contest the classification, then they were free to take up the case with the Ministry requesting the evacuation, and this might be the Ministry of Supply or Board of Trade, or one of the Service Ministries. But they would have to be jolly quick; we knew our rights and would brook no delay. I was, in a word, uncompromising, and this was a key factor in achieving the result for which we were known: getting the targets out fast. HQ T-Force knew this, and if occasionally they had to do battle with branches of the Control Commission whose objectives ran counter to ours, then so be it.

One such target consisted of a couple of storage tanks constructed from a special high-grade alloy, and designed for the storage, in the last months of the war, of hydrazine hydrate, a propellant for the V-2 rockets in their assault upon London. Warlike stores if ever there were any. After hostilities ceased, the tanks were put to use for storing milk—in itself a laudable objective, but not so laudable as to override the right of the Service Ministries to examine the tanks and test their resistance to corrosion and pressure. The objection to the evacuation was instigated by an officer of the Control Commission whose undeniably praiseworthy interests were in facilitating the supply of milk to a starving civil population. In the first few months after April 1945 these tanks would have been whisked off without a qualm on anyone's part. But by now enough time had passed for the heat to have cooled, and for some of the civilian officers to have 'gone native', tending to see matters more from the point of view of the prostrate enemy. I, on the other hand, remembered too well the death and destruction so recently wreaked by the V-2 on our civilian population, and I allowed myself to become emotionally engaged. I was still haunted by memories of those victims stripped naked by the blast and drowned in the gutters by the burst water main outside the Natural History Museum in the Cromwell Road. I thought, too, of the lady whose hand, severed at the wrist, reposed neatly on the chest of a friend of ours who lay unconscious in the road. It was the first thing he saw when he recovered consciousness from a blast which had left him otherwise unharmed. I was instinctively unsympathetic to any attempt to stall the evacuation of equipment which had been put indirectly to such lethal use.

One of the prerogatives of officers of T-Force (indeed of anyone bearing the T-Force pass signed by Montgomery's Chief of Staff, Freddie De Guingand) was to requisition without hindrance property bearing or containing a T-Force target—above all in cases of 'warlike stores'—and to keep off those premises any other persons not so authorised. It required an officer of the rank of brigade commander or above to countermand this right. The objecting officer in the case of the tanks had enlisted the support of Colonel Beasley—merely a full colonel—and I was obliged to explain to the Colonel that he would have to involve his immediate superior, Brigadier Barraclough, if he wanted to prevent the evacuation. He couldn't, but he did say that I was the rudest young officer it had ever been his misfortune to deal with. I don't think I was personally rude to him, however chagrined and thwarted he may have felt. My guardian angel at HQ T-Force, designated to pick up the pieces, may have had to bear the brunt for me later, but I never heard any more about it. The tanks went out, the milk found other means of storage. Nobody went without milk as a consequence.

Anyway, did Beasley not know that the Germans had been offered a choice? No, two choices, the first by Goering: 'Guns, or butter?' And they had chosen guns. Then famously by Goebbels, at the Sportpalast in February 1943: *'Wollt Ihr den totalen Krieg?'* ('Do you want total war?') And they bayed their approval. Indeed, Goebbels went on helpfully to describe to them the implications of total war, so that they should be quite clear what they were letting themselves in for.

'If necessary, do you want a war more total and radical than anything that we can even yet imagine?'

'*Jaaa-a-a-a-a!*' they howled.

'Now, people, arise, and let the storm break loose!'

And they arose, and made their high-grade alloys, and their special tanks, and their hydrazine hydrate, and used them to loose their rockets on London. Later, I saw to it that they lost their tanks, and their formulae for the alloy and for the hydrogen peroxide/hydrazine hydrate blend, but somehow they got their milk anyway, and even a very little butter. But, as I said, I did not enter into any controversy.

Capt. M. Howard R.B., H.Q. No. 1 T-Force, B.A.O.R.

20th October 1946

Darling Mama,

My leave vacancy is booked for the 4th of November for 18 days, and I don't think that there will now be any alterations in that. I am booked to play in the Army squash championships on the 18th, but I don't know that I shall perform. Dicky and a friend of his in the 'Phantoms' and I went down to the Mülheim Officers' Club this weekend and played squash there, both on Saturday evening and Sunday a.m. Both times I was on the court I was called away by an urgent call from Rhine Army—such is the price of fame!

I shall probably spend the first day or two of my leave up in London, buying the odd thing or two—a pair of shoes, pants, etc. Luckily my bank balance is quite healthy, and I am now owed about £40 back pay from July 24th as a Captain. I am still only being paid as a Lieut., it takes so long to come through.

The new Colonel arrives tomorrow—he is certainly pleasant as an individual. As a C.O. one cannot say until he takes over.

We are having quite a spell of real autumn, with a spot of mist in the morn-
ing, but lovely warm sunny afternoons: it all puts off the rather depressing
feeling that winter is here—it's such the hell of a long winter in this country,
and the people look miserable enough anyway without being cold too.
All for the moment—thanks for socks, dye and the book.
All my love,
Michael

Despite having had a fortnight in June and a long weekend for the wedding, I was apparently due eighteen days' leave from 4th–22nd November.
The Army Squash Championship was being held at the Lansdowne Club in
London, just off Berkeley Square, from Monday 18th onward, presumably
to finish on Saturday 23rd, when I expected confidently to be back at the
unit. A certain number of the places in the last sixty-four had been allocated
to the Army of the Rhine and, by dint of winning a couple of eliminat-
ing rounds in Germany, I had one of these places and was due on court
on the Monday at 1.30 pm. This at once posed a problem—two, in fact. I
felt I had to go and see the senior tutor, Roy Lubbock, at Peterhouse about
the possibility of getting a Class B release in time to go up to Cambridge
in October 1947, as all the signs were that under ordinary procedures my
group would not be out until at least the end of that year. The only time he
could see me was at noon on the 19th, therefore it was imperative (even if it
was also likely in any case) that I should play no further part in the proceedings after the 18th. How could I ensure this gracefully? I speculated that
I might arrange skilfully to hit the upper part of the tin on the important
points, cursing just enough. Then there was the even more important question for anyone going on court at that hour: do you lunch before or after? If
after, and it went to a fifth game, surely I could easily faint from hunger? So
lunch before it was, and on Monday at noon I was on a bar-stool at Bentley's
Oyster Bar in Swallow Street, W1, ordering a dozen natives and a schooner

of Williams & Humbert's dry sack. By twenty past I had disposed of the lot, and since they were rather small, ordered the same again. Then another half-dozen, and more sack. By the time I went on court there was no need of artifice. Honour was satisfied with four points in each game, which liberated me after a restorative hot shower to do as I pleased the next day. My opponent, an engineer, was rather short and tubby, and was annihilated in his next round.

At Peterhouse the next day Roy Lubbock explained that there was simply no room, the place was full of scholars who had been in precisely my position, but got there first by means of primogeniture. However, quite a number of those returning from service felt, after a brief vain attempt, unable to get down to academic work again, and I was told that if there were any drop-outs from October there would very possibly be a place for me. He told me also that my service would have been long enough to count four terms toward the nine required for the residence qualification, so that I would be able to take my degree in June 1949. I was secretly not at all sure about that; I had in mind an extended period of recreation while I made up my mind what should follow. Five terms seemed too few.

We had already had a look at our postulant commanding officer, Lieutenant-Colonel R F Nason of the Seaforth Highlanders, when he came for a couple of days to visit Peter Brush; they had become friends during the time they spent together as prisoners of war. We gathered that Nason had been very sick at one time, and that it was Peter who had nursed him back to health. Later we would have a better opportunity to decide whether Peter had been well-advised, but first signs were quite promising.

Peter was a great horseman. His book, *The Hunter-Chaser,* was very well received in equestrian circles in 1947. He took us to the races at Dortmund, where his good friend Peter Peel was to be riding 'Stolzenfels', the best horse from the Rifle Brigade string. (Several of these horses were later returned to their French owners, once those owners had been identified.) Peter himself had acquired a very fine German mare called 'Geruta', and his imminent departure on retirement posed the question of what he might do with her. He told me that he would love to have her in Ireland, and said that he had heard that his friend Lieutenant-Colonel Harry Llewellyn (gold medal winner on 'Foxhunter' at the 1952 Helsinki Olympics) had smuggled a horse out by giving it a knockout drop, and putting it in an empty Hercules aero-engine power-egg crate, and getting it flown home by the RAF from Bückeburg. (This was indeed the route by which we flew out some of our urgent, small, high-value items.) He looked at me in an enquiring sort of way, and I managed to look sufficiently appalled to avoid him suggesting straight out, if indeed it had been in his mind, that I might be able to arrange anything of the sort. I never heard what became of 'Geruta'.

To be called from the squash court twice to answer a telephone call from headquarters was not so much a measure of celebrity as of our plain commitment to attend to the demands of our task, come what may, within the least possible time. If an important operation was taking place, then I would let HQ T-Force know where I would be and how they could get hold of me. Nowadays one would just play squash with a mobile phone in one's pocket. The 'Phantoms' were a special branch of the Reconnaissance Regiment, the GHQ Liaison Regiment, where other Riflemen found themselves 'otherwise occupied' in those days.

Capt. M. Howard R.B., H.Q. No. 1 T-Force, B.A.O.R.
31st October 1946

Darling Mama,
a) To report the theft of my watch at once, so that an insurance claim can be put in. The leather strap broke on Monday morning, and I put it in the drawer on my dressing table until I got a new strap. My house is locked, and also my room but I have nevertheless had fags stolen when the room was

locked. The lock cannot be all that difficult to pick. When I came back to my room after lunch I noticed it had gone. I told the police to warn all the watchmakers to look out for it but have had no word of it. It will be miles away on the Black Market by now.

Colonel Peter Brush left today to retire from the army: I am sorry to see him go—he was a good C.O. and very kind to me. Before he went he hauled me aside and said that while he had known me I had been the greatest credit to the regiment and of the utmost service to the unit, and that I was doing a superb job of work; all of which went to my head at once. I put it all down on paper, his exact words as it is an opinion I would value more than most people's. He is a person for whom I have a terrific admiration. And at the end of 27 years soldiering it was nice of him to bother to say that. He has recommended to his successor Col. Nason that when Dicky is demobbed at Christmas I should take over the job of Adjutant: which is about the highest honour he could give me. I didn't tell him that I would rather stay on in my own infinitely more interesting job, as it would have hurt his feelings, but I shall ask Col. Nason if he would consider letting me stay on as I.O. He also said that he had put in a very strong recommendation for me for a C.-in-C.'s certificate for distinguished service, but of course there is no guarantee that I will get one as there are only 250 names on the New Year list. Still, it was nice of him to do that much. So at the moment I am fair wallowing in a trough of self-satisfaction.

Yesterday I went to Hanover (110 miles) and 'acquired' about 35 records, which I shall either bring with me or send in advance by post. They include the following:

Beethoven's 3rd, 4th and 6th Symphonies with the Berlin Philharmonic, Beethoven's 5th Symphony with the Dresden Philharmonic, Mozart's 41st (Jupiter) Symphony with the Turin Philharmonic, Beethoven's Moonlight Sonata and Schubert's Trout Quintet—and all at a ridiculously cheap price. I hope to bring home some rather moderate liqueurs and if we don't come to

drink them as they are, they make a good base for cocktails.
No more news that won't keep until I see you—6 days now.
All my love,
Michael

It was slightly unnerving to realise that one's personal possessions were not secure, even in a drawer in a locked room in a locked house. That I had previously missed cigarettes in such circumstances implied that the thief was probably German, because no member of the unit would regard cigarettes worth stealing since they would have access to their own supply. Those civilians who had access to my room in the course of their employment, Tuppence and my Hungarian batman,[22] could not afford to have suspicion fall on them—their employment brought them pay and a hot midday meal, so it was too valuable for them to put it at risk. It remained an unsolved riddle, and the watch was never recovered. Watches were at a premium in the civilian market, available only at black market prices or from the Officers' Shops—and those not very good ones. Alarm clocks were available through the watch and clock trade at normal prices in Rentenmarks, but only for miners, who had to rise early to go on shift on time. Bill White had, for reasons I have already touched on, some difficulty in waking and rising in the morning. Having little German, he asked me to go with him to the watchmaker in the square and help him acquire an alarm clock. We were both in uniform. *'Sind Sie Bergarbeiter?'* asked the watchmaker drily. ('Are you miners?') I translated to Bill, who replied: 'My dear, I'm too, too *Bergarbeiter.'* We didn't get an alarm clock.

In our loosely structured set-up, Peter Brush had been the one fixed point. Born in 1901, he was more than twice my age. We did not know it then, but it was the many trials that he had been through at the Defence of Calais and as a POW that had made him a man carved in rock. Had he not been taken

---

22 I apologise to any reader startled by the sudden appearance of a Hungarian batman. I knew very little about him and his history at the time, and now remember almost nothing.

prisoner, he must surely have achieved high command, a fighting brigadier at least. We young officers admired him enormously. It was typical of him that he would not go without first calling me in to thank me for my services. He had kindly put my name forward with a strong recommendation for a Commander-in-Chief's Certificate in the Christmas honours list. This was not for 'distinguished service', as I then described it, but for 'efficiency'—about all that was open to me. I didn't get the award, but his mention of it, about which I knew nothing, spurred me into putting forward the name of Sergeant Wigg. Wigg did get the award and so he should have done, and it did him more good than it would have done me.

For Peter, as for any young regular soldier, the peak of his ambition as a junior officer had been to be selected Adjutant, an ambition which Peter himself had achieved, and had taken pride in. In recommending that I should follow Dicky as Colonel Nason's Adjutant he was paying me a compliment, despite the kind words he had found for my work as Intelligence Officer.

I had no real impression of the depth of Peter's Irishness, I did not know then that his fourth given name was Howard. My father was only ten years his senior and born at Dungannon not twenty miles as the crow flies from Drumnabreeze at Magheralin, County Down where Peter lived, as did his father George Howard Brush. So we never had occasion to explore the possibility of a common ancestry.[23]

---

23 In retirement he was always busy in Territorial Army affairs, and in 1954 became chairman of the Territorial & Auxiliary Forces Association in County Down until 1965, which brought him the award of the CB in 1966. He was also Deputy Lieutenant for County Down for twenty years from 1953. Frustrated by the lack of political progress in the Province, he lent his support to Down Orange Welfare, a cover organisation for a loyalist paramilitary force which he led clandestinely, and in 1975 he claimed to be able to put an army of five thousand in the field at a moment's notice. Shocked as I was to read about this in later life, and though I would never have been comfortable with his politics (and of course politics, and particularly Irish politics, were never a subject for discussion in the Mess), nothing could have diminished my admiration and liking for the man.

We learned from our opposite numbers in No 2 T-Force, whose HQ was at Bad Nenndorf some twenty miles from Hanover, that Deutsche Grammophon there were in full production of records—seventy-eights, of course—and that they were only too happy to accommodate customers at the rate of three cigarettes per disc as between a willing buyer and willing seller. I found a quiet day and beat my way up there in a Humber 4x4, returning triumphant with a pile of symphonies and chamber music. The transaction involved no negotiation, the ground rules were known on both sides; it left me feeling only slightly sheepish. The discs were terribly heavy and, because there was no-one in the Mess who shared my tastes, I carried the considerable load home on leave.

Life in the Army of the Rhine had lent a certain air of unreality to my perception of the place of liquor in life on civvy street. My supposition that rather moderate liqueurs would be a useful basis for champagne cocktails was founded on extensive experience while waiting for posting from 54RHU at Osnabrück. There, several new varieties were explored in good company, and the predilection did not entirely leave me until I had completed the education I enjoyed at Cambridge at government expense, and long since spent my gratuity. I don't think I have made a champagne cocktail for fifty years.

Capt. M. Howard R.B., H.Q. No. 1 T-Force, B.A.O.R.
24th November 1946

Darling Mama,

I have settled right in after a most enjoyable leave—much as I enjoyed it, I feel no pangs at settling down to this again, which I now take as my normal existence. I never cease highly to congratulate myself on the combination of circumstances which placed me here—I could hardly have been more fortunate.

Robin is with me—he restores the balance in a Mess which tends to be humourless and saves it from being just a vulgar brawl. Luckily the Colonel rates the value of his company as highly as I do, and would be most reluctant to post him elsewhere.

I am now almost certain not to be made to do Adjutant. The case arose when I was on leave, and the G.2 had the kindness to say that whereas there were others who could manage the job of Adjutant, he did not know of any who would be able to do I.O.—and so I have been left where I am.

I enclose copies of photos taken at our Farewell dinner for Col. Brush. These are just two of which I have more than one copy—the others I shall send later. Some of the last photos I took indoors came out well, and one only of the front of the house, I shall send copies as soon as possible.

My journey over by sea was not so much of an ordeal as it might have been, as we set off so late that I was safely in my bunk by the time that we really started rolling—as indeed we did.

Germany is hungrier than ever—food was stolen from two of our houses last night. I don't blame them, even though it has got to be stopped. We now have 'Mob Squads' organised, but we don't anticipate real trouble here.

The weather is remarkably clement considering the time and place—nevertheless I have got hold of a real pair of skating boots which I have attached to my skates.

All my love,

Michael

During my leave I visited Cambridge and Rugby in my mother's car, a Humber Super Snipe with the same engine as 1 Bucks' Humber scout cars, and quite powerful. I had sold my little red J-Type MG 'Tosca' in anticipation of getting a new MG TC-Series from Stewart and Ardern in Berkeley Square. By the time I was demobbed about a year later, there was quite a waiting list. That I was able to afford a car in the first place was due to the prescience of my grandfather who, when gold was first discovered in Fiji, bought for my sister and myself a share in the mine. An Australian who knew a little geology and mineralogy had pitched his tent (so the story goes), set up a hammock between a couple of coconut trees, hired a Fijian labourer, said, 'Dig, you black bastard, dig,' gone to sleep in his hammock, and lo! the Fijian struck pay-dirt really quite quickly. The Australian incorporated his mine, and my grandfather bought a handful of shares which, as an administrative officer, my father was debarred from doing. Over the years the investment had appreciated in value to the point where selling the shares enabled my sister and me each to buy a car, something we could not otherwise have done.

The arrival of Robin Smyth was the greatest amelioration of the lot of all of us in the Mess, and fortunately Colonel Nason took to him straight away and decided that he did not want to push him on to one of the outlying detachments. So Robin was for the time being lodged in A Detachment in Kamen, and hence a member of our Mess. Nason had discovered that Smyth Senior was a distinguished and much decorated soldier who had commanded a brigade at Dunkirk and a division in Burma, and consequently calculated that it might be wise from a social point-of-view to keep Robin handy. Quite right too: Robin was always original and amusing, and a great asset to the Mess. Even Ronnie Coe seemed to find him personally unobjectionable, even though Robin added to the number of subalterns whom Ronnie was convinced had been born with silver spoons in their mouths. It was a Howard family saying that such-and-such a person would 'lend a tone to what might otherwise become a vulgar brawl', and this was something that Robin's influence would certainly do for the T-Force Mess at Kamen. 'Live graciously,' he would admonish us.

I must try to remember who else was in the Mess at that time. Apart from our new Colonel, and Ronnie Coe, and Jack Griffiths the Quartermaster, and Dicky Muir, A Detachment was now commanded by a most agreeable officer, Major Charlie Lambert, an older man from a Corps where physical fitness was not a requisite. In civilian life Charlie was a musician and musicologist, and a conductor; it was mere coincidence that he was a contemporary of the more famous Constant Lambert, composer and conductor, but we called him 'Constant' anyway. Amiable, hard to provoke, educated, and knowledgeable, he added another dimension to the Mess. It was now possible to have a serious discussion about classical music, a subject upon which we were all capable of learning more. His second-in-command was a rather wishy-washy cavalry captain—so anonymous, in fact, that his name escapes me. I do remember that his wife was Maltese and they had married quarters, so he was not often in the Mess. I had no business dealings with him, and hardly noticed when he went.

John Bayley was to be with us for another ten months. He had more inner resources perhaps than any of us, he was self-contained and unobtrusive—and better read than the rest of us. He believed that the more exercise you took, the more you needed; it was a risk he preferred not to run. After dinner one evening, Robin and I said, 'Come on, John, let's take a walk round the block.'

'What?' he said, shocked. 'N-not the *whole* block?'

Probably the least obtrusive Old Etonian I have ever met, he never to my knowledge wore the tie. His unjustified self-effacement was part of his considerable charm. When, a couple or so years later, he was introduced by Lord David Cecil as the Newdigate Verse prizeman, to read his prize poem before a distinguished audience at Oxford, he started off, 'W-well, it's n-not very g-good, b-but h-here it is!'

More obtrusive (though still not very) was Johnny Pepys Cockerell, recently come to us from the 60th with whom he had seen action at the end of the war. Having had a platoon of Cockneys, he enjoyed a perfect command of Cockney slang which he used freely and with an absolutely authentic intonation. He was entirely at home in that vernacular and could be as foul-mouthed as any of his soldiers, but he could then switch seamlessly to classic Old Etonian. He also rejoiced in an effortless mastery of all the filthiest of the common soldier's filthy songs, but sadly he really only had the chance to trot them out on the evenings when a handful of us went over to the Sergeants' Mess for a drink after dinner. Even they were shocked. Tall and unathletic, and by no means an intellectual, he nevertheless had a place waiting for him at Oxford, which he took up in September 1947. He never missed a night out when a party of us went to a club for dinner, and in spite of his somewhat saturnine and even faintly sinister appearance, he always added to the gaiety.

Our third Old Etonian, Tony Chance had left by this time to read English at Oxford, but in the end his nervous disposition prevented him from sitting his final exams and he left without taking his degree. It made little difference to his prospects. Five years later we shared digs for a while in Beaufort Gardens; he was undertaking an art course at the Heatherley School of Fine Art in Chelsea and rather sweetly, I thought, expressed some shock on finding that the models at the life class actually took their clothes off.

Word was by now reaching high places back at home of the speed and efficiency with which our task was being accomplished. We were all amused to hear that, in the House of Commons, the Conservative MP for the Isle of Wight Sir Peter Macdonald had asked of the President of the Board of Trade, Sir Stafford Cripps, 'Who *are* these bright young men?' The reply was not retailed to us, but we liked to think we knew who they were.

One of my attempts at living graciously was the recruitment of a piano player who I hoped might 'lend a tone' in the Mess in the evenings. Like the Messerschmitt pilot, he was a man who stood out in a crowd, especially because of his imposing height at six foot ten. Again, I spotted him walking across the square towards us, and again I had the guard go and bring him to me. I asked him what was his occupation, and he said he was an unemployed musician. He had been the principal bass at the Dortmund Opera, but he was also a pianist. With the agreement of my Mess-mates I arranged for him to come one evening and play the piano and sing in the conservatory next to the ante-room and dining-room, and he did so very pleasantly. We paid him handsomely in cigarettes, at several times the going rate. He had an extensive, mostly classical repertoire, and we asked him to come again on a weekly basis, for the time being. After five or six weeks he asked to be allowed to play some of his own compositions, to which we readily assented, but it was not music we would have chosen. Naturally he began to exhaust his repertoire, and we brought the arrangement to a friendly conclusion. We had not been mean, and he had done well out of it. He must have moved on, for I did not see him in the town again. We did not further extend our patronage of the local arts.

In my absence on leave, Peter Brush's recommendation had been at work, and Nason made an attempt to move me over to replace Dicky as his Adjutant. My position was defended in my absence by Bill Adams, who was quite positive that I had become irreplaceable as Intelligence Officer, and would if necessary have produced the same opinion from HQ T-Force to dissuade the Colonel—or failing that, an order.

My sympathy for the hungry populace did not extend to letting them get away with stealing food from the Mess. None of the civil legal penalties would have any deterrent effect. Mob Squads were ordered to ensure that no-one caught stealing from our quarters should retain any inclination ever to attempt it again. This might involve a degree of rough treatment, but we had to feel secure in our own quarters. Life was hard, and in a sense surviving in gaol was easier than in the world outside (at least you were fed the minimum ration regularly), so imprisonment was no threat at all.

My experience of skating had been limited to an hour or two on the several miles of frozen fields flooded by the Medway between Forest Row and Hartfield during the winter of 1939/40 and then on the frozen swimming pool at Rugby in 1943. I was broadly incompetent, and regarded the occasional fall as part of the game. My Hungarian batman took great exception to this cavalier attitude, and insisted that it was not fitting that the *Herr Hauptmann* should be seen in an inelegant posture in public, even if only while skating. Our skating rink was a shallow pond a foot deep in front of the telephone exchange and only a couple of hundred yards from my billet. I found myself unable to heed my batman's advice about appropriate etiquette.

His rather prim view of the proprieties came to the fore again in relation to another of our sporting activities, badminton, of which Colonel Nason was rather fond. It was something he and his fellow POWs had been able to play in prison camp. In Kamen we could play in an indoor arena, a *Turnhalle*, and we could book it for our use pretty well whenever we wanted. But it was a public space and we had neither reason nor inclination to call for the area to be cleared while we played, usually in the early evening. The Colonel would be partnered by his second-in-command, Ronnie Coe, and Robin and I would play together. Although we were reasonably evenly matched, Robin and I invariably won, but there was no question of changing the pairings— Ronnie would never have relinquished an opportunity to prove the older men better than their younger subordinates. My batman approached me one day and asked if it was true that the junior officers were permitted to be seen to beat their seniors. I confirmed that this was the case. He shook his head reprovingly: 'It would never have been allowed in the German Army.'

Capt. M. Howard R.B., H.Q. No. 1 T-Force, B.A.O.R.
5th December 1946

Darling Mama,

Busy is a pathetic understatement for what we are at the moment. I don't get out of my office until 7.30 in the evening as a rule—we are at the moment averaging 60 letters a day. I gather that we are doing as much as possible under our normal procedure before the New Year, when increased activity starts on a speeded up clearance procedure: my job is definitely not packing up on me! I have written to Harrow in Malta telling him the situation about Anne and asking him to do his best.

Another dastardly attempt this week to make me Adjutant—again sternly put down by Bill Adams. Unfortunately all those tried so far have proved themselves incompetent. I haven't had the chance to prove that although I manage this job with an assumed air of efficiency, I would be as useless as the others as an Adjutant.

Your parcel arrived O.K., thanks. Did you see the photos—do you want any copies or have you got some? They turned out quite well considering the awful weather that day.

Robin's a treasure. He keeps us all amused: he makes the Colonel laugh like a drain. He is NO SOLDIER—as were so many of my platoon. I could not hope for better company.

Enclosed are photos of our farewell party to Col. Brush. I have written on the back who the various people are—an awfully good one of Col. Peter and Dicky.

The mildest imaginable weather here—though there are a few inches of snow 35 miles to the south.

No more news.

All my love,

Michael

Since my sister Anne and her new husband had no right to married quarters in the Valetta suburb of Sliema when they arrived in Malta, they might need help finding somewhere to live not far from the Grand Harbour, but who Harrow was and how he might have helped, I no longer remember.

Anyone reading my letters home might be forgiven for assuming that I regarded our daily tally of letters produced in the office to be an end in itself, but that was not so. An almost direct relationship existed between the number of letters we wrote and the number of 'serials' (items of equipment or documents) we evacuated. A count of those was kept as well, but that was not for consumption outside official circles—HQ T-Force, BIOS, and the several Ministries. Anyway, the intrinsic importance of the uninterrupted flow of equipment and documents would make little or no impression on public consciousness either then or in later years when, if ever, an account of the evacuation programme came to be written.

Certainly any account of what might be seen as the extraction of the gold fillings from the teeth of German military-industrial technology and intellectual property in the Ruhr would be spectacularly unspectacular—and that was precisely how His Majesty's Government wanted it. Any comparison with the almost indiscriminately rapacious parallel activities of the Russians in sacking German industry in their Zone was deemed undesirable. A later assessment was that the Russians had taken a thousand tons for every hundred of ours, even unto the water closets and urinals, those astonishing new appliances they were finding apparently in daily use. But that did not justify drawing attention to what we were up to by means, for example, of anything in the nature of a catalogue—especially in the light of the critical attitude we were adopting towards the Russians.

Room for a speeding up of the 'clearance' procedure existed primarily within the offices of the Control Commission, between the RDR Division who issued the Form 80G and the branches of the Trade and Industry Division responsible for all the different sectors of German industry. That was where any delay lay and, if they were able to speed it up, we would have no difficulty in coping with the consequences. We would simply have to work even longer hours, and put more people on it.

Dicky Muir, whose tenure of the office of Adjutant would end with his demobilisation soon after Christmas, did not find Bill Adams' assertion that almost any nitwit could do the Adjutant's job very flattering. Nor, presumably, would he have cared to concede that the Intelligence Officer's job which he had performed before my appointment had grown in the interim by an order of magnitude, which made it by virtue of its operational nature the more important of the two. He tried two or three of our colleagues as assistants and understudies, and rejected them all as incompetent and unsuitable to take over from him. He had allowed himself to be a little seduced by the aura generally surrounding the office of Adjutant—the most senior and influential position short of field rank—which he had grasped so eagerly. In the end an outsider was drafted in to do the job, Roy Smith of the Warwickshires, who was to fill the role unexceptionably for a few months.

For us the signs for Colonel Nason as CO were rather good; anyone who could laugh like a drain at Robin couldn't be all bad. Indeed, Robin's wry sense of humour and penchant for verbal wit lifted us all, and it had ensured that Robin had not been incontinently despatched to one of the outlying detachments where he would have been wasted. I had my eye on him at once as a potential assistant to myself, something the still-increasing volume of work had begun to justify. The demands on me personally in terms of hours of work and weekends spent in the office had been considerable, and I was beginning to feel entitled to some relief, as well as the confidence to ask for it.

Kamen stood only 210 feet above sea-level. It lay on the rather miserable, slow-flowing Seseke, which ran into the River Lippe near Lünen, which itself debouched into the Rhine at Wesel. Nearby to the south where the snow was beginning to lie, the Ebbegebirge rose to over 2,100 feet, by standard yardsticks a full four degrees Fahrenheit colder than with us at the lower level. Winterberg, sixty miles to the east and with its ski school on the Kahler Asten at 2,750 feet, is higher and colder still, and with another hard winter in prospect the milder weather in early December was a temporary relief. The cold would once again prove to be a killer in our grim, grey little town.

Capt. M. Howard R.B., H.Q. No. 1 T-Force, B.A.O.R.

15th December 1946

Darling Mama,

I know I am naughty—but as mitigation (there is no excuse) we have just had the most almighty flap. Someone thought that reparations deliveries were to stop at the end of the year and that gave us 30 days to do some 4 months' work. We were about halfway through that lot when we were told to relax two days ago. For the last twelve days I have been writing some 50 letters per diem, been rung up at all hours, and been to three conferences. The day before yesterday was the first time that I got to bed before midnight. The flap is now off, but we still have some £5,000,000 worth of machinery or 6.5 thousand tons to move—so my job isn't folding in on me at any rate.

Since I came back there have been three determined attempts to make me Adjutant. All have been successfully fought off. It is a full day's job with practically nothing to do, and I don't want it. The only way to tolerate the life out here is to keep busy. Robin is away for 10 days doing acting G.3 Equipment at H.Q. T-Force at Bad Oeynhausen, and so I have him at the other end of a telephone line: at any rate he gives the impression of understanding what he says. Dicky has managed to get his month's course at the University of the Army of the Rhine extended for another month, so we won't see him for five weeks yet—he is not bad company, but a bit of a strain, and the Mess is quite placid without him—he is always having rows with the 2 i/c. Snow here for the first time today, although one of our Messes south of here has had 6–9 inches for about a week. On Monday I have got to try to get through to Siegen, about 90 miles south of here over the mountains, but the snow may hold me up. I should get some good snaps of the scenery on the way. The people round here look sick already, so God knows what it will be like when the worst of the winter really hits them. Now the children are beginning to look bad, which is heart-rending. Even here, where we are in a more or less agricultural area, people are just folding up in the street—about three die every two days. We are giving a party to the children (300 of them) at Christmas; there are 2,000 destitute children in Kamen, and most of those chosen for the party will be so unaccustomed to eating large quantities of food, that their bellies probably won't be equal to the occasion. And the men, out of whose rations the food is being provided, probably won't even notice the cut.

The attached cuttings about the B.I.O.S. exhibition may interest you. I have been informed that if I happen to be in London between 10–19 December, I am allowed to go to see it—they don't give me a short leave to go over. 70% of the exhibits are jobs which I have hauled out, so I am a bit sore at not being able to visit it.

Could you manage to send my large red Cassell's German dictionary—they haven't got anything as good out here.

SUNDAY—27 degrees of frost last night and a cold dry east wind this morning, but now the clouds are piling up again for another fall of snow. If it freezes tonight like it did last night we shall be able to start skating—I wonder whether I can—it is years since I had the chance.

We don't get much here in the way of entertainment. We get two film shows a week, but it is not always that either are worth going to. This week however they are showing Dead of Night—very much worth going to see. Did you see that news flick with the film taken from a V-2 fired in the Mexican desert?

As I write, it is beginning to snow again—I am in two minds about my journey to Siegen tomorrow—the mountains are about 3,500 feet high, and the road pretty tortuous.

All my love,

Michael

There was constant guerrilla warfare between the powers of darkness on the one hand (T-Force, BIOS and the Chiefs of Staff), who insisted that Britain should have its pound of flesh by means of the evacuation programme, and the forces of goodness and light on the other (the Foreign Office, the Control Commission, and anyone else who thought that we should forgive and forget, or just put the Germans to work to feed and pay for themselves). It was a question of priorities, and these began to change with time. In the end there was the usual compromise, achieved by putting a term to T-Force operations, with no new demands to be made after 30th June 1947, but continuing evacuation of any serials approved before that date.

For ten days we had been victims of the latest false alarm: that everything had to be out by the end of the year. But after ten days of working pretty well night and day, I still had six and a half thousand tons of equipment valued at five million pounds to get out. Conferences took place at different levels— HQ Rhine Army at Bad Oeynhausen, HQ CCG at Minden, Regional HQ CCG at Düsseldorf—in order to rehearse, frankly, the same points. Robin was suddenly drafted in to plug a short-term gap at HQ T-Force where they were almost as busy as we were. In the end we secured what we considered to be our rights and were given the time we needed. I was able to resume a less frenetic tempo of life and go to bed at a normal time again, as were my sterling young staff, whose billets were above our offices. I never knew who had set that valuation upon the stuff due to go, probably its depreciated cost, but it was nowhere near the valuation settled on it in 1948/9.

Nobody had bothered to tell Nason that they were not going to let him take me away from my job, so the attempts went on. In a unit like ours there was nothing like a full day's work in the job of Adjutant. It consisted mostly of remaining at the Colonel's beck and call rather like a PA, and much of it could be done by the Orderly-Room Staff Sergeant. The situation was exacerbated by Dicky Muir taking the fullest advantage of the educational facilities offered by the Army of the Rhine prior to his own demobilisation, which of course left us short when we could least afford it. Having missed the beginning of the academic year at Cambridge in 1946, he had arranged to spend the spring semester and summer at the Sorbonne in Paris before going up to King's College Cambridge in Michaelmas term 1947. By the end we were not all that sorry to see him go. When the rest of us wanted to relax and have a bit of peace and quiet in the Mess, Dicky could not bear to pass up any pretext for picking a row with Ronnie Coe, who was of course equally quick on the trigger. Claiming to have been born a couple of gins below par, it was Dicky's habit to rectify the disparity before coming down in the evening for a more public drink before dinner, with a slight whiff of

Eau de Cologne about him—which was in itself enough to set Ronnie off. Testosterone overload.

Winter had arrived with a vengeance by the Saturday night, with fifteen degrees Centigrade of frost, enough to have a visible effect on the civil population. Apart from keeping them indoors in their cold houses, it slowed them down as they walked, and I found the condition of the thin, rickety and shivering children distressing. The regular parade of horse-drawn hearses plodded on past my office window. At such times you cannot help everybody; many had to be left to starve, some to die. It was a hard lesson to learn. By this time we were taking a small (frankly, hardly perceptible) cut in our rations in order to have enough to give a Christmas party to some of the children, many of whom were fatherless in the wake of the February mine disaster. But it was a palliative, a sticking-plaster only.

The trip south to Siegen posed the perennial problem: driving on snow and ice. Which was better, the Volkswagen or the Humber 4x4? In theory the latter, in practice the former, or so we learned by trial and error. I don't know where I got the idea that the mountains on the way were as high as Snowdon, I don't think any of our road-maps, including the one which hung on the office wall, had any altitudes marked. The road may have seemed that high, but in fact it was little more than half what I thought. One learned to drive on snow and ice, or not at all. Slip your clutch rather than your wheels, drive in the highest gear you can without stalling, never touch your brakes. It still works.

Twice a week the AKC (the eccentrically initialled Army Kinema Corporation—who ever went to a 'Kinema' outside Greece?) took over the local cinema in Kamen, and we got a fair assortment of the good, bad and indifferent. The *Pathé News* kept us up-to-date with what was being shown to our families in the UK, a very important link with at least one view of reality. *Dead of Night* was a film distinguished from the ordinary by the spine-chilling episode where Michael Redgrave's malicious little ventriloquist's dummy takes him over. During the summer the public cinema had shown the film of the liberation of Belsen, widely believed among the civil population to be a propagandist fabrication, and thus widely boycotted. I asked the unwilling Kunsemüller family to go; they were genuinely appalled.

The BIOS Exhibition in London was open to all comers, and displayed what we had managed to extract from German industry so far. I thought it a bit rich to be sent permission to visit if I happened to be in London. Presumably they realised that I would be busy extracting the rest; or perhaps they thought that all those targets trotted out of their own accord?

Capt. M. Howard R.B., H.Q. No. 1 T-Force, B.A.O.R.

20th December 1946

Darling Mama,

I have been waiting in the hope of being able to pick up some small present to accompany my wishes that you will have the happiest of Christmases. All the sorts of things one can get out here are pathetically tawdry, and not the sort of thing one wants in any case. I know you will appreciate the difficulty, and as I lay my hands on the things I have in mind, I shall label 'Xmas' on them.

Christmas threatens to be unexciting. We have of course to serve the men with their midday meal, and we are dismissing the German staff after they have served us with ours. I then anticipate going down to our Mess at Lüdenscheid in the hills and achieving extreme mellowness with Robin and one or two others. At the moment we are having the most vile weather. After the first fall of snow, about an inch, it froze hard, and it has not touched above 10°F below freezing point for some days, and has been as low as 28°F below. Skating is near at hand. I have tried twice and am going later this afternoon. I have a warm room with hot water, and a bar downstairs, so I have no complaints.

We gave our Christmas party to 340 poor children—most of them had never seen anything like it, poor kids. Some of them were sweeping the breadcrumbs into their handkerchiefs.

Thank you darling for the shaving brush, a lovely soft one, and not inclined to moult—also many cigarettes. The Swedish Red Cross has given every man in the unit 2 dozen Havana No. 2 cigars—I hope Daddy can cope with them—all I want is one to convince me that I don't really like them.

All my love,

Michael

My 'Happy Christmas' letter home underlined the difficulty in shopping for anything much more than the bare necessities. We did not even have access to an American Post Exchange much short of Frankfurt, and even then they were barely more elaborate than the Officers' Shop at I Corps HQ at Iserlohn. I should of course have thought about presents while on leave in November, but Christmas seemed too far into the future then.

A Detachment had operated an Investigators' Mess in Lüdenscheid since early 1 Bucks days. It was handy for targets in Iserlohn, Witten, Hagen and Siegen—never a very large number but they needed to be catered for. The Mess was looked after by a sergeant and a couple of lance corporals, with civilian staff to do the cooking, waiting, and other menial work. We warned them by phone when we were sending anyone down to them, so that they could indent for rations and other supplies. Otherwise they were on their own, and we had to rely on using some of our best and most reliable NCOs on such a remote detachment. They made themselves very much at home there. I don't think we looked very closely into matters (their love-lives, for example), but at least no scandals ever emerged, and the occasional inspections revealed no deficiencies. They were appreciative whenever we dropped in, as I did on a couple of occasions on my way to and from targets in Siegen. But this time I didn't make it down to Lüdenscheid as planned. The roads were like ice—and ice, in fact, they were, for gritting had not been invented. It was thirty-five miles south to Lüdenscheid, and we had not been expecting to stay strictly sober. The prospect, which we could not entirely ignore, of spending the night in the ditch in fifteen degrees of frost held little charm for the sake of a brief change of scene and more exclusive company. The freeze was on and, bar one momentary thaw, was to last for fifty-six days before we were to experience the dizzy heights of zero again.

I cannot think what possessed the Swedish Red Cross to give every man of ours two dozen Havana cigars. Perhaps it was to assuage a sense of guilt over Sweden having remained neutral in the late, great conflict, and if anything favouring the wrong side by meeting the majority of their need for iron ore. Still, I suppose it had suited us all to have a couple of neutral intermediaries in Sweden and Switzerland. But two dozen Havana cigars for men whose currency was cigarettes? Perhaps that was why.

Capt. M. Howard R.B., H.Q. No. 1 T-Force, B.A.O.R.

28th December 1946

Darling Mama,

Just a note to add my love and good wishes for the first of January. I hope your daughter and son-in-law will be handy to sip a tot with you.

We had a conventional army Christmas—not much sleep, and an excess of alcohol. We played the usual game of fancy dress football in the morning against the men, and then served them their lunch. Our own Xmas fare we did not consume until Boxing Day.

I spent Christmas evening with the Grevel family, and dined with them. On Boxing morning I had the doctor's three children (23, 21 and 20!) round here for mid-morning coffee, and for sherry. All highly illegal, but it made it more like Christmas.

Tomorrow the Colonel and I start a tour of North Rhine and Westphalia provinces to find hotel accommodation, and should see some interesting spots on the way. The snow has gone, and it is quite temperate again, in spite of four inches of ice on the ponds still.

In a confidential document I saw, the value of T-Force to the country in the last year was given as not less than £100,000,000, but it said that it will take years to judge the full value. If you can lay your hands on the Daily Express of 9th October, I believe there is an article of interest in it on the subject.

Wireless reception in this spot is superb and one can always get good music—one of the few ways of staying sane in a Mess where subjects for conversation seem heavily restricted.

Three more R.B. officers on the way from England—no buddies of mine, though one I know vaguely.

All my love,

Michael

My parents' wedding anniversary was on New Year's Day, a hard one to forget.

It was a new convention to me, the officers playing the other ranks at football on Christmas morning in fancy dress—anything exotic would do, cross-dressing preferred but hard to get hold of in Kamen. Then we and the sergeants served the men their 'Christmas dinner' at lunchtime: turkey and all the trimmings, Christmas pudding, mince pies, claret, port and brandy. A great effort had been made to provide a 'traditional' Christmas for us all. The sergeants had their dinner in the afternoon, and had devised their own entertainment for the evening. Having donned side-arms, they proceeded *en masse* to the prison, requisitioned the keys, locked the warders in a couple of cells, then set the prisoners free and corralled them into the canteen, where they were served soup and a meat stew. The sergeants then took them back to their cells, locked them up again, and finally liberated the warders and returned the keys. The action was not highly publicised; everyone stayed schtum and there was certainly no complaint from the German side. It was as if nothing had happened. Goodwill to all men at Christmas, courtesy of the Regimental Quartermaster Sergeant. Jack Griffiths probably knew perfectly well what was up, but it never reached the Colonel's ear.

The Grevels had invited me for a meal in the evening of Christmas day. The scruples which had earlier not allowed me to eat as the guest of a German family inhibited me no longer, perhaps because I knew more by then about their personal circumstances and accepted their assurances, i.e. that they would not themselves suffer deprivation by giving me a meal. I was the only guest of the four of them—Mutti and all three young women; it was a signal honour. For me there were two presents from Marianne, and both were books. In one there was a pressed, dried flower and the inscription, *'Für Dich, Michael, unsere zweite Friedensweihnachten in Deutschland.'* ('For you, Michael, our second Christmas at peace in Germany.') The other was an anthology, entitled *Der Deutsche (The German)*, which described and praised the virtues of the good, true German—a relic of the Germany of Josef Goebbels. It, too, was inscribed by Marianne, this time with a quotation from the 17th century sage and aphorist Angelus Silesius: *'Freund, so Du etwas bist, so bleib doch ja nicht stehn: man muss von einem Licht fort in das andre gehen!'* ('My friend, if you are to be anything, don't just stand there, you must go forth from one light into the next!') This was to be, after ten months, the watershed, in the nature of an implied ultimatum from giver to receiver, and perhaps it was only natural. Cooped up in those small premises in that depressed and drab little town, Marianne was younger, brighter, livelier and more beautiful than her two sisters. With the few young males in the area who had survived war, displacement and the Bergkamen mine disaster left without work and metaphorically impotent, I may have been seen as a potential *deus ex machina* come down from the still threatening clouds to lift her up out of all that. It was not a role that I envisaged for myself, and the next time we met a couple of weeks later she will have realised that I was not about to take the hint, and that nothing had changed. For she asked me straight out if I could give her a job, admitting quite frankly that she could do with the extra rations courtesy of the midday meal which came with employment with T-Force. Her command of English certainly equipped her more than adequately for work as an interpreter, but there was no way I could have her working for me. I already had two interpreters whom I hardly used, and since our friendship was known at least to some, the move would at once be misinterpreted. I did say that I would put the question to A Detachment—the principal employer in Kamen—in case they had a vacancy for an interpreter, and that I would recommend her. Happily, A Detachment did indeed need an interpreter, and they employed her at once to work for Don Cropper. It was not long before I became aware that a close personal relationship was developing between them. I doubt whether I saw myself deprived of the friendship of a beautiful young woman without a slight bruise to my *amour propre*, but it was a superficial wound.

I never visited the Grevel's house again, but I knew that Don did. There was never any discussion between Don and myself on the subject; our relations were entirely civil rather than cool, but we had never been going to be exactly buddies. He had always been very reticent about his personal circumstances and there was no reason why it should not stay that way. By the time I was demobbed, Don was still working for A Detachment in the Evacuation Office, and Marianne for him, but when I went back to Germany in 1949 he was no longer with the rump of T-Force.[24]

While I was not courting any emotional entanglement, the possibility of exposure to one existed nearer home—that is, in the doctor's house which we

---

24 He found other employment in Germany into the 1960s, both with the Control Commission and elsewhere, and Marianne stayed with him throughout that time. They married when he became free to do so. In the early 1960s they came to live in London and Don became Secretary-General of the National Association and the International Confederation of Employment Agencies. In 1968 they had a son, John, whom they later sent to school at Oundle. Eventually, they retired to the Fens of Lincolnshire. A happy end to a story which began not without complications at a time when in Germany, and above all in the Ruhr, the outlook was bleak.

occupied. In the morning on Boxing Day we, that is Robin and I, entertained our contemporaries the doctor's three children for mid-morning coffee followed by a glass of sherry. There was an argument, a little specious perhaps, that the doctor was a prominent local citizen, that T-Force was occupying his premises illegally, and that using coffee and sherry in *demi-tasse* quantities was performing a useful service by keeping them all sweet. We did not try to justify ourselves—it would have been a little disingenuous.

Colonel Nason took it upon himself to make a formal search for more accommodation for our BIOS investigators, though no-one else seemed to notice any shortage. The basin of the Ruhr and its environs, which provided more than eighty per cent of our targets, extended only about fifty miles from north to south, and the same from east of Dortmund to west of Düsseldorf, and the area was already fairly well packed with our investigators' Messes and hotels. Travelling another five or ten miles to their target each day was a matter of another five or ten minutes in the plentiful transport we provided—hardly arduous. Nason made no attempt to tell me why he wished me to accompany him when he knew I had other priorities. The tour was cursory and produced no result whatever, but it might have made him feel useful, which was desirable from a social point of view. And it did enable me to get to know him a little better. He was a man without imagination, but largely without inherent vice or malice either. He must at some stage of his career have had the ability to take decisions, but this faculty had been drained from him by those terribly hard years as a prisoner of war when the scope for freedom of action was highly circumscribed. It was a war he had entered as a major, so he was without experience in command of a battalion (which was how No 1 T-Force was ranked in terms in terms of its establishment of officers and men). Six months with us was for him in the nature of a freebie, a nice easy step toward his retirement as a lieutenant-colonel. He was also rather charmingly unsophisticated. At breakfast our staple diet began with porridge, but one day he found himself faced with half a grapefruit, and a facer it was too. Goodness knows where *they* came from in 1946. Anyway, watching the technique of his neighbour at table, Nason attacked it with vigour, managing only to squirt a good deal of juice into his right eye, effectively disabling it for the duration. Dabbing his closed eye with his napkin, he returned to the fray one-eyed, and perhaps predictably managed to disable that one as well. Blind, helpless, and groaning, he was rescued by his ever-attentive Adjutant Dicky Muir, who quickly stubbed out his Egyptian cigarette and led Nason upstairs by the hand to wash out his eyes. Our Colonel was never to risk such an insidious attack again. Returning eventually to the table, he enquired plaintively, 'Is there no porridge?'

Nason was a keen shot, and had a pair of 12-bore with him. One spring evening as it grew dark, he heard the sound of quacking coming from the ponds between us and the railway line. 'Aha,' he said. 'Duck.' Upstairs went he for his gun, and then he set off with evident intent in the direction of his prey. Suddenly silence fell, no ducks rose, but the noise would start up somewhere else. He would set off again in the new direction, only to be greeted again by silence. Eventually he trailed back mystified, thwarted, and duck-less. It later emerged that the quacking had been croaking; the ponds were home to no ducks but to many frogs who, on the approach of an armed colonel, wisely held their peace.

Coming under fire in some quarters for its very existence, T-Force had a vested interest in putting figures to the results of its work, an extraordinarily difficult and complex calculation. The figure that I mentioned, current by December 1946, might have covered evacuation up to, say, the end of October, but will have referred only to tangibles, i.e. machinery and equipment, upon which it was possible to hang some sort of price-tag, and which were seen as reparations. But what about the intangibles, the intellectual property? A figure produced in 1970 from German sources, for the value of appropriated patents alone, was of the order of £250 million in the coin of post currency-reform (June 1948). On top of these were to be added: 'sharp' battlefield weapons and the means of producing them; industrial processes and the documents and drawings which described them, over the whole field of industry; the knowledge obtained by British scientists and industrialists from their interrogation of their German counterparts and of academics; and access to the records and archives of all of these. I was not shocked or entirely surprised by the figure of £2,000 million quoted privately to me in 1949 by the last remnants of T-Force who had been tasked with making such a valuation (Rufus Harris and Wigg and a handful of others, by now with G Branch, Research Division of the CCG). I regarded it as the price of losing.

Access to good broadcast classical music was always a consolation, and my Telefunken wireless reproduced it admirably. One night when I had turned in early I picked up a performance, probably a recording, of Mozart's *Marriage of Figaro*. Since Robin had told me that he had never been to a performance of *Figaro*, I picked up the phone by my bed, rang him in his bed in the other building, and bade him listen while I placed the telephone handset close by the radio. Thus he listened to the whole of the last three acts. Though the sound reproduction must have been terrible, it introduced him to music with which he later became entirely familiar. We were not burdened with phone bills.

The Greenjackets by now viewed No 1 T-Force as a convenient spot in which to tuck away younger officers for whom they no longer had anything to offer. This little ruse was to bring us Tony Scolding and John Bendit, both of whom had seen some action, and went down to join Roddy Bennett at D Detachment at Leichlingen, Ken Wilson at C Detachment in Ratingen, and Lincoln Stuart Hallinan who remained with us at Kamen, all of them of the Rifle Brigade. Thus Leichlingen became a little Greenjacket sub-enclave, under the command of Major Richard Simpkin of the Royal Tanks. I am not sure how he had got shunted, at best sideways, into T-Force; he was, I suspect, at any level probably a difficult subordinate. He remained in the army as a regular, and reached the rank of brigadier. His obituary in the *Times* referred to him as 'one of the foremost military thinkers of his time'. He may have done some of his thinking at Leichlingen, where he would not otherwise have been stretched, and where he seemed to be both moody and taciturn. He was an advocate of professional soldiers among the more senior ranks spending some time in industry, but not the other way round. Maybe his experience of the investigators to whom he gave shelter, the lieutenants rather than the captains of industry, persuaded him that an infusion of soldiers into their world might smarten them up a bit. Perhaps he did not pause to wonder whether the soldiers might bring with them instincts which might be alien, even deleterious, to the industrial environment. Of the reverse attachments, the T-Force experience demonstrated that this would almost always have been true. For the more senior figures borrowed from industry, the equivalent rank of full colonel which they were granted went to their heads in a predictable and disagreeable way. One day, seven of these pseudo-military heroes marched solemnly into my office and surrounded me. Upon my appearing somewhat less than awestruck, the ringleader barked, 'Young man, I will have you know that we are all full colonels!' I called Sergeant Wigg. 'Sergeant, deal with these people would you? I have to be somewhere else.' Wigg was more than equal to it.

CHAPTER 5

*Two big guns and a howitzer – A drunken Pole and a
deranged Hungarian
– A budding romance – A court martial*

Capt. M. Howard R.B., H.Q. No. 1 T-Force, B.A.O.R.

3rd January 1947

Darling Mama,

*This letter rather by way of being a pot-boiler, as I haven't written for some
days. New Year—a bit belated owing to Summer Time,[25] we saw in rather
dismally with the sergeants, who were unable to raise much enthusiasm, as
they would all rather have been with their girl-friends.*

*Nothing much happens here—we get up in a temperature of 25°F, which
rises to about 29° during the day and falls to about 5° at night—and the
most bitter east wind persists.*

*The Colonel goes on three weeks' leave today—a good thing as he is getting
on everybody's nerves owing to an incapacity to make up his mind. We can
seize the opportunity to get things done.*

*When our three new R.B. officers arrive, Robin is being attached to the
H.Q. to help me and the Adjutant when required—a step in the right
direction.*

---

25 Double British Summertime was in effect in summer 1947, and Summertime for the rest of the
year, a sensible—in my opinion—relic of wartime practice.

I had a quiz for the 'Intelligence Section' today. One bloke misspelt his C.O.'s name, didn't know his O.C.'s name, spelt the P.M.—Atley. Spelt 'murdered' wrongly, thought Churchill was C.I.G.S.? and spelt Malteas for Maltese. Still, he is quite good at his job, so no matter.
All my love,
Michael

I note that I didn't make any exception among the sergeants when assuming they would rather have been with their girlfriends than inviting the officers into their Mess to see in the New Year. Several of them I knew had relationships, for the rest I guessed. Sergeant Hancock, who managed the investigators' 'Red' Mess, had a girlfriend whom I knew by sight. He would close the bar at night with the words, 'Well, now I must go and get married'— which he did on a nightly basis. It was curious to see how his pretty blonde friend, although not *enceinte*, grew ever plumper as the days went by, while he grew ever thinner in an almost direct ratio. The regime clearly suited her, but he must have lost a stone in the time that I knew him, and she have put it on.

In asserting that nothing much happened, I was referring to the lack of recreational activities outside our very busy working hours. Indoor badminton in the evenings continued, but I was getting tired of skating very badly, and didn't keep it up with no-one to show me how or keep me company. We were less keen than before to drive thirty miles for a game of squash, and skiing was still a little way into the future, though hockey would soon re-start on hard pitches. The winter was bitter; as with almost everywhere in Western Europe, the east wind swept 'straight in from the Urals', but I was getting used to it—I never wore a greatcoat, rather a sleeveless leather jacket over my battledress. Night-time temperatures fell to –15°C or below, and even daytime temperatures never rose above freezing. Our air-cooled Volkswagens thought nothing of it, though our breath might freeze on the insides of their windscreens.

The Colonel was shirking no decisions that had anything to do with the proper working of the evacuation programme; such decisions did not fall to him. It was the little things to do with personnel and staffing, billets and the like that exasperated us, so a period when these things could go ahead and be settled without him was welcome. Before he went I squeezed out of him an agreement that Robin, who was nominally on the strength of A Detachment, was to move over to HQ to assist me as well as be available to support the Adjutant if needed. In fact he was to be styled Assistant Intelligence Officer, I was to have first call on his time and he was to have his desk in my office. Although there was no extra pip in it for him (not yet, at any rate), I could not really regard him as a subordinate. We worked together. This was no less true of my other brother Riflemen who remained lieutenants. In the Regiment rank was not made much of anyway, except where formal situations required it.

Although I attempted to entertain my mother by quoting those examples of slight deficiencies in literacy and general knowledge betrayed by my clerk, I couldn't get very worked up about his shortcomings. He did much of the filing and did it very well, he shepherded the investigators, he was willing to turn his hand to anything except writing our letters. So not all our private soldiers were literate. One of our despatch riders, Private Hutton, was decidedly not. But if you marked his map with his destination, and recited carefully the names of people and formations to whom he should report, he would memorise the details and deliver his despatches without fail. He came to me once to ask to be sent on a 'basic education' course which had to do with literacy.

'But Private Hutton,' I pointed out, 'you have done this course three times already.'

'Yes, I know, Sir,' he replied, 'but I do enjoy it so.'

He duly attended his fourth course and was no nearer reading at the end of it. He was still a good despatch rider.

Capt. M. Howard R.B., H.Q. No. 1 T-Force, B.A.O.R.
10th January 1947

Darling Mama,

I must have started to write a dozen times in the last fortnight. I have three efforts on the desk in front of me now. I don't seek to excuse myself—it should be so easy to put a few words on paper and drop them into the post-box, and why I never get round to it is more than I can explain. I dread the arrival of the next letter from you, and rightly too.

The weekend after Robin joined me in the office, we had two days' skiing. No sooner had we got back when the G.2 got involved in a shooting accident which will put him out for two months. Sgt. Wigg went on leave. Then Robin caught flu and collapsed on the bathroom floor and, minus his two front teeth, went off to hospital. Two more clerks went on leave, and another lost his voice. I have been staving off flu myself, and all this chaos coincides (a) with the return of the Colonel, and (b) the first appearance of the new Deputy Commander, a full Colonel, who put his stupid head inside my office, and wouldn't go until I had told him all I knew about T-Force. Three other officers have flu, and the weather and roads have just about doubled our difficulties. So you can see that I have been a trifle harassed. To be honest, I never even sit down to a meal without being called away to the phone twice, and the whole has an unsettling effect to say the least: that still doesn't account for why I can't finish a letter.

Did I tell you that Sgt. Wigg got his C.-in-C.'s certificate? Rightly or wrongly I took it as a bit of a pat on the back for myself—presumptuous, maybe.

Winterberg was great fun. We learnt enough (Robin and I) in two days to be able to potter about with a certain degree of confidence. The first morning was pretty terrifying as we couldn't get hold of an instructor, and could only stop by falling, which we did frequently. Then in the afternoon we acquired a genial blond giant to instruct us, and learned a few of the tricks of the trade. Enclosed are a few snaps I took. I had the good luck to win a camera in the raffle, it is a Voigtländer 'Brilliant' for which one would pay £40 in London nowadays: I paid 49/- for it: luckily it is almost foolproof.

I have reason to believe that my pay as Capt. will be coming through soon. I have already received 7/- extra for 7 days' Field Allowance at 1/- a day from June 24th–31st, when the allowance was abolished. The rest should be following soon. I took half a dozen snaps of Margret, the doctor's daughter. She doesn't 'take' well, and hates being photographed. It was only the third time she has allowed herself to be taken since she was twelve. Two of them were quite good—I shall send copies when I can get them done. What makes her attractive doesn't come out in the photo. She is very good company, and the rest of the family is pleasant too. I don't kid myself that I'm what one calls 'in lurv' with her, and in any case in a country like this one can't afford even to let such thoughts cross your mind. But at any rate I am very fond of her. She is coming over to England to see relations as soon as such things are made possible, and I hope she will come and see us then. They have extended a great deal of hospitality to me, which it is impossible to repay out here without breaking some regulation. Must close now and really send this—I do try.

With all my love,

Michael

I must have felt very keenly the occasional reproofs I received from my mother for not writing regularly. I manage to present her by implication as some sort of harridan, which was far from the case. I found it hard to put in the post anything with which I was not satisfied, either with what I had said or how I had said it, and after an abortive attempt would sit down and start again, sometimes more than once. It is a failing, as a correspondent, of which I am still not entirely rid: vanity, in part.

Skiing at Winterberg! Our trouble was that we had arrived after the beginners' ski school had gone out for the morning and we would not be able to
catch up with them. So we drew our kit and dressed the part, and sallied
forth without guide or mentor, intending to rejoin the other learners at
lunchtime having picked up in the meantime some of the rudiments by the
light of nature. We found a convenient groove carved in the hillside which
we thought it would be rather fun to follow down to the bottom. Building
up rather more speed than a pair of beginners might prefer, we found we
could check it only by falling, which we did regularly and spectacularly.
When, mercifully, we reached level ground at the bottom, we stood up a
little shakily and looked up to the hotel at the top, where there were figures
on the balcony waving, apparently waving at us. We waved back. The trudge
back up to the hotel was exhausting. In the bar before lunch we found that
we had achieved a certain notoriety. In tones of awe, we were asked, 'Were
you the chaps who skied down the bob-run?' Without realising it, we had
found the pre-war toboggan-run, neglected and temporarily abandoned. We
nodded insouciantly and chose not to disabuse them of what was a gross
overstatement of the case. Neglected the course may have been, but it was
still very fast.

Thankfully, that afternoon and on the Sunday we joined the other beginners and were taken in hand by a group of four ski instructors, all of whom
had been NCOs at the German Army Ski School at Winterberg. Skilled
at teaching the rudiments to tyros, they encouraged us to take risks with
manoeuvres and to tackle slopes which at first we thought were quite impossible—the only way to make progress, I suppose. On Sunday night we drove
back to Kamen elated.

Our rough-shooting G2, Bill Adams, had been joined in Germany by his
wife, and they were allocated for their married quarters one of the four houses
in that block which we had requisitioned, which lay between the Mess and the
doctor's house. It belonged to the Schulze-Westen family, and their descen-

dants still live there today. Bill used to go out shooting hare, which were plentiful, but this time he had made the classic *faux pas* of shooting himself in the foot (the leg, actually), thus making himself the target of much inevitable merriment. Sadly, no longer did the occasional jugged hare add variety to our diet after that.

Given that there was a bug going round which had laid low the Intelligence Section by one means or another, for Wigg to have gone on leave left us very thin on the ground. Robin recovered and was given some excellent dental bridge-work at the same time, and was not away for too long. The arrival of the new Deputy Commander at HQ T-Force, a full colonel, Colonel Cousins, had not been received with undiluted enthusiasm. He was sent down to visit us, and of course went in to see Colonel Nason who had just returned from leave.

'And just what do you chaps do?' he enquired of the Colonel.

Nason took the only sensible evasive action, and sent him downstairs to see me. Cousins poked his red hat round my door, and tried again. Satisfying his curiosity took three-quarters of an hour of my time, which I could ill afford to give him at that moment, and I soon discovered that I had wasted my time anyway. Within three weeks he had disappeared from the scene, never to be replaced. Many years later I asked Brigadier Ted Grylls what had become of Colonel Cousins, his Deputy Commander. 'Never had a Deputy Commander,' he said. 'I worked directly to David Edwardes, my G1'. So poor Cousins had disappeared completely from the Brigadier's radar screen; he had been an aberration of too little importance and too brief duration to have caused a lasting blip. He seemed to me a very dull-witted chap. It would have been foolish to interrupt or dilute a chain of command which was working so well. David Edwardes was effectively Grylls' deputy, and Grylls let Cousins go.

Grylls himself came to see me in my office only once and, as is the usual way of these things, he appeared unannounced during one of our more apparently eccentric episodes. It happened that late one morning I had suddenly decided that I needed a haircut, but I was too busy to leave the office. So I had a barber brought to me instead, and a bar-stool was conjured up for me to sit on. While the barber set to, Sergeant Wigg brought to me some documents whose contents were sensitive and secret. They needed to be destroyed. I had Wigg position a metal waste-paper basket in the middle of the floor, fill it with the documents, and set a fire. Just as the smoke was curling nicely up to the ceiling, Grylls walked in and saluted. Teetering atop my stool, I found I was not in a position to return his greeting. Hastily, I explained the apparently disorderly circumstances, which he accepted without demur as being in keeping with the demands of the service. Since things seemed to be going pretty well, I also took the opportunity to introduce Wigg, who was hovering over our little fire. I had persuaded the Brigadier's subordinates at HQ T-Force that it was quite in order to deal with Wigg on the phone at any time that I were not in the office, and all of them up to and including Grylls felt able to do so with confidence.

My new camera went with us to Winterberg. In a raffle, I had won the right to buy the Voigtländer 'Brilliant' from the NAAFI at forty-nine shillings, a snip at that price. Fired by its potential, the first thing I did was try to get a decent photograph of Margret, who was camera-shy and thus resistant to the whole idea. I don't think I ever got a good photo of her except when I took her with her baby niece, Christa's daughter Ina-Maria, when Margret imagined that the object of my attention was the unfailingly photogenic infant. If the photographs were to be developed and printed in Kamen, the poses had to be entirely uncompromising—no glimpses of thigh or cleavage if my subject was to retain her reputation. Not conventionally beautiful, her attraction was in her bright eyes, her mobile face, her vivacity which congealed hurriedly into a fixed and embarrassed grin if ever she felt she was the object of my camera's attention. I was at pains to reassure my parents that there was no romantic attachment, when it must have been plain to them that one was developing nevertheless.

Capt. M. Howard R.B., H.Q. No. 1 T-Force, B.A.O.R.
21st January 1947

Darling Mama,

I have been and gone and been naughty again. I don't think I have written for about twelve days. Many letters I have started but few have blossomed forth and produced the finished article. I find I can't settle to writing in the evening—I have just given up trying to write in my room. Robin finds the same thing too, and he is usually a brilliant and prolific letter writer. So today, now that he is working in my office we are taking advantage of no mail having come in to write letters at each other over our respective desks. He has taken over the documents section from me, and sundry other small things.

On Saturday Brian came and saw us. On Sunday we went up to the 1 Corps skiing resort at Winterberg, about 2 hours' drive away. There was only about 4 ins, but people were performing nevertheless. We only had time either for lunch or an hour on skis, so we had lunch. Next Monday, however, the three of us are going up for 48 hours. It has snowed since, and should be enormous fun. A most comfortable hotel at the club—and the most lovely view. One becomes reasonably proficient in quite a short space of time—we hope to make several visits.

Enclosed are assorted photos—some good, some not so. If you want any more copies of particular ones, let me know.

Unfortunate in that particular case, but no missives from Auntie Miriam at all. Some mails never reached here at all and some mails from just before Christmas are still arriving. Bill Adams yesterday got a letter posted on 22nd December. All I can do is to write at once.

I have as yet had no chance of getting in touch with Pat Hallett. It is a part of the country I visit seldom. She probably goes down to Iserlohn sometimes, and I can ask her to break the journey for a meal here.

Your son did not feature among those on the New Year's Honours List for a C.-in-C.'s Certificate, but my Sgt. Wigg got one purely on the strength of my own recommendation, which took a whole afternoon to write out. So that is at any rate something in the way of a recommendation for the establishment I run. If I were Anne, I should be quite content with £385 for Gloria.[26] That covers just about all she ever spent on it, so she can hardly complain.

My promotion as from 24 June was published in Routine Order on 7th January. So I should be raking in £32 per month now, and should get back-pay to the tune of £60 in the near future.

Two R.B. and one K.R.R.C. officer arrived last week and Lincoln Stuart Hallinan, who has just forfeited his deposit as the Conservative at the Aberdare by-election is arriving this evening. We have so many officers we hardly know what to do with them.

We have had ten days of not inclement weather—not much below freezing: but it is now beginning to snow again, and I think we are in for a spot of real winter—though the last spell was realistic enough.

You know I tend to grind my teeth in my sleep—well I have just split another. I shall go down to Iserlohn tomorrow and have it out—with gas! The prospect disturbs me—I must go and drown my sorrows in alcohol!

All my love,

Michael

It was something of a comfort that Robin, though a natural communicator, also found that his room was not a good place in which to attempt to write letters, and that the office surroundings were more conducive to the task. We had placed Robin's desk up against mine, so we sat facing each other, and on that quiet day we both sat writing home, as if competitively.

If Robin was to take some of the work off my shoulders as well as assisting me generally, then the best way to divide the work was for him to take over the handling of the evacuation of documents, leaving me with the machinery and equipment, and the personalities. That was the way it was split at HQ T-Force.

---

26 David had been posted to Malta, and Anne was unable to take her Triumph 'Gloria' with her.

A staff captain or equivalent handled each of the three main activities—in both halves of the Zone—although by this time more than three-quarters of their business was with us at Kamen. Thus Robin dealt mainly with Roger Underhill at HQ, whom he liked and got on well with.

By this time I had probably forgiven Brian Lascelles his long-standing habit of borrowing anything of mine which he needed or fancied (including money) and failing to give it back until put under the most intense pressure. He had been posted to the 1st Battalion The Rifle Brigade, then at Osnabrück about sixty-five miles to the north of us, and came down over the weekend to visit Robin and myself. He was his usual amusing self, and we took him to have a look at Winterberg with a view to a future visit together. I had become quite keen on the sport, and seemed to have some natural aptitude; of course, I was very pleased when my instructor told me I had 'an eye for country', that is, which path to follow and where to make my turns. Seven years later damage to my back, developed while playing hockey and squash, ruled out skiing for good, and it was that above all other sporting pursuits which was my most keenly regretted deprivation.

When the list for the Commander-in-Chief's Certificate for Efficiency came out, Sergeant Wigg's name was on it. Was I perhaps too eager to believe that his award reflected well on myself? I was very glad that it had fallen to me formally to recognise his outstanding ability and the depth of his commitment. While he always observed the niceties called for by the difference in rank, for me he was more a companion in an interesting and exacting venture, as well as a friend.

The KRRC officer was John Laurence Pepys Cockerell, whose actual arrival I anticipated earlier. The closeness of our regiments (since the Peninsular War, since the designation before WWII of both regiments as Motor Battalions, since Calais, and by inter-posting throughout the war) made him instantly 'one of us'—we were both already Greenjackets.[27]

---

27 Johnny's father Frederick William had been a soldier, a lieutenant-colonel, but Johnny was not regular officer material. After leaving Oxford he devoted his life to fisheries in the Pacific.

Lincoln Stuart Hallinan, a lieutenant from the Rifle Brigade, by then twenty-five, was a bird of passage for a few months only. He was another who had been at school at Downside—the regiment had perhaps a shade more than its statistical share of Roman Catholics. He had lost his deposit in the 1946 parliamentary by-election in the constituency of Aberdare in Wales while representing the Conservative interest. His foray into national politics meant that he had ceased to be engaged in military service for a period before the by-election with the consequence that, when he returned to duty, he was still a lieutenant at 24. He seemed to me rather charmless and lacking in the common touch so, while his failure to appeal to the voters of Aberdare may have puzzled him, those of us who knew him were perhaps something less than astonished. He stood again unsuccessfully for Cardiff in 1951 and 1959. My relations with him got off to an uncomfortable start. One evening before dinner I found him on the bridge over the canalised River Seseke just forty yards from the Mess, deep in negotiation with a thin, scruffy and hungry-looking civilian, from whom he was buying three eggs in exchange for cigarettes. We were perfectly well fed, so why he felt the need to supplement his rations I could not imagine, nor indeed how he proposed to get the eggs cooked for his private consumption. I warned him that if I ever caught him at it again, I would throw him into the Seseke (which was pretty foul because in those days it carried effluent from a tannery upstream). Apparently I drew a moral distinction between buying eggs and buying gramophone records; but perhaps he had been buttonholed by the poor man whose need for cigarettes was even greater than his need for eggs and, for all I know, had I not happened along Lincoln would have dropped the eggs in the water—or just given the man the cigarettes. Maybe I was too hard on him. Lincoln became a Recorder of the Crown Court, Mayor of Cardiff, and was knighted in 1971.

I considered pay and allowances of £32 per month to be 'raking it in': £384 per annum, food, board and lodging, free cigarettes and concessionary rates

*25. Tony Scolding and Robin, disturbing the
peace at Zons*

*26. US grenade damage to pews of the chapel
of Sts. Peter and Paul, Petersberg*

27. John Bayley and the four huge Rhine barges

28. A day's excursion down the Rhine: L/R: Tony Scolding, Tony Lucas, John Bayley

29. The collapsed Rhine bridge at Remagen – the gateway to Germany

30. Johnny Pepys Cockerell by the Planschbecken

32. The bomb nets on the Möhne dam

*31. John Bayley and Sgt Wigg, looking up at the
Möhne dam*

33. Still standing on the skyline half a mile away, the southern wall of the Bochumer Verein steelworks

34. The son of Cpl Fox's girlfriend,
poorly clad, freezing cold, smiling in
anticipation of a little chocolate

35. Town centre, Dülmen

36. Bomb damage takes different forms - apartment blocks in Hamburg after the firestorm, July 1943

37. *The empty shell of Krupp's iron and steel works at Borbeck, from which 74,000 tons of machinery had been taken as reparations to the Soviet Union, by the Russians in our care at Heisingen*

38. *Krupp's 15,000-ton forging hammer evacuated to Yugoslavia as reparations: note the figure for scale*

39. *The Villa Hügel, Essen/Bredeney, confiscated from Alfried Krupp von Bohlen und Halbach, whose residence it was*

40. *Cologne, the cathedral and railway station, and the Excelsior Hotel Ernst, still standing among 30.2 cubic metres of rubble per head of population*

41. *"Trümmerfrau" - a "Rubblewoman"*

42. *Margret at university at Bonn, 1947/8. Medical, and other students were obliged to spend their first term salvaging bricks from the rubble*

44. *The Wiggs, a belated honeymoon, skiing at Winterberg*

43. *Dicky Muir and Tony Lucas, Paris, July 1947*

45. *A light lunch? A day's rations, of 1,250 calories: in the Ruhr it sometimes fell, for extended periods, below a thousand*

46. Jean Hughes-Gibb (Julia Draper) almost hidden behind her huge desk at HQ T-Force, Bad Oeynhausen

47. The lady of the violets, Elli Kumperlink – "Tuppence"

48. Johanna Kenzian – "Hanni"

on liquor, in today's coin an income of perhaps £10,750 at age twenty. My first job on graduation in 1950 paid me £400 per annum, equivalent to £8,900 today. The difference in terms of discretionary spending money is clear. No wonder I felt well off in the Army.

Pat Hallett was still in Germany with the Ballets Jooss, and I appear to have felt some obligation to look her up. Where they were I am not sure, but in a part of the country I apparently visited rarely, which could have been Berlin (which I never visited), Hamburg, or Hanover. Anyway, I wasn't making much of an attempt to get in touch with her, and in the end I never did. I wasn't sure that I would feel entirely at home in the ballet *milieu;* the ladies of the ballet were probably used to the attentions of handsome young officers with far more *savoir-faire* than I could muster.

The prospect of any dental operation made me nervous. Since the age of eight I had gone unwillingly to the dentist, especially as the dentist in question had been my mother's, the formidable Sir William Kelsey Fry at Guy's Hospital. His stern manner and apparent complete indifference as to whether he might be inflicting pain, made the whole business an ordeal. It took about fifty years for me to recover psychologically from having been his patient at an impressionable age.

After my letter of 21st January, there was nothing in my mother's cache of my letters from Germany until 24th February, an interval of just under five weeks, and in the later letter not a word of excuse or apology, which was unusual. I can only assume that she must have mislaid one, or even two, and not that I omitted to write to her over such a long period.

It was during that month that we had another 'high-level flap' which demonstrated that liaison between the quadripartite teams and T-Force remained less than perfectly coordinated, and hence called for urgent action to get us out of a difficult situation. As before, it started with one of the phones by my bed ringing at about one o'clock in the morning. Again, an incomprehensible codeword was muttered in my ear. It was the G2 at HQ T-Force, Denis

Gilson, who then had to risk the security of the whole operation—the risk was not very great—by telling me the details 'in clear'. Again, a quadripartite team of British, US, French and Russian investigators was coming down to visit Krupp's in about three days, this time to inspect the gun shed. Three huge pieces of ordnance still resided there long after they should have been taken out, and it was imperative that the Russians should not be allowed to see them in case they laid a claim to them. There were two guns, one of which had a barrel which I judged to be sixty feet long, and a howitzer with a bore of about fourteen inches. Getting them out before the Russians saw them was to have absolute priority.

I got onto Fred Bonney at B Detachment at once; the guns were practically on his doorstep. Between the shed and the public road there stretched about a hundred yards of rubble, and the guns were in no condition to be towed. In the first place it would be necessary to fix up jury-rig axles and wheels for towing purposes and, secondly, to bulldoze a path between the gun shed and the public road. Thirdly, towing vehicles had to be found which were strong enough to cope with the weights involved. Partly by bullying the people at Krupp's, and partly by his own ingenuity, Fred managed to accomplish all this within the three days available. Up in the north of the Zone near Oldenburg we found three Scammell low-load trailer towing vehicles, normally used to tow tanks, and got them down to Essen. With barely a few hours to spare, the guns were out on the road, and I went down to Essen on a motorcycle to act as out-rider to the threatening but motley-looking column. Very slowly I led them to Kamen (where nobody would have thought of looking for them, it being a small Westphalian mining town of no importance) and there they 'rested' for a few days while the quadripartite team completed their inspection and inventory back at Krupp's. The local citizenry came out of their houses whose front parlour windows the guns were overshadowing and gazed at them, nodding sagely and observing that all their barrels were pointing to the east—which by chance they were.

Once the coast was clear the guns were towed up to the T-Force Evacuation Depot at Geesthacht and shipped over to England. They were consigned to the Royal Army Research & Development Establishment (RARDE) at Fort Halstead in Kent—on the north-west skyline from where I am sitting at this moment—but no doubt physically delivered somewhere else where they could be inspected and assessed.

That cold February, with its piercingly bitter nights, brought yet another early morning interruption to my sleep. Whenever there was trouble in the town, which was not often, the Provost Sergeant, Stevens, tended to ring me, whether I was Duty Officer or not. This time there came the joyous news that a drunken Polish DP was running amok in the streets at one o'clock in the morning. Was he armed? Stevens didn't think so, but wasn't sure. What were the police doing? Nothing, as usual; they thought it was an army lark. I strapped on my Luger and met him in the square. By this time the delinquent Pole had broken into a butcher's shop a couple of hundred yards away. We went to have a look, and found that he had hurled a huge paving stone of a weight that I could not have even lifted, straight through the plate-glass window of the shop, perhaps in the hope of finding a side of pork. Evidently he had cut himself badly on the broken glass and was bleeding like the stuck pig he had been seeking, so we followed the helpful trail of blood down the street for another couple of hundred yards, right to the door of a house. The armed Provost Sergeant, flanked by a couple of men from the guard equipped with rifles, burst in and found their quarry, insensible either from drink or loss of blood or both, slumped in the arms of a lady whom he seemed to have met before in happier circumstances. No side of pork was evident. Deprived of any opportunity for heroics, I left them to convey their prisoner to the hospital under armed guard, and went back to bed. Comic though such an episode might seem, the fate of Max Patterson, murdered by our Pole's compatriots in an uncomfortably analogous situation, had never been entirely absent from my mind. But by three o'clock I was asleep again.

It was another example of a tendency which had grown up in Kamen, when there was any sort of a commotion or trouble at night, to assume that the police would do nothing—not even attend—and to come to us for help instead. And so it was that I was called again one night by Sergeant Stevens who took me to a tenement where the cause of the trouble was on the third floor. Stevens had been sought out at about three o'clock in the morning by the wife of a Hungarian cabinet-maker. The happy couple lived, with all their in-laws, in one huge room which, since there was a cleft in the family, had been partitioned in two. The cabinet-maker, swarthy, short and stocky, drunk, noisy and abusive, had suddenly been able to stand the strain no longer and let rip with the leg of an unfinished cabinet. He had smashed through the partition and fairly laid about him. When his poor wife had phoned for help there were no less than three people lying insensible and bleeding around her; she herself had a broken collar-bone and was bleeding from a head wound. The police had been called but declined to do anything about it. After I had surveyed the scene there was nothing for it but to put the man under restraint. Stevens and his two men were by now practised in this sort of thing. As I was too angry to trust myself, I then called my interpreter Sergeant Wallace and had him order the entire town police force to turn out. The Chief of Police and four constables finally sloped along to arrest the Hungarian. The police then assembled in the market square, and I told them through Sergeant Wallace that in future, if it came to their attention that a man with possibly murderous intent was putting others in fear of their lives, and committing actual and grievous bodily harm, it was an essential part of their duty to answer the call and attend the scene, even if it appeared to be 'only' a domestic disturbance. They must protect the vulnerable and defenceless and prevent violence. I dismissed them at about five o'clock. It had never been done before, and probably not since.

Capt. M. Howard R.B., H.Q. No. 1 T-Force, B.A.O.R.
24th February 1947

Darling Mama,

Excuse the official paper but (a) I am in my office and (b) it is pleasanter to write on than anything I can buy as writing paper.

I enclose some enlargements of the Winterberg snaps: they came out so well that I shall soon have difficulty in reaching any other decision but that I am the best photographer I know. Also an enlargement of the first one I took with the new camera, a most peculiar one of myself in the mirror, revealing a large boil on my cheek. Sgt. Wigg says I look very annoyed in it, as if I were trying to creep up and surprise myself from behind. I can show it to you when I come on leave, which should incidentally be on or around the 17th of May.

Darling—I don't want an enormous 21st—I know it's regarded as rather a special occasion, but with Anne in Malta and most of my friends scattered over the globe, or else I haven't seen them for so long, it all seems a little empty. That sounds rather apathetic, I'm afraid, but I mean rather to say that unless I could have a party with all the people I would like to ask, which would under present circumstances be impossible, I would rather have something quite quiet and homely.

The bitter cold has been maintained and it has snowed the last three nights in succession. There is now enough for us to ski locally, which we did on Saturday and Sunday. Quite fun. We are going to be flooded out here when the thaw eventually occurs.

Robin and I have been particularly busy recently, and in addition I have had a Civilian Transport Coy put under me for 'operational purposes' and that has added to it all. In addition, the C.O. is being more vacillating than usual—why can't he make his mind up? He can't decide if we are to go to Dortmund or Lünen, or just stay here. He can't decide where he is going to have his own married quarters. And he can't decide where to have his

Messes. It makes it such a strain for everybody else. I am very comfortable and well dug-in here, and would be loath to move at all.

The Colonel went away last Thursday to tour the detachments and was due to return on Saturday evening, but in the morning we got an odd message saying 'Send me a bottle of gin: will be away till Monday night.' So today it was almost more than we could do to refrain from sending him another bottle with a message—'Stay away till Wednesday.' During his absence no less than four people have turned up for interview, to whom he has more or less promised a job as detachment commander. How four of them are going to share the vacancy, which doesn't occur for six weeks anyway, I just don't know. Last week he kindly asked me out to dinner and the theatre, but by the time we had talked shop for an hour, and I had gone through the embarrassing experience of being asked my opinion of my brother officers, I was pretty fed up.

The blokes coming back off leave seem pretty browned off. They assure me that it is as unpleasant and cold over there as it is here. I hate to confess that I have electricity, hot water, and central heating ad lib. Luckily the mine here produces electricity, and we have not yet been cut.

I have written to tell Jock Harrow not to bother about accommodation for Anne. I have not had a squawk out of him on the subject—only a Christmas card from his home in Scotland. I don't even know if he is in Malta yet. Later—The Colonel returned this afternoon from his tour, and now wants us to move to Hagen. Why, I don't know: this place is far more convenient. Somehow I think his little plan will miscarry (a) because he is the only one who wants to move (b) because all further requisitioning will cease in three days from now, and (c) his wife is arriving in ten days. Anyway I nattered at him for ten minutes this evening, and with any luck I may have made his mind up for him. No, it was a man in Martin's garage who put Cotcher onto my car. I don't think we owe old stick-in-the-mud anything really, except to retain his goodwill, perhaps Tosca was in his garage when Cotcher first saw it.

I have now at rather long last done my stuff over the Golf Club. There is this year a clause saying that members who are abroad for over nine months will pay a subscription of two guineas only, and as my yearly leave only totals six weeks, I am asking to be included under this heading.

Momma—some yeast tablets please, of any reputable brand. I feel they can do me no harm. Also the History of German Literature—a large red book, in my bedroom, please. And the number of Auntie Miriam's new flat—I have just written to No. 26, which I have a nasty feeling is the old one. And all Uncle Barratt's initials.

Bill Adams now has his foot in plaster, and is being allowed back home for tomorrow night for his 26th wedding anniversary.

Thank you for an understanding letter re Margret. I do appreciate the points you raised. I find that I can talk to her, and she to me: in the evening after tea, she comes over to her father's surgery, which is on the ground floor of my billet, and we sit and natter for an hour or so. I find it restful and refreshing and it makes a change from the incessant matters military discussed in the Mess. I won't pretend that she isn't attractive, because although she is by no means good-looking, she has a way about her which is rather special. And I am very fond of her. But apart from the points you raised (a) about the financial angle, and (b) the social stigma, there is also to be considered the fact that for any girl in Germany, by far the most attractive prospect which can offer itself is that of marriage to an Englishman. And if ever it were in any way a possibility for me, and even if my experience of life in general amounted to anything more than a mere two years in the Army, it would hardly be fair to make any offer to her until she too had had the chance of meeting a few more men of her own generation and nation in times which don't seem so hopeless. I have made and will make no promises. They are easy things to make out here, and as easy to break. She knows how I feel, and I have a good idea of her feelings. And if in a few years' time we both think the same way, all well and good. I have had to apologise to so many

225

girls for the behaviour of my ex-brother officers that I am not prepared to
do a thing which might hurt Margret. Having had your letter, I know you
understand—quite a load off my mind.
I also enclose some more snaps of Winterberg—a rather better lot than the
last.
Must close now and really send this off.
All my love,
Michael

Mondays tended to be quiet because no one would have written to us on
Saturday or Sunday; broadly, nobody worked the long hours we did. My
letter, one of my longer ones, must have taken all of forty minutes or
more to write. Perhaps I felt entitled to the luxury now that I had Robin to
share some of the load. I was still having a field day with my new camera.
I had been particularly fascinated by the shutter delay mechanism, hence
the self-portrait in the mirror, even though I had a boil on my cheek—
hardly flattering.

I now had a date for my next leave—17th May, just over a week before
my 21st birthday—and clearly my family were preparing themselves for a
traditional twenty-first, really the last thing I wanted. Perhaps they thought
it would be a marvellous opportunity to introduce me to some English Rose
who might serve to take my mind off the distractions I had found on my
German doorstep, but I had no taste for celebrating an unimportant rite
of passage with a crowd of relative strangers. My own contemporaries and
friends were all scattered at His Majesty's pleasure round Germany or Greece,
Palestine or Japan. The only toast I would care to drink would be to 'absent
friends'.

As this was still the time of maximum inflow of BIOS investigators to Germany, and to the Ruhr in particular, it made sense that I should be in control
of the transport to take them to and from their targets, rather than having to

request it. I was therefore given operational control of a CCG Car Company (No 12), plus a few of the larger and roomier Austin 16s, and the ubiquitous Volkswagen. This occasioned very little extra work for me, but the certainty of the instant availability of transport was a relief, and the allocation of that transport was delegated to my NCOs. It was a measure of the confidence that HQ felt in our ability to operate a smooth-running show. The car unit was located at Buer near Recklinghausen, twenty-five miles down the autobahn from us, so we could whistle up a car in thirty minutes. We still had our own transport for personal use in Kamen.

Poor Nason was still rehearsing his Hamlet tribute, his resolution sicklied o'er with the pale cast of thought. Our premises in Kamen met our requirements fairly exactly, and a move at that time was the last thing we needed, but he had his eye on Lünen, a small industrial town north of Dortmund, a dozen miles to our north-west. Less accessible to the main road system, it was unsuitable from every point of view but I believe there may have been a certain amount of military barrack space available there, and he would certainly have felt more comfortable in a barracks. It was what he was used to, and he was a creature of habit. However, the more he vacillated, the more certain it became that nothing would come of it, which suited us after all. His wife was due to join him shortly—where would he put her? This weighed with him far more heavily than operational considerations; he didn't fancy any of the available accommodation in Kamen as married quarters. The danger was that he would do something sudden and irrational. I believe he was profoundly aware that he was making no mark on his command, that the intelligence operations proceeded very nicely without him, and that the officers commanding the detachments ran the Messes and hotels without needing to refer to him. He lacked any perceptible usefulness, so the only way he could assert his authority was by moving people around willy-nilly.

Charlie Lambert, who commanded A Detachment, was due for demobili-sation at the end of March, leaving a major's command to be filled in six weeks' time. So Nason had an appointment to make, a favour to dispense. It went straight to his head, and he went hog wild, promising the job to anyone who was half-way suitable and inviting them to come and discuss it. Four of them arrived in his absence and had to be persuaded to go away. It reminded Robin of the story about his father who, when a subaltern at Quetta, proposed to a young lady at a dance, and then decided almost at once that he had made a terrible mistake. He was young, handsome, intelligent, amusing, athletic and brave (he had a VC *and* an MC)—quite a catch. His exit strategy was inge-nious: he quickly proposed to three other young ladies in quick succession. All four met when powdering their noses.

'The most marvellous thing has happened to me,' said the first. 'Jackie Smyth has just proposed to me, and I have accepted him.'

'But he has just proposed to me!' chorused the rest.

He had to marry none of them, but he did have to be posted somewhere quite different. Sadly, we could not think of a way of using Nason's prodigal largesse to get him posted elsewhere. For me, Nason's least attractive feature was his inclination to invite my opinion of my brother officers while I was his guest. It made me wonder which of them he was quizzing about me, but he knew by now that he was saddled with me. Perhaps it was another aspect of his difficulty in making up his mind, of not being able to trust his own judge-ment. Did he think my judgement might be better than his? Did he think I would dish the dirt? In fact, I gave everybody a good character, even if they had none. His sudden yen for gin was surprising, not least because scotch was his drink—we had never seen him have a gin. And at any of the three outly-ing detachments he had been visiting, they would have given him all the gin he wanted, no questions asked. We assumed he wanted a whole bottle to use as a return for some service or favour received, perhaps to do with his fishing at the weekend.

It was now a year since the mine explosion at the Zeche Monopol at Berg-kamen, and some coal production had recommenced in other shafts, although our supply of power had continued uninterrupted since the disaster, anyway. Now the supply was in local hands again, generated at the mine, and apparently controlled from the municipality. This essential transition back to local control of course created a potential weak point for an occupying force. It was imperative to ensure that disaffected elements did not get the chance to exploit any opportunity to cause widespread disruption. One afternoon without warning there was a power-cut which brought some of the operations of No 1 T-Force to a halt, a circumstance calling for a robust reaction. The Quartermaster sent an armed guard to bring the Burgomaster and those responsible at the Rathaus to his office at once, where they were informed simply that the occurrence would never be repeated. It never was.

By the time of the Colonel's return on Monday evening, he had forgotten all about Dortmund and Lünen, and we were told to expect HQ to move to Hagen, another large and suitably bombed industrial town on the River Ruhr south of Dortmund. No reason offered, the same arguments applied: there must have been either a barracks or a trout stream, or perhaps a nice house for his wife.

Bill Adams was being allowed out of hospital for the first time, in plaster, but not very mobile. He had been married to a German lady in 1921 as a member of the occupation forces in the Rhineland. He had seen it all before, except that T-Force itself was something which knew no precedent.

My continuing relations with Margret, something short of a 'relationship', were now, to my relief, out in the open as a matter for discussion. My mother's concern had been first that I would not for some time be sufficiently financially secure to consider marriage to anyone and, secondly, that however much Margret might be 'of good family' she was still a German, and that continued to carry with it an unacceptable stigma in the society in which we moved. Unwritten but nevertheless understood, for my mother, for me, and surely for Margret as well was the fact that pregnancy would mean marriage. And since an English officer was seen as being a desirable catch, pregnancy would at once be interpreted as a naked attempt at entrapment. To allow yourself thus to be ensnared would be folly. My confident assertion that marriage to an Englishman would be by far the most attractive prospect available to a girl in Germany sounds suspiciously like a reinforcement of the view that to be born British is to have 'drawn the winning number in the lottery of life'. But it was no more than a reflection of the reality of the situation at that time and in that place, at least in the short term.

Our trysts in her father's consulting room, where Margret went in the evening ostensibly to study, were by no means a daily occurrence; my duties made that impossible. However, when we did meet, we had the chance to talk about just these things in tranquillity, and we both recognised the realities of the situation. Her desire to follow in the profession of her parents and siblings would require years of study at university and beyond, in her own language and hence in her own country, positing a finishing line some years off. I was committed, after what I recognised was a slightly heady interlude, to taking up the place I had won at Cambridge and equipping myself to earn a living. This did not mean that our relationship would not in the interim be allowed some physical expression. However, we would both survive my sojourn in Germany as *'demi-vierges'*—a condition which we both felt we could just about tolerate. We were not, apparently, in the grip of an entirely uncontrollable passion.

Kamen
10th March 1947

Darling Mama,

Thanks for the letter; the things have not arrived yet, but parcels always take a good bit longer, and your letter only took 40½ hours to reach my hand—they must be flying the mail over once more.

We were accused by H.Q. T-Force the other day of inefficiency in the evacu-

ation of documents. Luckily we managed to prove that the inefficiency lay in the filing system at H.Q., and the whole affair finished with a personal letter from the Brigadier conveying the thanks of the B.I.O.S. secretariat and the Board of Trade, for the excellent work done recently. Also the Brig. sent his Staff Capt. down to see us today to see how it should be done! Robin and I are having a positive orgy of self-congratulation, as he is now learning how to do the docs side for me.

I heard the other day from Mike Corbett (Capt.), second in command of the camp of the British Military Mission in Athens. He says he has now grown so fat that he is no longer capable of playing rugger, and only an old man's game of cricket! Three months at Cambridge should change all that. He writes a delightful letter.

Most of my contemporaries are now abroad, and about a third of them have wangled their third pip. Brian Lascelles, to whom I occasionally speak on the phone, assures me that all the least deserving cases have been promoted. I am soon going to try putting the idea of a third pip for Robin to the Colonel. Unfortunately he thinks that any officer not employed on strictly military duty is not really doing a full day's work, and not earning a subaltern's pay even. The fact that we often do work until dinner impresses him not at all, and when we sometimes tell him we haven't time for a game of badminton after tea, he looks most puzzled at us. His wife has now arrived, and there is now a less strained atmosphere in the Mess, as he lives at Unna, 5 kilometres down the road.

Great Expectations I have yet to see. A Matter of Life and Death I found unsatisfying, but none the less charmingly done, and good entertainment value. We get two flicks weekly here, roughly in the proportion of one British to three American, and the same proportion of good to bad films. Have you seen The Strange Love of Martha Ivers, or Dark Corner? Both I can recommend. I have seen two German films recently—one of them a nonsensical musical extravaganza, but with a Hungarian actress of extreme beauty, and in the most exquisite colour. Another, called Damals, most excellently handled, but too heavily in every detail, for my taste at any rate. This one possessed a Swedish actress with the most lovely low pitched voice.

Last Sunday afternoon it was quite warm, and Robin and I had an early tea and went for a walk to a nearby village, where there is a lovely old moated country house: both of us in grey flannels etc. I was rather tickled—Robin said that if we didn't talk as people passed us, they might not realise we were English. He was rather hurt when I told him it stuck out a mile anyway.

Within five weeks from now we will have double summer time out here, which will give us the chance to have an early dinner, and then go off for a walk before it gets dark. Or even run off to the Möhne See at tea time to sail, supping at the Officers' Club there.

The running of the Zone is being put more and more in the hands of the Germans. It is strange to get correspondence in, as we now do, from the German 'Minister of Economics', or of 'Finance' or something. They work on the same system as the French, that only stupid people are honest. You couldn't really hope to run across a finer set of sharks.

Darling—I wasn't surprised to find that you understood about Margret, but merely thankful. I don't under-estimate the value of the virtue of prudence, and shall conduct myself accordingly, for the sake of all parties.

Almost all the snow has now gone, here: and tonight warm rain is falling. Spring breaks out pretty quickly in this country. It should be upon us before we know where we are, thank God.

All my love,

Michael

Something had gone wrong with the normal flow of document evacuation. Of course, headquarters was by definition right and the subordinate formation, ourselves, wrong, but we bit back and found that the deficiency was in the filing system at HQ, for which Roger Underhill was responsible.

I received a letter from Brigadier Ted Grylls, drafted for him of course by David Edwardes, expressing the gratitude of the BIOS Secretariat at 32 Bryanston Square (which meant that of Lieutenant-Colonel Derek Ezra[28]) and the thanks of the Board of Trade for the good work we were doing in getting the documents out for them. Rather eating humble pie, Grylls also sent Roger Underhill down to us for a couple of days to see how it should be done. There was nothing that couldn't be settled in twenty minutes, it was simply a matter of procedure. But Robin and I enjoyed having him with us for a couple of days, he was sparkling and amusing company.

It was good to have a letter from Michael Corbett, whom I had so wished to have posted to us. He was bored and under-occupied in the administration of the Military Mission camp in Athens, with food, drink and nicotine doing no good to his waistline. As I predicted, that would all be rectified within three months of his going up to Trinity College Cambridge in October 1947, where he distinguished himself on the rugby field. He later went on to play at county and divisional level.

Brian Lascelles' assertion that only the least deserving got promoted was perhaps coloured by the fact that he did not. It was hard to keep tabs on all those who were commissioned with us, to see who had been promoted, and I knew anyway that it could be a matter of luck or influence. They were scattered round Germany, Palestine and Japan, and it was only later that I was able to verify from the Army List of 1947 in the National Army Museum that only a third of us had managed to wangle a third pip. I had been the first, and luck it was. But no such luck for Robin, at first, anyway. Nason, like Peter Brush and John Nicol before him, did not consider T-Force to be proper soldiering, and one could very easily sympathise with their difficulty in reconciling the promotion given so early to these young officers with the years they themselves had spent as regular soldiers waiting to achieve the same rank, and with the absence of promotion they had suffered as

---

28 Ezra became Chairman of the National Coal Board, and later a Member of the House of Lords.

prisoners of war—although Peter with his generosity of spirit had been an exception, in my case at any rate. Robin would have to wait until the intelligence function began to run down later in the year, and he could be spared to do the job of adjutant which carried the third pip more as a matter of course. To him, the prospect was so uncongenial that he would rather have done without the extra pip.

The film *Damals* had been made in Germany in 1943, and the Swedish star with the beguiling low, dark voice was Zarah Leander. At the outbreak of war she had had to choose between a career in Sweden or in Germany, and for good commercial reasons she chose the latter. At that time the industry was the plaything of Goebbels, and he kept the studios and the acting profession busy. But in the long term, it was the wrong decision. She found work elsewhere hard to get—she had been tarred with Goebbels' brush.

Given all the chat about moving the HQ and the Mess, Robin and I thought we should do a little reconnaissance of our own. If we had to move, it might as well be to somewhere agreeable. We drove a few miles and lighted upon the Haus Reck, a charming *Wasserschloss* with a moat round it, in open country to the north rather in the direction of Hamm. In a single secure site it could have housed our offices and support services, as well as the Mess and our living accommodation, with room for our transport in the inner courtyard as well. But, ideal from that point of view though it was, we could not in all conscience have made a bid for it given the housing situation in the province. We saw no-one to talk to, but there must have been at least a hundred people living there who would have to be evicted had we been allowed to requisition it. It was no more than a nice fantasy, and requisitioning was coming to an end anyway. Even with our grey flannels and our mufti, I had to disabuse Robin of the idea that we would not be identified as Brits from our mien alone; he was rather crestfallen. We did not make credible Mofs.

Our correspondence with the Regional hierarchy at ministerial level generally concerned matters of detail only, not of principle or policy. When the

Economics Minister, Land Nordrhein/Westfalen, Erik Nölting, attempted to intervene to obstruct the evacuation of a machine from a factory in Oberhausen, I had to warn him of the consequences in a directive written in German and English, with the latter the authoritative text. The penalty for contravening provisions of the Additional Terms of Surrender as set out in Proclamation No 2 of the Allied Control Council could, by implication, be death—probably by firing squad. Nölting withdrew and the machine went out. However, a year later when I was gone, and following the reform of the currency, there was unrest at the same factory, during which the 1st Battalion the Manchesters had one of their Bren gun carriers overturned by the workforce. The Manchesters still had the same sanctions at their disposal, but probably lacked both the knowledge and the confidence to impose them. The workforce had the right to strike, but not to cause civil insurrection.

My mother had been reassured and was content with my account of my relations with Margret, and my assurances of prudent conduct. I was perhaps secretly less sure. Spring was suddenly in the air.

> *Capt. M. Howard R.B., H.Q. No. 1 T-Force, B.A.O.R.*
> *Monday 31st March 1947*

Darling Mama,

Been naughty again, I know, and nothing to plead as excuse except to say that I have sat down to do this half a dozen times, and just never finished. Played hockey on Friday against 55 Anti-Tank Regiment, and lost 3–4. I bagged one goal and made the other two for Roddy Bennett to score. If we had had a goalkeeper who had played before, we would have won. This Friday we play the 1st East Lancs in the Corps shield game.

The Colonel, remembering the days when he used to command a company, is having the whole unit on parade every morning at seven o'clock. None of these regular soldiers can quite grasp the fact that you can't treat a specialised unit like this as you would an ordinary battalion. The unit has now got the hell of a good reputation almost solely because those officers, N.C.O.s, and men who were doing the special job were prepared to spend a great deal of their own free time in the evenings and at the week-end doing the little bit extra which made the difference. I shall hardly feel inclined to go back to the office in the evening if I have to be up at six in the morning, and I can't expect my staff to either. But I suppose if one points this out to the Colonel, it sounds like an ultimatum. Even the O.R.s say they have never yet been in a unit where every officer was on parade at 7 a.m. I wouldn't mind taking my turn when orderly officer, and drilling or giving P.T. to the unit until we were all blue in the face, but getting up at that hour for the privilege of being told that I could 'Fall out' is more than I can bear. And all put into force by an Adjutant whom I first gave a job as an Evac. Officer, and then suggested to take my place as Adj. I suppose I should have taken the job myself. And the immoderate glee with which he announced that the unit was in future to do Redcoat instead of Greenjacket drill. The only people who didn't give a tuppenny curse either way were the R.B. officers.

Robin and I paid our call on Mrs. Nason one day when he was up at Rhine Army, but unfortunately she was indisposed, and in bed. Anyhow, we were invited out to dinner last Wednesday and everything went off very well. At any rate he managed to keep off his pet subject, discussing his officers.

The chief of the B.I.O.S. Documents Section paid us another visit the other day to say that the Board of Trade and Ministry of Supply were more than satisfied with the rate at which documents were being evacuated.

I went over to Soest last Sunday and took snaps of the churches and town hall there. It is an ancient pilgrimage centre, and all the churches are built of green stone: it isn't as marzipan as it sounds. Some of the snaps were really quite good, I am having copies done for you.

I got the M.T.O. to give me an official driving test, (which I passed), so I hope that on the strength of that I can get a permanent licence.

We have moved our headquarters out of the square, but still in Kamen. Sgt. Wigg and I both get smaller but brighter offices, and the 5 clerks now have two large airy rooms, where they before had one small dark one. My room has a projecting window with glass on three sides, with a raised ledge underneath. I had the ledge extended, and we both have our desks up in the window.

Robin goes on leave on the 7th and as soon as he gets back, Sgt. Wigg goes: on Wigg's return, I go.

The first spring flowers are out now, violets in my room today for the first time. The only tree which has leaved so far is the weeping ash outside my windows, but all the fields are a fresh green; the temperature has been at 55°–60° for some days now, and yesterday one could easily sunbathe out of the wind.

No more news for the moment.

With all my love,

Michael

Nason must have been feeling the impotence of his position even more keenly than we had supposed, because he suddenly gave an order that the entire unit at Kamen—officers and men—should turn out on parade at seven in the morning, every morning. Enforcing this order was the responsibility of the Adjutant, Roy Smith, and he and the RSM would then drill the men for a while before dismissing them. The guard and other details had always used Rifle drill, because the majority of our men had come to T-Force from 1st Bucks and were accustomed to it. Smith did not have the great good fortune to be a Rifleman (he came from the doubtless admirable Warwickshires), and the resentment latent in the Colonel and in the Adjutant of the use of Rifle drill was revealed by the decision that the drill to be used on these occasions would be Redcoat drill (that of the ordinary infantry of the line), which obviated the necessity for the Adjutant and some others to learn new tricks.

Soest was a pleasant cathedral town thirty-five miles to our east in the direction of Paderborn. It had been the scene of furious fighting during a German counter-attack twenty-three months previously. The town was set in rolling country which became well used by the Tanks for manoeuvres. The cathedral, built in the 12th century of a local green sandstone, was dedicated to the French Saint Patroclus (of whom we had never heard) and hence was known as the 'Patroklidom'. The other great church was the Gothic *Wiesenkirche*, Mary of the Meadows. It was my only visit to the town other than to the Officers' Club.

Passing the driving test was a pre-requisite to being commissioned in the Rifle Brigade, and this covered Bren gun carriers and scout cars and 15-hundredweight trucks, as well as ordinary cars. I can't think why I did not already have a permanent driving licence; it must have been an administrative oversight. The Quartermaster also acted as Motor Transport Officer; he did what he was told and formally passed me. I still have a licence to drive vehicles steered by their tracks on the public road. Even tanks!

Since 1 Bucks first arrived in Kamen, our headquarters had been at number 11 Am Markt, which had been an inn known as Biermann and is now the Hotel Stadt Kamen. In recent years I had lunch in their restaurant at a table placed precisely where my desk had for so long been, and with the same broad view of the market square that I had enjoyed. The tramlines crossed the square diagonally from beside the Rathaus in the far left-hand corner

into Am Geist on our right. At No 3 Am Geist there had been the Hotel Konig von Preussen, named for Frederick the Great of Prussia, where we now moved our offices; it offered better accommodation really, except for the loss of my view of the comings and goings in the square.

First among the flowers of spring to register on my consciousness were the scented violets in an eggcup back by my bed, thanks to the indefatigable

Robin Smyth at his desk in the 'König von Preussen'.

Tuppence. To keep them so fresh she must have denuded the countryside for miles around. An attempt to thank her brought only blushes and confusion.

Capt. M. Howard R.B., H.Q. No. 1 T-Force, B.A.O.R.

9th April 1947

Darling Mama,

Down to the grind again after Easter. I had to work on Friday morning to finish off before the holiday. In the afternoon we played hockey against the 1st East Lancs, in the Corps Shield, and beat them 4–2. They, a regular battalion, were very hurt at being beaten by such a motley crew, and were quite sure the better side had lost. I got three of our goals. The win puts us in the last eight, and if we win against the Cheshires we shall be in the semi-final.

After the game Robin and I drove down to our detachment at Leichlingen, near Cologne. We spent a quiet and rather exhausted evening there with Roddy Bennett and Tony Scolding, another Rifleman who has just joined us. On Saturday we went into Cologne, and I took some snaps of the cathedral, not a bright day, but they should be passable. Then on to Zons, a small walled town on the Rhine, on the west bank between Cologne and Düsseldorf. My Baedeker assures me that it is the best-preserved example of a mediaeval walled town in the Rhineland, and it certainly is delightful. I took 10 odd snaps there.

Lunched in Cologne, and then on down the Autobahn as far as König-swinter, where we climbed up to the Kaiserhof hotel, where Chamberlain and Henderson used to stay. From up there you can see up to Coblenz and down to Cologne, and you get a lovely view of the Rhine valley, which I again recorded photographically. Also a small but very ornate little chapel up on the hill, not very old, but beautifully if vulgarly decorated internally, in the Baroque style. Exquisitely and richly painted gold, red, and silver wood carvings all over the place. I took another 6 snaps inside there, and they should be fun. Then more snaps as we were crossing over in the ferry to Bad Godesberg, where Hitler used to hang out, in to Bonn, where we had tea by the river, up to Cologne (more snaps of the cathedral) and across the river to Leichlingen. After dinner there, in to the Officers' Club in Düsseldorf, where we sipped 'brandy flip' and watched a mediocre cabaret. Nothing went wrong in the whole 300 miles, no wrong turning, no puncture, and Robin and Tony are very good company. Altogether a most refreshing weekend. We were back by lunch on Sunday to take over while the others went off for 48 hours.

Robin went off on leave yesterday, which means more work for me again: under these conditions one feels less and less like getting up at 6.30 and going on parade. I suppose it does settle the problem of what to do in the evening—one just goes to bed.

Daddy—golf balls are like gold out here. There are only some nine courses, mostly nine-hole, in the British Zone, and consequently no golf balls to be obtained from German sources. The meagre supply in the country is obtained through N.A.A.F.I. sources, and as you may well imagine there is already an enormous black-market for them. My chances of laying my hands on any are remote.

Our M.T. sergeant who married a German girl about a year ago (in a church) has today been told that all his papers are now in order. He is being married by a British padre on Saturday, and I am going down to Düsseldorf with him on Monday finally to fix it up with the German civil authorities.

We have had the most awful gale for the last four days. Apart from the fact that my new office is miserably draughty, a high wind is always so tiring. The day before yesterday two men fainted on our early morning parade through sheer cold, so this morning I dismissed them as soon as the inspection was over. In the absence of the Adjutant on leave, I have the doubtful privilege of taking the parade. This evening however the wind has dropped and the rain clouds cleared completely, with one of those lovely orange-to-midnight

blue sunsets, which usually betoken a cold night with fine weather to follow.
Bill Adams is now back at his desk, his leg still in plaster and an iron.
He will always be lame, but he was extremely lucky not to lose his foot: he
is just getting a grip on the problems of the moment before going down to
Düsseldorf to act as liaison between T-Force and the Control Commission.
We had our riots here last Thursday too, but all quite orderly, and organised
by one of my interpreters. I had to drive (in the C.O.'s Snipe) in to Unna,
where there were 10,000 strikers, and go and liaise with the I.O. at the Bel-
gian brigade there. I had horrible ideas of the C.O.'s Snipe being overturned,
and me on my head inside—but they all behaved very well. Some of our
civilian employed received permission from the Q.M. to strike in sympathy,
which they did. Their first strike since Hitler came in, and an idea so alien
to them that they use our word for it. It is a fact that some weeks they only
get 900 calories per day, and a ration of 800 will starve you to death in nine
months: few of course, live on their ration alone, but not many can supple-
ment it up to the scale of 1550 per diem which it is supposed to be.
Our stock stands lower now then ever: one notices it even just walking along
the street, and a lot of the girls who are openly going round with our men get
beaten up by gangs of youths. One of our tougher types got loose among some
of these the other night and laid three of them clean out. He was reported
to have 'maimed' another in the arm. Robin, who was Duty Officer, asked
the orderly corporal what was implied by the word—was the arm broken, or
just bruised? 'No sir,' came the answer, 'just maimed.' So he was no further
on than in the first place.
Partly because the anti-British feeling is running high, and partly because
they have, I think, a perhaps understandable suspicion of me, Margret's
parents forbade her to see me, about a fortnight ago. This didn't stop
it however; but last Sunday they relented and asked me to tea, which I
accepted. They are pleasant people, but I have remarkably little in common
with the menfolk. The mother is an extremely pleasant person, and the eldest

daughter charming, but not as lively as Margret—understandable perhaps as her husband is P.O.W. in Russian hands. However, they have heard that he is in a Communist propaganda camp, which means that he should be back in a matter of months now. He, poor fellow, has never seen his daughter, nor knows of her existence—she is only eighteen months old, and it is two years since he was taken prisoner, and he has not heard from Christa since that date.

I was asked over the other evening to see Margret's first long evening dress, and her first high heels—struggling hard not to appear self-conscious; but sweet. She is such very good company: I only hope you will get a chance of meeting her one day. It is on the cards that in a year or two when that sort of thing is allowed, she will come over to England to visit relatives. Having been more or less shown by her over the show places of Germany, I would like to show her some of the lovelier bits of England. And London is something which is quite beyond the imagination of most foreigners. Still, time enough for all that. In the meanwhile I am grateful enough for her companionship. She and the perpetual good music one can get on the wireless out here, between them keep me from drink, which is where most of the others have gone. I won't say that I have gone teetotal, but bar the odd spot of table wine, which harms nobody, I now don't have half a dozen gins a week even, and find it quite simple to knock right off it for a few days. There is even some danger of your having a 100 per cent teetotal son when he comes out of the army!

I keep pegging away at Peterhouse, plaguing them to get me out.

A pat on the back for this missive please. No virtue in it really—this evening it comes easily from the pen.

With all my love,

Michael

P.S. So far this evening the Bruch Violin Concerto, Haydn Sinfonia Concertante, Beethoven's 9th and Mozart's 40th Symphonies.

The court martial adjourned the previous autumn in which the Colonel had asked me to prosecute one of our men who had injured a civilian had now come up. The incident had occurred one night when Robin had been Duty Officer. Our man was undoubtedly guilty, but the only witness to the assault other than the victim had been passing on the other side of a poorly-lit street, and after some questioning by the defending officer about the limits of visibility, and the uncertainty of identifying the assailant, the witness appeared confused and the court found it impossible to convict.

Working on Good Friday morning meant that I could go and play hockey in the afternoon with a clear conscience. We owed much of our success to our Belgian civilian, an interpreter from B Detachment and a pre-war international who, with Tony Lucas, held things together behind and fed Tony Scolding, Roddy Bennett and myself up front to score the goals. By this time we had retrieved our goalkeeper, which gave us a chance again after our previous defeat. After the match Roddy and Tony went back to Leichlingen, and Robin and I drove down to join them for a couple of nights. We had to be back at Kamen by midday on Sunday to let the others (John Bayley and Johnny Pepys Cockerell) off for the next forty-eight hours. Our exertions on the field of play suggested that a restful evening involving a quiet drink or two and a chat in the Mess would be in order. It was the first time that Robin and I had spent any time with Tony, who was a lively and agreeable addition to our number. Commissioned a year before us, he had seen action in Germany briefly before May 1945. He was to remain a friend of mine for years after we all went home.

Cologne was still a mess. The centre of the city had been terribly damaged and although the rubble had all been tidied up, the streets cleared, and some repairs effected, it was still a shocking sight. However, the area round the cathedral was clear, the railway station was functioning normally, and the virtually unscathed Excelsior Hotel Ernst, traditionally one of the best hotels in Germany, was open and functioning as an Officers' Transit Hotel, and re-establishing its former reputation for excellent cuisine. We lunched there, Robin and Tony and I, after a mildly cultural excursion during the morning to Zons, the Roman *Sonsium,* which lay a couple of hundred yards back from the banks of the present course of the Rhine. In Roman times, of course, it had been directly beside the river upon which it later served as a toll and customs point. Its walls and towers now encircled the little fortified village. Built in red brick, it presented a mainly fourteenth-century face, undamaged and unspoiled. It lay to the east off the road between Dormagen and Düsseldorf and was isolated from the commercial traffic—and from the T-Force investigators, particularly those from Courtaulds, who showed continuing interest in the huge IG Farben works at Dormagen. In uniform, and in an army vehicle, we were objects of curiosity in this self-contained little community which the Occupation largely bypassed, and we felt rather out of place.

Our excursion up the Petersberg behind Konigswinter to the Kaiserhof hotel had as its purpose to enjoy the view, and also to prospect the facilities of the hotel which had been converted into an Officers' Club. It had been the lodging of Neville Chamberlain when he came to see Adolf Hitler across the river at Bad Godesberg in September 1938 in the vain hope of dissuading him from entering Czechoslovakia. The hotel was magnificent,

The Hotel Kaiserhof on the Petersberg, from the nearer bank of the Rhine.

and the terrace on its west front, at an elevation of a thousand feet above the Rhine, had views down-river to Cologne twenty miles away and up-river to Remagen. We went to have a look at the little chapel opposite the entrance. This part of the Rhineland had been taken in 1945 by US forces and, to make sure that there should be no ambush from the chapel, they had tossed a grenade through a window. The explosion had torn holes in pews and other wooden furnishing and decoration. No attempt had been made to repair the damage, but the locals had redecorated the interior, painting carefully round the ripped and torn woodwork as if to draw special attention to the savagery of the barbarians who had caused the damage. As it happens, there had been no-one in the chapel, but the Americans weren't in the mood for taking chances.

We crossed by ferry to Bad Godesberg and on to Bonn with its pleasant villas, a few with gardens running down to the water, and one requisitioned to provide tea and quiet recreation for the likes of us. Back to Leichlingen for dinner, to give us the stamina—which had not yet been fully tested—for the cabaret in Düsseldorf, fuelled by brandy flip, whatever that may have been. An admixture of cream and perhaps an egg, I expect.

My father had resumed his membership of the Royal Ashdown Forest Golf Club at Forest Row, famous for its lack of sand-traps, but the fierceness of the deep heather rough. Golf-balls were hard to acquire and easy to lose. Any enquiry in the clubhouse as to what you had scored would elicit not the number of strokes you had taken, but the number of balls you had lost. It was good to get round in three. The course was not yet back to its pre-war best. My father used as his caddy Mrs Mitchell, widow of the great British golfer of the 1920s and 30s Abe Mitchell (he who is depicted atop the Ryder Cup), who lived in a cottage on the course. She had a pack of four or five spaniels who were trained to look for lost golf-balls, but the dogs remained at home while she was working, so if you hit one into deep rough while going round, her search for it at the time would tend toward the perfunctory. In the evening or the next day, however, she would be back with the dogs, and would then sell you back your own golf-balls at sixpence a time. Golf had been a minority game in Germany before the war, which was a shame because it is a game which obliges everyone, except the very expert, to laugh at themselves from time to time—not a very German trait. It would have been good for the pre-war German soul; just think what it would have done for Goering and Goebbels to play golf badly.

The Motor Transport Sergeant, Sergeant Pyle, had stayed with us from 1 Bucks, and very good he was, and a very nice man—tall and handsome. His pretty lady friend, whom he had married in church locally but to whom he was not yet legally married, lived in Iserlohn half an hour away, so a couple of times I had given him authority—which I should not have done—to use 'my' Volkswagen in the evening to visit her. They had a child together, and I was very glad that his papers were among the first to come through so that they might regularise their situation. I helped him to deal with the German authorities, who recognised a ceremony in front of the British chaplain. This would allow the new Mrs Pyle to come and live in Kamen. During their wedding breakfast in the Sergeants' Mess, at which I was placed next to her, she excused herself to go and feed the baby.

If we had to have an early morning parade, which I doubted, I was prepared to do my bit and take it from time to time, but if someone had to stand in for the Adjutant it seemed to be too often myself. I was not prepared to keep the men standing out in the bitter cold, and dismissed them to their barrack rooms. Insensitive as Colonel Nason was, even he eventually recognised that the parade was causing a good deal of disaffection without contributing positively in any way to improved performance. Perhaps his second-in-command Ronnie Coe got through to him at last, or maybe it was HQ T-Force to whom we aired our grumbles in the course of our daily telephone conversations. Anyway, after a few weeks the 7 am parade was called off.

Bill Adams' role had been liaison, that is, to oil the wheels between HQ T-Force and myself, and he had been superfluous for a while now, since the relationship was good anyway, and frankly we had not missed him. But it was liaison between ourselves and the RDR Division at the CCG Regional Headquarters which was going to need tending from now on, because of the increasing feeling in the Control Commission that our activities should by now have been brought to an end. Bill would save me personally from a good deal of bother arguing with them.

Labour unrest had been a possibility for a little while, since the right to strike had been brought in as a measure of democratisation and re-education. The first time it reared its head in practice was when Erich Braatz, one of the interpreters at A Detachment, asked permission to come and see me. He had been directed to me on account of my responsibility for internal security. An educated man, he had lost an eye fighting on the Russian front, and I knew him a little and liked him. He had been deputed to speak for the miners on the subject of their grossly inadequate rations.[29] The interview went like this:

'Yes, Braatz, what is it?'

'Captain Howard, we wish to have permission to strike.'

'Braatz, I cannot give you permission to strike. You have the *right* to strike.'

'Yes, I know, Sir, but I would still like to have permission.'

'No, Braatz, I cannot give you that. You have the right.'

'But if we do, Sir, what will you do?'

'I expect I shall be in the corner of the square, with a few men.'

'And then, Sir?'

'Nothing, Braatz, unless you behave in a disorderly manner or cause a breach of the peace.'

'So may I have permission?'

'Braatz, go away!'

In fact the strike meeting was to be held down the road at Unna, where the Kreis headquarters was. I was detailed by the Colonel to liaise with the Intelligence Officer of the Belgian Brigade in 49 Division, who had a battalion at Unna, and were the occupying power for these purposes. I was not at all sure that they could be relied on to behave sensibly and not mount a provocative show of force. They had a reputation for toughness, but in

---

29 Braatz was also Secretary of the local SPD.

the event they were quite discreet. I had been given the Colonel's Humber Super Snipe tourer (with balloon tyres, a relic of the desert war) and we tucked ourselves away pretty well out of sight. In Kamen, some of our civilian employees were assured by the Quartermaster, rather counter to the line I had taken with Braatz, that they might strike for a few hours in sympathy. Failures in food distribution had left some of them very short—down to starvation rations—and we could hardly deny them the chance to draw attention to it.

This lack of food was the fount of some anti-British feeling in the town at that time, but we did not allow violence toward girls who went with any of our soldiers to pass without some remonstration. However, one could hardly blame Margret's parents for forbidding her from seeing me in such an atmosphere, a matter over which actually they had little influence. Once the strike season was over, they asked me to tea to show that it was nothing personal. I was invited over to their quarters in the hospital late one afternoon to see Margret, wearing her first long, blue evening dress and high heels, a sort of private view. Telling my parents that she had shown me over some of Germany's show places was an exaggeration; perhaps she had pointed me in their direction. She had never taken me anywhere, nor I her. I was preparing my parents for some future visit.

News came from returning prisoners of war that Christa's husband Eberhard Haller was in a Russian communist propaganda camp, being indoctrinated prior to his return to Germany. Exposure to brainwashing seemed a small price to pay for the chance to come home, though he was to return to a rather different Germany from that which he had left. His home-coming was delayed by his catching spotted typhus, but he survived and reached Kamen after I had returned to England.

I listed the classical music I had just heard over the Telefunken radio in my room; it was an important factor in keeping me away from the other pastime available in the Mess in the evening—drink. Half a dozen gins a week plus table wine was a moderate amount, and I didn't feel too bad about it. Robin was moderate in his habits, and so was John. Most of the others drank too much.

Kamen

2nd May 1947

Darling Mama,

I've been and gone and not written again, I know. At least I have compiled a more or less meaningless missive which has been lying on my desk looking futile. But here is an answer to yours at any rate.

My apparent aversion to a party was not really as strong as it might at first appear to have been. It was just that I felt that to collect together a whole lot of people, few of whom I know at all well, and few of whom know each other, and to tell them all to get together and be happy just because I am 21, all seemed a little bit futile. I suppose the logical answer is that it is an excellent chance for me and them to get to know one another better anyway. I think your plan as suggested sounds very pleasant, thank you darling; two worries though. In a party of those numbers I feel that a preponderance of young men to the tune of about four or five is desirable if there is to be any dancing; and secondly, I feel it is the hell of a long way for most of them to come for just a cocktail party. But still, I will accept your judgement on those matters.

I think I shall now probably aim to get home nearer the 16th than the 20th May, and am wondering a bit which would be the best day on which to have the party. Anybody who has any distance to travel is hardly going to feel like travelling between about the 23rd to the 27th on account of the holiday crowds. Would it perhaps be better to have it all on the following Saturday the 31st?

I am still taking photos like mad. I snap things indiscriminately with the result that I produce rather a lot of chocolate box effects with nothing in particular to recommend them, except as a record of things done and places visited. Some, however, have been really surprisingly good, though I say it. Recently I had about 5 postcard-size enlargements done—two of them a three week old foal,

249

which were delightful. Two portraits, John Bayley and Sgt. Wigg, and a close-up of a bunch of daffodils. I won't send any, as they can so easily be damaged in the post, but I will have a fine array to look at when I come home.

Robin is back and settled in after his leave, which makes life more tolerable. I was able to greet him with the gladsome news that we have both of us missed Class B release for the next academic year by 13 days. The clause says that anybody who has completed 3 years' service by 31st August is eligible: as I was instructed to join on 13th Sept 1944 instead of earlier, I miss it by just that much, and so does Robin. Considering that I first volunteered at the end of November '43, signed on 3 Feb '44 and was told by a grateful nation that my services would not be required until September, I feel that we are being a little hard done by. Also as our juniors by one year are escaping with twelve months service at the age of 21, after their university career! Oh! Exasperation overcame us at lunch time yesterday, and a sympathetic Mess celebrated our glad tidings with us. In short we threw a cocktail party which lasted 90 minutes, crept into lunch at 2.0 o'clock, and staggered back to the office to reactivate T-Force at 3.15.

This means that unless we can persuade somebody in authority that we are getting a raw deal, somebody who is prepared to do more than just sympathise, we shall go out with our group in FEBRUARY 1948—*all very good for the rising generation, I suppose, but all very jolly good and tedious. Another winter out here—ugh!*

Our employees are growing less and less popular with the rest of the populace, who are growing gradually more impudent as they become better-fed, not that they are much. What with all our bright boys trying their hardest in Moscow, the chances of the problem of Germany being settled in the next four years seems remote. The running of the country is being put gradually back into the hands of the Germans which, I suppose, is a good thing for the British tax-payer. But it is making life complicated for me at the moment. Especially as, if you give them an inch, they aren't content with anything so paltry as a yard!

After all these long months, I suddenly discover why the name 'T-Force' has never appeared in the press—evidently the security value of it is such that H.M. Government cannot even afford to recognise its existence! You will have to dig a deep hole for me, if the Russians ever get wind of us.

I must send this off or I won't—
With all my love,
Michael

I was due for another fortnight's spell of leave, and it looked like being right at the time of my birthday on 26th May. The fact was that from the outbreak of war until I joined the army, I made no close friends of my own age of either sex, other than at school. Wartime restrictions made it difficult. After joining the army I made good friends of half a dozen of my contemporaries, but none of them was by any means accessible in England at the time that I happened to reach my twenty-first birthday. I tried to appear more accommodating to my mother than I had the year before, and left it to her in the confident expectation that she would see my point and keep the whole business low-key.

I started to use my new camera to attempt portraits, John Bayley being the nearest and easiest subject, and one who betrayed no trace of self-consciousness in front of the camera. The one of him sitting on my bed, immersed in the *Faber Book of Comic Verse* without a hint of a smile on his face, is one which I later treasured—particularly after he had been awarded the Newdigate Verse Prize at Oxford. I enjoyed the implication that I had helped to set him off on the poetic path. Wigg had a patently intelligent,

John Bayley reading my Faber Book of (fairly) Comic Verse.

handsome face, but was more elusive, and found it difficult to take the process seriously.

News came which settled our hash as far as Class B release was concerned. New conditions were introduced which by a narrow margin ruled out both Robin and myself as far as Michaelmas term in early October 1947 was concerned. Since our Release Group (63) was still scheduled for February 1948, it meant another winter in Germany with a unit which had effectively finished its job,and still there would be a gap of eight months before going up to Cambridge. Our colleagues in the Mess felt our disappointment keenly enough to hold a sort of wake over lunch-time, fuelled by a bucketful of 'gnomes' blood'.

Here we were two full years after the surrender, with no apparent amelioration in the lot of the ordinary German, and the further we moved away in time from the military collapse, the more the civil population began to show their dissatisfaction with their lot. The gradual attempt to place government up to regional level back in German hands tempted them to try their luck wherever they saw an opening to exploit. An unendearing but perhaps understandable trait of the Germans of that generation was that they understood two relative positions only: either you had your heel on their neck, or they would have their heel on yours. An attitude of mutual tolerance and collaboration was not one they understood, nor had much natural talent for. Our civilian employees rather got caught in the crossfire.

His Majesty's Government had apparently such a bad conscience about the 'price of defeat' which T-Force had become the instrument for exacting, that not even our name was allowed to appear in print, although in the early days after the collapse of Germany some stories of what we were up to were leaked into the press. But at the same time no real attempt was made to keep our activity completely under wraps. As already described, the BIOS Reports on our targets, written by the investigators whom we had shepherded round German industry, were published and on sale in HMSO and available to anyone walking in off the street with the money to pay for them—including not just our allies but our late enemies as well as our new enemies in the east. You did not have to show your passport or other identification to buy one in HMSO in Kingsway. Many of our industrial and other companies had participated in the interrogations of scientists and technicians, and were not sworn to secrecy. So, it was a sort of open secret, the product of a split mind in government. Exhibitions in the UK of the product of our activities drew further attention to them.

It was clear that the enemy was now the Russians, and all the cases in which we were called upon for strong urgent action involved keeping them away from targets we did not want them to have. We were unsure how far they were aware of the acts of interdiction of which they had been the victim, or of the identity of those of us who carried them out. Nevertheless, when I came up for release I was warned that for the foreseeable future it would be unwise of me to find myself in Russian hands.

From about 1948 the Control Commission for Germany began to destroy their files and documents, and this continued until 1956 when the remaining 240 tons were brought back to the UK. Then the Foreign Office set about them, employing mostly retired officials who had been given a brief, the details of which were never disclosed, but which did not leave much to chance. Today, less than two tons of those documents remain. It was a deliberate attempt to make the task of writing a complete history of a unit whose very name was not to be voiced in the public domain very difficult. Great care has been taken to prevent a cataloguing of what we took out, and above all to avoid setting a monetary value upon it.

CHAPTER 6

A body in the kitchen – A bride at the Möhne Dam – A trip to Paris – Some very drunken Russians – A farewell dance turns into a flood

H.Q. No. 1 T-Force Unit, Kamen

Sunday 10th May 1947

Darling Mama,

Your admonishment, the fags, and your last letter all arrived safely in that order. I hardly dared open the first—every word of it more than justified. I tell myself just what you said every day, with paralysingly little effect, as you will have noticed. Don't think that I have changed, or 'gone bad' or anything—I haven't. Don't think that I don't worry too, because I do, though that may sound funny coming from this end. It isn't really that I have lost the ability to finish things off either—I know that from my work. It may be that in the last year I have of necessity been too far submerged in my job—which I am sure is a bad thing, and something I always intended to avoid: I saw what it did to Alec Bateson and Alan Cowan and some others. I haven't gone all military-like and lost my sense of humour as they did, although it might appear so from all this introspection. It is hard not to get absorbed in a job when one realises that one is holding down a difficult job, and doing it well: that may well sound a trifle self-satisfied to say the least, but on Friday one of the staff officers from H.Q. came down to tell us that it was realised that the new C.O. wouldn't be interested in the work, and that as before all the work would be done, and the decisions made, in my office: and that we could continue to count on their support of anything we chose to do off our own bat. And that one of my last letters had been taken up by the Brig. with the Deputy Military Governor!

I am trying with scant success to grow a moustache. I have skipped shaving the upper lip for the past three days—and have acquired a fair downy fur which can be observed in favourable light from close-to. I shall leave it on until I come on leave, and then make the big decision on whether to keep it or not.

I am due to come on leave a week today—Sunday 18th. I get in to London at about ten on Monday morning—I can go to Pulford's for my fitting for my suit. You hadn't told me about the offer of Uncle Tom's dinner jacket— no fear of it being too small! Would it be possible to have it left at Pulford's between now and the 18th?

A new and very pleasant major is in our midst—quiet, not humourless and fortunately tolerant. The new C.O. is from the Scots Guards—name of Grant. Not an idea in his head, but, I believe, a considerable aptitude for fly-fishing. He is quite content to let us carry on just as we are—which suits us right down to the ground. We were rather amused that during his first week he came into the office once only, and then to see if the floor was dirty! He has since come in and asked what goes on, but walked off before we had a chance to tell him. Early on Saturday he runs off over the Rhine to fish near Cleve; he lives in Unna, the next-door town, and the only time we see him is for lunch—as long as you don't talk about blowing up fish with grenades he is more than happy.

I was in the garden the other evening when Christa, Margret's sister, came rushing in bristling to tell me that the evening before she had been at a party consisting of her contemporaries at school and university, and a few others, and that the officers were discussed in detail, and that Robin and I were considered the only two not drunken nor dissolute nor corrupt—or all three! So I may dare to re-appear in Kamen in years to come; it is a dirty, smelly little town, but I have become quite attached to it, and I don't much want to move the H.Q. now. I have slept in the same room now for seven months, and fed in the same room for fourteen months.

I have hopes of being able to bring a bottle of Cointreau with me! We have devised a most pleasant but potent cocktail which is no more than an ordinary White Lady with a trace of French and a vestige of bitters in it:- we'll be able to try that one on some of our more staid acquaintances. You haven't given me a lead as to what else to bring but I think a spot of German gin for me, and a spot of Gordon's and a bit of fizz for you should meet the case. My camera I shall also bring, and plenty of film, and I shall photograph incessantly, all the things such as Mou-Mou and Battle which I meant to do last time.

I am contemplating, on about June the first, fixing a duty trip for myself with B.I.O.S. secretariat: to go to Vienna and/or Munich, where I would spend the rest of my leave. I feel that it is an opportunity which I should perhaps not miss, and I won't always get H.M. Government paying my fare. Still, I can decide when the time comes nearer.

The weather has been superb, if not infrequently punctuated by thunder storms. We usually get out in the sun for an hour in the late afternoon, and although I thought I didn't sunburn, I am told that I have turned what is technically known as a 'healthy tan'. Usually when I get home it is implied that I look like death and need a good bit of rest and lots of feeding up—I think you'll find me in good shape this time, but I can never tell by just look-ing in the mirror.

As I sit here making my little and rather belated effort, at believe it or not, twenty minutes past midnight, I can hardly hear myself think for the sound of the nightingale in the garden, only a few feet away!

I am not a little shaken by the prospect of going on doing this until February 1948, but it is no use feeling in any way grieved. But I can't afford to ignore

any possible channel through which I might get released by October. Robin has put his papa on the job, and John Bayley has given me a string I can try to pull while on leave, and that with a visit to Peterhouse and a pathetic appeal to our M.P. would appear to be about the lot.
Must close down and send this off. Until Monday then.
All my love,
Michael

It would have been wrong of me to have been critical of my mother for laying such emphasis upon regular letters. My parents' separation from their children over the four years when they had been in Fiji and we had been sent to England for our education had been hard for her to bear. She was entitled to more consideration.

Nason's term in command had run its course, and we had to accustom ourselves to his successor, P C H Grant, Scots Guards, a process which enabled us to see some virtues in Nason after all. We were presented, as far as I could discern, with a commanding officer without charm or any perceptible intelligence, or any adaptability. I suspect that these characteristics had also been quickly detected by HQ T-Force, who in the circumstances—i.e. having in No 1 T-Force an intelligence mechanism which ran like a Singer sewing-machine—were ready to assist in the laudable process of easing the way of such gentlemen out of the service in which they could have no worthwhile future, with honour and the honorary rank of lieutenant-colonel. To avoid the risk of a revolt of the peasants, they will have told the new Colonel that he could safely leave operations to run themselves. Denis Gilson, the G2, went so far as to come down to Kamen to see me personally, to tell me that everyone (the Brigadier, the G1, and himself) realised that Grant would not be interested in the work of the unit—actually, I suspect they told him not to be. The work would continue to be done and the decisions made in my office, and we (Robin and I, along with the estimable Sergeant Wigg) could continue to count on their support for any decisions we took without reference. This was an astonishing state of affairs, to the point of irregularity—but then we were irregulars. It could hardly fail to induce in us feelings almost of contempt for Grant, but we were trusted not to let it show, and to accord him apparent respect even if it were only a veneer. We would have to treat him like a difficult child. As the days went by, Grant lived up to his billing. He checked on the cleanliness of the floors, asked us what we did, remembered that he was not meant to ask, then turned on his heel and walked away. He would disappear early on Saturday to exercise his talent for fly-fishing some ninety miles away near the Dutch border, then return for lunch on Monday. He was a sort of spoof Colonel of the Guards.

By the end of the month I would have come of age. Perhaps I thought that sporting a moustache would lend me a year or two. My account of my efforts (which were never repeated) showed, I think, that I had not lost the ability to laugh at myself—something I feared. Alec Bateson and Alan Cowan were two friends who had preceded me from Rugby into the Rifle Brigade and appeared to have become so single-minded about soldiering that they had indeed lost, or at least temporarily mislaid, their sense of humour. Years later I got to know Alec again and, if he had ever lost his sense of humour, he had certainly by then fully recovered it.

I wish I could be sure about the identity of the 'new and very pleasant major'. He would have been the officer commanding A Detachment, hence joining the Mess in Kamen. Robbie Cooper, Royal Tank Regiment, was in that spot for my last six months, so I think it must have been him. Thirty-something, always good for a laugh, always good for a drink too, Robbie also had an eye for a pretty face or a shapely leg, as the Mess servants would soon discover. One day at lunch, just as the waitress was walking past Robbie's chair, the Colonel's Labrador, Tioram, greeted her from behind by laying his cold nose against her upper inner thigh, of which a certain amount was exposed by her shortish skirt. The waitress promptly slapped Robbie's hand.

We laughed, she and Robbie blushed. We decided that Tioram should no longer have the run of the dining room at mealtimes anyway, as he was a hazard to hygiene. We were told that 'Tioram' was the Gaelic for 'dry', and that the dog was so named because he was always thirsty.

Christa was bursting to inform us—Robin and myself—of the verdict delivered upon us by her coterie of girlfriends (she was by now 24). They decided that, of all the T-Force officers in Kamen, we were the only ones who behaved decently. We were interested and surprised to discover that we figured as a subject for discussion among the local young women of better class. We were seldom exposed to their observation, so was the source of their information perhaps somebody on the inside? Christa would have spoken for us, of course, but could they have depended on the testament of 'Hanni the Honeyblonde', the Shakespeare enthusiast who served us at table and had the opportunity to observe us at play in the Mess? Furthermore, we thought their judgement a bit hard on John Bayley, who lived a blameless life and could on no account have been thought drunken, dissolute or corrupt, as Christa herself could testify—unless when he went out for his German lessons he got up to some quite uncharacteristic tricks. And even Johnny Pepys Cockerell, our other Etonian, hardly qualified as a rake, despite never missing his round. Nevertheless, it was a boost to our egos that we had been found to be of good reputation by the Germans of our own generation.

By May, I was becoming aware of the opportunities for travel for rest and recreation at His Majesty's expense, and aware that I might not have much more than six months in which to avail myself of them. The work of T-Force and BIOS offered many such opportunities, and I let it be known that I was open to suggestion. The appeal of Vienna, as yet still known as the home of Schubert and Lehár rather than *The Third Man*, was very strong for me, but nothing came up immediately.

At some time between the turn of the year and May, and for reasons of which I was not informed, I had to move my room to the Schultze-Westen house between the Mess and the doctor's house at number 8. My new room was pleasant, with doors leading out onto a flat roof or verandah, over which hung the outer branches of a huge peach tree. Later in summer some of the peaches would dangle within easy reach, and I would call for champagne so that we could enjoy the luxury of peaches and champagne without straying from my room. It made the best of breakfasts on a Sunday morning, but twice was enough. Some time after the end of April the nightingales, which had spent the winter in Africa, returned to Europe and were present in numbers in the Ruhr and Rhineland. One of the males had settled for my peach tree, and I first became aware of him one night when my sleep was shattered by his incredibly loud territorial song, which seemed to last until dawn. Giving nary a thought for the role that the song of the nightingale had played in European literature and music, I repeatedly urged my new neighbour to be gone and sing elsewhere, but every night he maintained his position resolutely on that same branch twenty-five feet from my pillow. Eventually I drew my Luger, marched out onto the verandah, took aim, and ordered him straight to shut up. He didn't even budge, he just sang blithely on. It occurred to me that if I roused the neighbourhood with my own territorial song—a gunshot— tiresome explanations would inevitably have to follow. There was no way I could let it be known that I had just shot a nightingale. Anyway, I would probably have missed; it is a very small bird. The very small bird prevailed. I put up my weapon, withdrew from the field and tried to block my ears. Exhaustion got me to sleep at last.

Kamen
10th June 1947

Darling Mama,
It surprises me how easily one can slide back into one's skin—I'm holding all the reins again. I was met by Robin at the Dutch frontier, whence we

drove home. Robin was never a fool, and always quite capable, but now he has become businesslike into the bargain.

I hope to go to Paris on the 8th of July with Tony Lucas. I don't intend to lose any of my chances for entertainment between now and the time I leave the army.

We are in the middle of a slight 'crise' within the unit. The house in which I used to live was the doctor's, and he used to use three of the downstairs rooms as a consulting room and surgery—and six officers and two batmen were billeted upstairs. The Colonel has thrown us all out, and is taking the whole house for himself and his wife. In addition, he is telling the doctor to clear out. He is quite incapable of understanding that in a country where there are only 230,000 houses for 6 million inhabitants, it literally is morally wrong for two people to occupy a 32 room house. There is positively no alternative accommodation for the doctor to set up his surgery and consulting room: and this in a town where the men and women with all manner of diseases lie crowded in the same ward. The doctor is the leading expert on miners' diseases in this province. I have told the Colonel what I think—as had Robin and John before I returned. The Colonel was so childish as to ask me to try and prove that the doctor had been an ardent Nazi. When I told him that I knew the old boy quite well, and was quite certain that he had not been one, he was a bit taken aback. The doctor of course lodged an appeal, which met with some success at first, but has later been turned down. The Colonel has given him a month to clear out, and 'forbade' him to make any attempt to get his house back. The stupidity of it—no wonder the people get a bad impression of us.

Later—very!

Up to my old tricks again—I must post this at once and write again. Had a spot of 24 hours flu but am fit and well again. Photos not ready yet.

All my love,

Michael

It was always nice to be met at the Dutch border when returning from leave, because after that the Rhine Army 'Express' meandered south into the Ruhr, and through Essen and Dortmund before passing through Kamen where one could hijack it and get it to stop to suit one's convenience. It seems unlikely that I based my assessment of Robin's new-found business-like qualities purely on the strength of his having brought a car to meet me at the right place at the right time.

All became clear concerning my sudden move to the Schultze-Westen house. As had been the case on and off really since I had arrived in Kamen, the occupation of the doctor's house at Sesekedamm 8 was a bone of contention. It had come to a head during my absence on leave, with Colonel Grant deciding that he would like the house for himself as married quarters, and proposing to throw the doctor out of the three rooms he had been allowed to use for his practice for the past year. Dr Kunsemüller appealed again. Though not always well-advised in the manner in which he pressed for the return of his property, he did so with genuine justification, not least because he and his family were occupying space in a severely overcrowded hospital; conditions there for patients were unacceptable. And, of course, the original requisition had been illegal anyway. The figures I quoted for the number of houses against the population figures were for the Ruhr area as a whole, and were for undamaged houses. But people were also living in homes which had been bomb-damaged to a greater or lesser degree, and some were even living in ruins and cellars which were decidedly unfit for human habitation. For a house of such a size to be occupied just by the Colonel and his wife (and later their daughter, alas of marriageable age) would have been atrocious, and I told him straight that it would be plain *wrong*. From the look of absolute puzzlement on his face, I judged that this was perhaps a concept with which he had little familiarity. I was pleased to discover that, when this matter had come up while I was away a few days previously, both Robin and John had used the same word to him. He must have begun to feel that there might be something in it, if we all used it—or perhaps it was a conspiracy? In order to demolish the doctor's case, the Colonel asked me to prepare what might these days be termed a 'dodgy dossier' in order to prove a rabid Nazi past for the doctor. Grant appeared to consider it something of a betrayal on my part when I could show him only that the exact reverse had been the case, and that the doctor had conducted himself in such a way as to place himself personally at risk from Party discipline and worse. The Colonel was more than just taken aback, he was livid. He gave the doctor a month to get out of the three practice rooms, but much was to happen in that month.

By June, with the prospect of no new intelligence targets after the end of the month, and existing 'serials' pending evacuation beginning to run down, it was felt that my exemption from participating in external courts martial could very well be lifted. It was agreed that I should initially attend a court as 'officer under instruction' in order to refresh my memory of procedure. The first case to come up was very close to home. Discipline at C Detachment at Ratingen had remained a problem, even long after Major Powell had been spirited away to avoid what would inevitably have been a high-profile court martial. A very slack regime had developed, though this was not immediately apparent during brief visits from HQ. With that history, and in those conditions, a scandal was simply waiting to happen.

A little after midnight one Saturday night, when the members of the Sergeants' Mess had gone to bed, a woman who was known to be the *maîtresse-en-titre* of Company Sergeant Major Weir let herself in as she was wont, and made her way upstairs to his bedroom. There she found not only that Weir's door was locked, but that there were audible signs of another woman within. She went downstairs quietly to the kitchen and turned on the gas oven. When the sergeants came down to breakfast in the morning, there she was, stretched out on the table. They thought that she was merely drunk as usual, and the morning bustle continued around her for a while. There was a whiff of gas, but no-one connected it at first with the woman recumbent on the table.

Finally, somebody noticed that the poor woman was dead. The Duty Officer was nowhere to be found, and none of the right procedures was followed in the meanwhile. He eventually showed up around noon. I later learned—he did not tell everyone—that he had spent the night on the wrong (west) side of the Rhine, in the company of a lady who had represented her country at breast-stroke in the 1936 Olympics in Berlin. Apparently she was still in terrific form.

Sergeant Major Weir was placed under open arrest on more than one charge, including that of 'conduct to the prejudice', and kept for the time being confined to the Sergeants' Mess at Kamen. It so happened that Weir's was the first and only court-martial at which I was to sit as officer under instruction. Several German witnesses were called, including the lucky new lady, and their evidence was given in German, which had then to be translated into English by a German interpreter. I had a seat behind the Members of the Court. In the course of translation, the interpreter made what I considered to be a mistranslation prejudicial to the interests of the accused, and I made a written note. Several others followed, six in all. It could hardly be accidental. When the court was considering its verdict, I could bear it no longer and intervened. I was asked by the president of the court to read out my notes. They felt they had no option but to dismiss the case. I was reminded of Maurice Healy's story of the Kilkenny judge dismissing the obviously guilty accused with the words, 'You have been acquitted by a Kilkenny jury, and you may leave this court with no *other* stain upon your character.' There must have been something aphrodisiac about the air in Ratingen because Weir went straight back to enjoy it.

Kamen
22nd June 1947

Darling Mama,
I enclose copies of the last two films I took while at home. Not one failure,
but the one of Bob standing is a little bit blurred. I am particularly pleased
with the one taken from my bedroom window looking toward the kitchen

garden—it has a lovely warm effect about it. The photographer says that owing to a shortage of printing paper he is unable to do me any more copies, so I also enclose the negatives of the snaps of the girls, and of Bob. I think Clark would do as many copies as they might like.

Bill Adams is away in England this week, and so I am running his office for him in Düsseldorf, which means that Robin and I are being more or less run off our feet. In addition, we are having to make all the administrative arrangements for running a taxi service of 200 Volkswagens for allied businessmen in Germany!

Nevertheless, we took yesterday off and went down to Duisburg-Wedau, an internationally-known spot for rowing, and watched a regatta in which Ronnie Coe was rowing. He was the only Englishman in the race, and when at one stage they announced that he was leading by a clear length, we thought we were going to have to run for it, but when they announced that he had caught three crabs in quick succession, was steering crooked and was three lengths behind, this appealed enormously to the German sense of humour, and they laughed uproariously. When Ronnie came in second by six lengths, the air of tension was completely relieved. Coe gave us all dinner chez the town major of Essen, in a transit hotel. But by ten o'clock after a first-class meal, the party was becoming so alcoholic, and the set-up looking gradually less and less savoury, that Robin and I pushed off home.

The struggle for the doctor's house has become intensified. The Colonel has, like an ass, told H.Q. T-Force that if he loses the house, he will be forced to resign his command. The public health authorities in Düsseldorf have declared the requisition of the house illegal in the first place, and the Coal Control, and the Miners' Trade Union, both influential bodies, are backing the objection. And as my acquaintance with the family is not unknown, I can hardly afford to appear in the slightest degree partisan.

One is becoming increasingly more convinced that summer fell on a Wednesday again this year.

The enlargements of the dogs are not yet ready. When are we to be a mother?
No more news for the moment—I must get this off.
All my love,
Michael

Manning Bill Adams' liaison office in Düsseldorf in his absence had become important now that growing confidence was emboldening German industrialists to challenge the evacuation programme. Such challenges were not made directly to us, but by approaching the head of the branch of the Industry Division of the Control Commission responsible for their sector of industry at Regional level in Düsseldorf. It was better that they should do so there, rather than bothering us in Kamen. Bill was a practised and conciliatory intermediary, and he saved us a lot of aggro. His absence meant that for a week I had to start my day in the office at Kamen first thing in the morning, endure a fifty-minute slog on the autobahn, spend four hours in Bill's office in Düsseldorf in the middle of the day, endure another fifty-minute slog back home again, and then work in my own office until last thing in the evening. It was a fairly punishing routine, but it was only for a week.

We took Saturday off, and went to support Ronnie Coe sculling at his regatta at Duisburg/Wedau. It would have been intolerable to the German crowd in the grandstand around us if he had won; fortunately, Fate intervened and, as the commentator told us, *'Der Englische Major versteuert, und verliert sein Platz.'* ('The English major has steered crooked, and has lost his place.') The news was received with a great cheer from the crowd, and this relieved the tension. He came in second by a distance—just as well, or we might have had to scarper. Ronnie was livid at being beaten by someone who was (a) younger, (b) German, and (c) having to train on less sustaining rations. His many weekends in Essen and nearby Baldeney had led to a good relationship between him and the Town Major of Essen, who flew his flag from the Essener Hof Hotel in the centre of the town. He stood us all to dinner in the hotel, and very good it was—rather ironic in an area where it seemed to me that rations were lower and hunger greater than anywhere else. We noted the quality of the cuisine for future reference. Ronnie's lady-friend had been pointed out to me at the regatta, but she was not of the party. It was as if she did not exist, so at least we were spared the embarrassment of enquiring after her husband's health, especially as we saw more of him than she did. The party got very drunk, and we had to drive home. Ronnie had only a mile or two to go to fall into the arms of his *inamorata*, and the Town Major merely to climb the stairs.

Grant was determined to make an issue of his intention to take over the doctor's house as his living quarters, to the point of making it a resigning matter. We were very much inclined to tell him not to be silly, but remembered that we had to treat him with consideration. In the end he vented his spite on the doctor by designating the premises as the offices of the Intelligence Section rather than his own married quarters, and I was therefore obliged to move my people into a space far larger than we needed. However, at least the doctor was allowed to continue his occupation of the three rooms he used for his medical practice. The increasing transfer of local government into German hands had the effect of politicising the whole affair. The doctor was well known and respected by the miners at the Zeche Monopol in Bergkamen for treating their sicknesses and injuries. They made representations to their trade union, which pressed the case with the British North German Coal Control, who took the miners' part. However, at the end of the day no-one was prepared to risk trying to keep us out of premises required as offices, specious though the excuse was. With regard to Grant's living quarters, HQ T-Force had indeed told him not to be silly, and he went to look for something he liked in Iserlohn eighteen miles away. It was a blessing in disguise.

Once we had moved our office into their house, the Kunsemüllers were still allowed the fairly free run of the garden, and little Ina-Maria, now two, went where she pleased, including my office. Sometimes, when I had been working in my office on a summer evening, the infant would see me through the open window and we would wave at each other. She would toddle busily off to the other end of the garden where the wild strawberries grew, and bring me a handful as I sat at my desk. As a reward, I would let her use the telephone to ring up her mother or Margret, or even one of the clerks in the next room. She used to stand entranced as she listened to the voice coming out of the machine.

Kamen

28th June 1947

Darling Mama,

I hope the last lot of photos got safely to you. Enclosed are a couple of enlargements of each of the dogs, with two of the great man himself, one in attitude of repose and the other as for work—note 2 telephones. I also had some done of Roy, John and Robin all of which turned out well, but as I had of course to give them the spare copies, you will have to wait until I next come over.

On Tuesday I go to Paris for a 72 hour short leave—Tony Lucas is coming to keep me company. Then when I come back Robin is going. Then at the end of the month we shall both do a weekend at Winterberg—where we went to ski in the winter. In August we shall take it in turns to go to Prague, leaving Vienna until September, and doing the trip by road both ways.

Michael Corbett never came on leave—he is too near his release date. He appears to be leading an entertaining if slightly debauched life in Athens.

For the last four days we have been having the most amazing weather, with the temperature anything up to 105°F. In the evenings and over the weekend we have been lying as dead men in the sun, toppling at frequent intervals into the handy pool in the garden. It is about 18 foot square, and four foot deep.

The Colonel felt that he hadn't quite got a grip on the business of the unit, and instructed me to send up for his approval every letter emanating from our office. The first day we sent him up 93, which took him the whole morning to wade through—in the whole week we managed to turn out 370, so we hope that soon he will be heartily tired of the practice, and give it up.

When Robin heard that he was destined to become Adjutant in August he immediately wanted to rush off and get another job, but I think he is resigned to it now, and we have agreed to more or less share both jobs.

The Colonel now appears to want to live in Iserlohn, the late Corps head-quarters, half an hour's run away in the car: a good respectable distance. There is now no need for a Colonel in the unit—there are only 200 men to command, so the less he disturbs us the better. In any case he goes fishing on Friday every week, coming back on Monday.

Thank the Lord we went back to single summer time last night—it means that one can get to sleep by about midnight now—and all the best wireless programmes are at a more reasonable hour.

More cherries and strawberries than that—this is a great country for fruit—the advantage of a genuine continental climate I suppose.

Christa's (Margret's sister's) child, of whom I have I think already shown you some snaps, is growing into the most delightful infant. During yesterday afternoon it was toddling round in and about the swimming bath, and I took another dozen snaps of it—one of it laughing horribly, sticking its little belly out, and yelling the German equivalent of 'Fat Tum'.

This evening (Sunday) it has cooled off a bit, and thunder is rolling round the hills to the south—and in the plains to the north, but we seem to have escaped it. How clever of the weather to know we don't need a storm here—the air is quite clear, and the atmosphere not in the least oppressive.

My sergeant Wigg has today completed six months from his day of application to marry his girl—so as soon as his papers come back with 2nd Echelon approval he will be free to marry her. I have as tactfully as I could suggested that she should now stop working in the Sgts.' Mess, where she looks after him, as any less well-informed and more suspicious minds might smell a 'set-up'. He took it well and she stopped working there the day the papers went forward for approval.

No news else—will write when I get back from Paris. I phoned Dicky there
this morning on our new international service to book accommodation.
All my love,
Michael

T-Force had priority in various fields, transport was one, and communications was another. Telephones were in short supply, therefore to have one telephone line—let alone two—on one's desk was a status symbol. But to have had two telephone lines to my bedside as well was a particular mark of distinction. Robin had only one of each, but this still constituted an unusual sign of favour. The demobilised Dicky Muir had been of some practical assistance to us: he was by now at the Sorbonne in Paris, so we made international phone calls from our desks asking him to make a hotel booking for Tony Lucas and myself at the Hotel Chateaubriand-Balzac in the Rue Balzac, which ran between the Champs Élysées and the Avenue Friedland, just two blocks from the Étoile.

In the hot weather those of us who had been billeted in the doctor's house made liberal use of the *Planschbecken*, the plunge pool in the garden, which in the late afternoon and evening became a focus for social activity. The pergola afforded some shade for conversation and discussion, even for argument. John, Johnny, Robin and I could often be found there, and often also Margret who might be taking Ina-Maria off her sister's hands. John Bayley and Margret had no difficulty in finding subjects for lively discussion and argument, often apparently passionate, probably literary. The water in the pool was kept at a level which was safe for the child. It stayed

Margret, deep in discussion with John.

271

miraculously clear, though there was no filter system. I suppose they must have used chlorine tablets to purify it.

Out of the blue, Grant suddenly felt a resentment of his isolation from the intelligence work of the unit, and wanted to be allowed at least to 'approve' our outgoing correspondence. The only thing to do was to kill him with kindness. Most of the first ninety-three letters were merely routine and he can hardly have read them all. He had no comment or suggestion to make on any of them. One day he was obliged to delay reading the day's offering until tea-time, which was when he usually left, and it took him until after dinner to finish them. There was never any discussion about anything he had read, we just humoured his whim. It took time and patience, but the new regime lasted a mere ten days.

The British Army of the Rhine, which was contracting in accordance with the reduction of its fighting strength, disbanded I Corps which had its head-quarters in Iserlohn. They had earlier requisitioned premises in keeping with the needs of a large formation, including married quarters for quite a number of fairly senior officers, and many of these quarters were therefore falling vacant. Grant kept an eye open for a house that would suit him, and fortu-nately found one that he liked. This enabled him to forget about the doctor's house in Kamen without losing face, and to move his personal centre of grav-ity to a location from where he was able still to enjoy his weekend fishing. His job was a sinecure.

Roy Smith, the Adjutant, heard that his Release Group was to be demo-bilised in August, and the finger of Fate fell on Robin. We could no longer maintain that the volume of work required the attention of both of us. Robin was convinced that working closely with Grant would be intolerable, and he swore that he would look for a job elsewhere, even though he had only five or six months to go. His influential father could have conjured up another job without difficulty, but I persuaded Robin to stay on the under-standing that we would share both jobs, but he would get the captaincy and extra pay and prestige that went with the post of Adjutant. He had by this time conceived such a deep dislike of Grant that he was only just consoled by this arrangement.

Double British Summer Time lasted only until the week after the summer solstice, which meant that it would again be dark rather before midnight, and that European continental broadcast concerts would be on air at a time which would not oblige us to stay up until the small hours to listen to them.

After an application went forward for permission to marry a German national, there was a 'cooling-off period' of six months to allow time for consideration as to whether the proposed marriage would be a wise course of action. After that, if the request were not withdrawn, agreement was just a formality. A little while after Wigg had become personally committed to Margarete, she came to serve as a waitress in the Officers' Mess, where she became friends with Johanna Kenzian, otherwise known as 'Hanni the Honeyblonde'. Then she moved on to the Sergeants' Mess to wait at table, and to look after Bob Wigg and also Sergeant Pyle who shared a room with him. Wigg and Pyle were the unit's pioneers in the matter of marriage with German women. I had suggested to Wigg that too abrupt a transformation for Margarete, from a position as servant in the Mess to that of wife of a leading sergeant, might appear unseemly, and they kindly allowed themselves to be guided by me. They married at about the same time as Sergeant Pyle and his lady, again with the help of my Volkswagen substituting as stretch limo. There was no immediate opportunity for a conventional honeymoon, so the next Saturday John Bayley and I offered to take them out for a drive, anywhere she would like to go. She had always wanted to have a look at the Möhne Dam, so I took them all down there. They wandered around and across the dam, and looked up at the protective hanging steel bomb nets from the flood-damaged valley floor down below. I photographed them together. Once she could be identified as the wife of a sergeant, she was socially entirely at ease with the officers at whose table she had for a while served. It was possible that she, and her people still living in Pomerania, came from a social stratum in which officers were not a rarity. Sergeant Wigg's marriage brought about a marked improvement in his nervous and physical health. Once he and his wife had moved into the flat on the ground floor of the Schmitt's house where by that time I had my billet upstairs, if Bob noticed that I had, for instance, cut myself (I once stapled two fingers together) or torn my shirt, he would see to it that Mrs Wigg would appear with an Elastoplast dressing, or needle and thread.

Kamen

8th July 1947

Darling Mama,

Paris is now past-history, and I am back in Kamen. A most entertaining, if financially costly week. Last Monday evening I went down to Heisingen in a 16hp Austin kindly provided by our H.Q., and spent the night—or most of it—at the V.I.P. Guest House. Tony Lucas and I rose at four on Tuesday morning, and after a hectic car journey, caught the Nord Express at Düsseldorf by the skin of our teeth. Our travelling companions were an English youth from some welfare organisation, and a girl of about 22 from the Consulate in Hamburg.

At about eight I was feeling a little peckish, and as I only had 84 Belgian francs, I didn't know if we could afford breakfast—but the waiter told me that it only cost 25 francs a head. So Tony and I asked the girl to come along and have breakfast too, as she didn't have a sou in Belgian money. So we laid into a really good feed, and were not a little concerned to be presented with a bill for 214 francs! However, after much argument we paid the balance in French money—to our financial detriment, as the Belgian/French exchange rate is bad.

Having had our passes and luggage perused by German, English, Belgian and French authorities in turn, and having lunched at a more favourable rate, we pulled into the Gare du Nord a shade before five. We pushed by a zealous porter into the Metro and were led to the Embassy, whence we found our hotel and the cashier, and phoned Dicky Muir. He had kindly booked tickets for us at the Comédie Francaise, a modern straight play by Mauriac: we fed very well beforehand (the show started at 8.15) and afterwards wandered back home—some considerable distance, sipping vermouth at the occasional bar.

Of the rest I can only say that for the next four days we had the most lovely weather, and visited all the sights of Paris and Versailles, and went to Tosca, Carmen and the Ballets Jooss, and one French film. I took photos like a mad thing throughout as did Tony—some of them should be terrific. You may walk into almost any restaurant and order what you feel inclined to—we had some of the most enormous steaks I have ever seen. The food was however unpleasantly expensive. Nevertheless, our money which we had changed for francs lasted nicely, and we returned to Germany with the equivalent of only 6/8 in our pockets.

One does not learn much about the French during a short leave in their capital: however I confirmed my suspicion that I would hate to live among them, and detected at any rate one admirable characteristic, namely, that they do not interfere in anybody's private affairs—you may do what are usually considered as unconventional things in public without anybody taking the slightest notice. In most instances I found this charming—if thwarting to the exhibitionist. Anne wrote to me about my watch—the officer they were depending on had his leave postponed, or something and so we are trying to find some way of getting it direct from them to me safely, but yet without paying exorbitant duty on it. I think official mail is the best bet.[30]

I envy you being able to watch the tennis—from all accounts the play was of a pretty high standard and not un-entertaining.

---

30 A twenty-first birthday present from my parents, the watch would eventually be conveyed from Malta on a journey facilitated by my brother-in-law, and deposited at my bank in Berkeley Square.

I am desolated about Mou-Mou, I confess that she seemed to be bearing her burden awfully well—all a hoax!

I heard from Anne—an entertaining letter describing the visit of the French carrier 'Arromanches' among other things.

My little typist is away for three weeks in Vienna, and for the seven days I was away no D.R. arrived at the H.Q. with mail. Consequently no sooner had Robin departed to Paris on my return than a D.R. arrived with eight days' mail. I was presented with 76 letters, requiring action from H.Q., and 35-odd from the detachments: and since there was only Wigg and me to cope with it, and as I have been doing Robin's work in addition, it has taken me the whole week working until eleven at night to catch up, which I have now, thank goodness, achieved. Things also are especially difficult now that we are handing a great deal of control back to the Bosch: my God how they have been quoting the Hague Convention at me these last few weeks: on Tuesday I am going to run one slimy customer in for breach of the Terms of Surrender which of course still apply—that should shake them and keep them quiet for a bit in any case. Also we have just accepted considerable new commitments which have entailed my issuing a long and complicated directive—so there at any rate you have my reasons but no excuses for the delaying of this letter.

Daddy's letter to the W.O. covered certainly every point that I can think of—it couldn't have been better expressed either. If that doesn't do the trick, I can't think of anything which will.

One thing—if you can lay your hands on any post-card size photo-printing paper, I could do with up to 100 sheets for any more enlargements I may want. Took two more enchanting snaps of Christa's infant. One really can't go wrong with it. It is the most engaging child I know. Christa has just heard from her husband again, who indicated that he was likely to be repatriated in the not-too-distant future. I don't honestly think that she will ever see him again unless he gets home inside three months.

Also took some sweet snaps of Margret during the last hot spell, which obvi-
ously have to be printed not too near to Kamen.
One snatch of music whose name I have been hunting for months—I heard
the other night announced—the last of a set of four piano impromptus, Op.
no 90 by Schubert—the most lovely thing.
All my love,
Michael

In exculpation for my failure to write, I was using an expression for which I was indebted to my father. When his brigadier, on an inspection, had lifted the lid of a swill bin and saw lying on top four pounds of wrapped pork sausages in apparently prime condition, he had demanded, 'What is your excuse for that?' My father had replied, 'There will be a *reason*, and I shall find it out, but there can be no possible *excuse*.'

My friends at HQ T-Force felt that after fifteen months in the hot seat with little in the way of perks, I deserved a little pampering. So they sent me down their best available car, a top-of-the-range Austin, to take me chauffeur-driven down to Heisingen for the night at B Detachment, and on from there with Tony early the next morning to catch the Paris train from Düsseldorf. Everybody wanted to look at our papers and our luggage, even the Germans—at which I bristled slightly, until I remembered that we were now meant to encourage them to run their own country. We went in uniform in hopes that it would serve to remind the Parisians that they once had gallant allies and that those allies were not all American. It didn't do us much good, except to excite the expectations of the little *café-au-lait* Martiniquaise on the corner of the Champs Élysées and the Rue Washington whom, alas, we felt unable to oblige.

The British Embassy, some distance from our hotel, must have seemed to us like a good launch-pad. After a 4 am start we had slept a bit in the train, and fed before the theatre: François Mauriac's *Asmodée*. Tony and I had learned French together since 1935, but neither of us had ever been in France before. It would take a day or two before our French comprehension was up to speed. We did all the tourist stuff, and took in three operas and a ballet. The one opera which I did not name in my letter to my parents must have been one of the first few performances of Poulenc's surreal *Les Mamelles de Tirésias* at the Opéra Comique where it had been premiered on 3rd June 1947. At the conclusion of the first act, Tirésias/Thérèse (a double part, she wore the same white dress, but added a false black beard for the former) appeared at the back of the stalls and advanced down the aisle toward the stage, singing and holding in her arms a symbolic white wooden lyre. Tony and I were dressed for the occasion, wearing our Rifle-green patrols. Our seats on the aisle in the front row meant that we were ourselves very visible to the performers, including Thérèse, who finished her aria as she reached the bottom of the aisle, within inches of us. Did she brush against me? Having no more use for her lyre, she bent over and very carefully placed it upright on the ground exactly between us—showing, with exquisite delicacy, no preference. Exit left, applause, lights, interval. Thus was a script, as it were, thrust upon us, daring us to take the lyre back-stage, and insist on returning it to Thérèse in person, saying, 'We think you must have left this behind by mistake.' Or perhaps we were supposed first to have tossed-up to decide which of us should perform this service. Unprepared in every way for such an adventure, we chickened out, and handed the object to an attendant. In the second act, even after a couple of stiff drinks, we hardly dared look her in the eye. Perhaps I did not recount this to my parents because I felt it did not reflect very well on either of us, and certainly not as Riflemen on patrol or reconnaissance, to leave such an advantage unexploited.[31]

---

31 The soprano playing the double part of Tirésias/Thérèse that night was Denise Duval who had premiered in the opera on 3rd June, and went on to have an international career lasting eighteen years and very much associated with Poulenc in *La Voix Humaine* and the *Dialogues des Carmélites,* as well as *Mamelles.* She was just five years older than us, but ten years more sophisticated.

I came to the firm conclusion that France was a marvellous place to visit, but no place to live. Robin, on the other hand, who followed us to Paris the next week, ended up living there for twenty years as the correspondent of the *Observer* and, alas, dying there too young twenty years ago. His health was never robust.

My mother's poodle, Mou-Mou, about whose health I had been enquiring, was meant to be having a family, and had all the customary fits of the vapours, etc. But it turned out to be a phantom pregnancy.

There was a deluge of mail to greet me just as I returned from my week away, and with Robin now in Paris I was having to cover his desk as well. Naturally, this was the very point at which our mouse of a typist chose to take three weeks off, but to be honest her productivity was so low

The soprano Denise Duval, in her Dior gown for Poulenc's Les Mamelles de Tirésias, *Paris May 1947.*

and her work needed so much correction that she was not an unbearable loss. However, it took a week of working until late in the night to catch up, something of which the Colonel was quite unaware since he was so seldom there to notice—and never after tea.

I wonder which articles of the Hague Convention those indignant Germans were quoting at me—possibly the Laws and Customs of War on Land, or the 1899 Prohibition of Bombing from the Air, perhaps? All such attempts were aimed at preventing the evacuation of equipment or documents, and in terms of practical politics the provisions of Allied Control Council Proclamation No 2, the Additional Terms of Surrender, were in the end more immediate and always more potent. I never had to resort to charging a recalcitrant German under Proclamation No 2, the threat was enough. For those who contemplated disobedience, their lawyer's advice was always in favour of discretion, despite any show of bravado.

Relations between Russia and the Western Powers, and that included the western Zones of Germany, were by now deteriorating so rapidly that I feared the repatriation of German prisoners of war, never more than a trickle, might come to a halt within months, even those who had been 'indoctrinated', like Christa's husband Eberhard.

I had been fortunate, listening at random, to catch on the radio the announcement of a piece of piano music which had been on my mind for a while without my ever having known what it was: the fourth of the first set of Schubert Impromptus. I was not musician enough to be able to recognise and remember the key signature, which happened to be A Flat Major, but I managed to get by with 'Opus 90, No 4'.

That July we ran into the third of a sequence of 'high-level flaps' calling for urgent and strong action, and exhibiting the same characteristics as the preceding two: first that it involved interdiction from the Russians, and secondly that it involved a target for inspection by a quadripartite team which included four Russians. This time, however, it did not involve my being woken by a phone call in the middle of the night with a mystifying codeword—some improvement at any rate. It concerned a quite new equipment 'serial', a whole section of the plant of the Vereinigte Aluminium Werke at Lünen just a dozen miles down the autobahn west of Kamen, a target which had been identified and requested by an investigator from the British Aluminium Company. It would have been evacuated in the near future anyway, but the usual lack of effective liaison between the Reparations Agency and HQ T-Force meant that we had again not been forewarned that a quadripartite team had now been scheduled, at the instance of the Russians, to come and inspect the factory and prepare the inventory as a prelude to a bid either for the whole factory as reparations, or for any part of it. The team was already on its way, and would be based at the 'Red' Mess in Kamen while going over the factory.

We decided that there was only one thing for it: a prolonged and spectacularly alcoholic bash. A party to celebrate the signing of an inventory by the four national components of the team, British, US, French and Russian, was routine practice, and the signing ceremony at the conclusion of the festivities was generally a formality. But this time the official inventory of the factory would make no mention of the equipment requested by British Aluminium, and our plan was that the omission would go unnoticed by the Russians at the time of signature thanks to their utter inebriation. The team was led by a Conducting Officer who in this case was, to our great good fortune, Charles Roger Middleton, a civilian officer who wore on his battledress blouse the ribbon of the George Medal, won when extinguishing a fire in a huge fuel tank during the Blitz in 1940. A cool man in a hot spot, then. I do not know whether he had been specially selected for what might be a ticklish job, but he was a man who exuded authority. Conducting officers were not generally men of his quality.

When the time and place were set for the signing (twelve noon in my office, now in the Kunsemüller's house) the Russians said they would like to contribute a crate of vodka, a kind offer which was at once accepted. Seventeen in the team, and seven or eight of my people, say twenty-five in all, half a bottle of vodka each—quite normal dosage for a Russian shindig. But I let it be known that we would match them with a crate of German *Edelkornbranntwein*, rough corn brandy, warranted at least thirty days old. We knew that on straight vodka they would probably see us off, but on a fifty-fifty mix, an unholy brew which could itself have fuelled a V-2 rocket, we would be on all fours with them. I pressed Corporal Weatherall, the Mess Corporal, into service for the occasion and he was to provide no other glasses but half-pint beer mugs with handles, and serve the brew ready-mixed. Middleton had identified which of the four Russians was the NKVD officer keeping an eye on the others (there was always one secret policeman in every team), and it was important that he should be at least as inebriated as the others. Middleton conducted the proceedings with great aplomb, persuading the Russians to drink up, and they themselves cheerfully encouraged the others. Middleton himself missed not a round, though I think there were only two, since two was enough to complete the job in hand. We introduced them to the game of darts, which became ever more lethal as they hurled the unfamiliar projectiles at the board and, once their eyes glazed over, we called a brief halt. The British contingent hastily signed the inventory first, followed by the Russians, then the others. Not one of them made any attempt to read the document through. Sergeant Wigg then spirited the inventory away, and the team was conducted via the footbridge over the Seseke to the 'Red' Mess for a late lunch, followed by several hours' sleep.

My head had remained clear, but our alcoholic concoction played the hell with my knees. Apparently, I was heard for some reason to give the order, 'Corporal Weatherall, place me on the window-sill.' I declared the office closed for the day, except for two clerks manning the telephones. The next day the team had gone. Within days the equipment in question, 120 tons of it, had been crated up, trucked up to the Evacuation Depot at Geesthacht, and was on the water on its way to British Aluminium at Monmouth. We never heard a thing more, never had a word of thanks. We kept what was left of the vodka.

Kamen
29th July 1947

Darling Mama,
Naughty again! This short note betokens something more worthy to follow soon.
I am well, happy etc.
Weather fine but oppressive.

I am saddled with the usual extra work while the Colonel is on leave—and lose Robin next week when he becomes Adjutant.
63 Group begins demob on 19th December!!!!
All my love,
Michael

We had at last received a date, December 19th, for the commencement of the demobilisation of our Group, number 63. There was no guarantee that Robin and I would be in the first batch to go, but at least it put a finite term to our service, and prompted us to take advantage of the remaining five months to enjoy all the pleasures that the Army of the Rhine had to offer, especially since at the same time we had to run the intelligence activities of T-Force down to almost nothing. Roddy Bennett, who had joined up with us and would normally have been released with us, was enjoying life in the army and in Germany, and decided to sign on for a further period. He had purchased out of his own pocket the first Volkswagen off the production line at Wolfsburg to be sold to the general public after they had fulfilled their contract to supply 20,000 to the British Army. Roddy took advantage of always having his own transport at his fingertips, and of being able to carry anyone he pleased in it. I never knew if he had any German friends.

One fine, hot Sunday morning, when Robin was Duty Officer and hence tied to Kamen for the day, I suggested to John Bayley, 'Why don't we take a car and go and have a little drive down the Rhine?' It was a trip which I had made earlier with Robin. Tony Lucas at B Detachment and Tony Scolding at D Detachment joined our party too, and we picked them up in our Volkswagen, with me driving. We took off toward the south, into the hillier country to the east of the Rhine in the direction of Coblenz in the French Zone, where on the uplands they were already beginning to get the harvest in on farm carts drawn by oxen. Wearing 'shirt-sleeve order', we

didn't present a very military appearance, and dawdled along enjoying
the pretty country and stopping to
take in the view from time to time.
Eventually we turned west, and came
down to the Rhine at the little town
of Linz, and then north to Remagen
where the failure by the German
army to blow the bridge had enabled
the US Army tanks gingerly to cross
the river onto the east bank. The

Getting the harvest in by ox-cart.

bridge had collapsed ten days later after the Americans had consolidated
their bridgehead and much of it still lay in the river, but it had been cleared
sufficiently to allow the river traffic, the tugs and barges, to continue on
their way up to Switzerland. By mid-afternoon we were able to negotiate a
snack of wurst and gherkins in Bad Honnef to keep us going, knowing that
we were headed for country where British officers were well catered for and
we could later eat our fill.

The two Tonys, not about to swim across the Rhine to Bad Godesberg.

Our next objective on that hot day
was to get down to the Rhine for a swim,
and we found a way across the railway
line and down to the water's edge, at
the foot of the Siebengebirge. It was a
most unromantic spot. The shoreline of
pebbles and shingle was not very invit-
ing and not very clean, but swimming in the Rhine was a challenge we were
not going to duck. At the very fringe the current seemed fairly gentle, but as
you ventured further out the pull of the water became positively fierce. The
strength of the current became evident when we looked across to the west
bank and saw a tug, apparently static in mid-stream, attempting to tow four

huge barges. Only by focussing on a fixed object on the other shore could we detect the tug's painfully slow progress. The Rhine was very narrow at that point, constricted by the hills of the Siebengebirge. I took snaps to record the adventure, including one of John Bayley sitting naked on the shingle.

When we had dried off and dressed—not very smartly—it was getting toward seven o'clock, so our next target was the Kaiserhof Hotel up at the top of the Petersberg behind Königswinter, where we were confident of getting a good meal at the Officers' Club. With a quick look first into the chapel at the grenade damage which had been left so conspicuously unrepaired, we went in to the hotel and tidied ourselves up a bit. The dress code stipulated that, because Tony Lucas was wearing blue games shorts rather than khaki ones, we must be served outside on the terrace rather than in the restaurant. We much preferred this anyway; the view of the Rhineland bathed in the evening sunshine was magnificent. Two bottles of Moselle consumed at a most leisurely pace complemented the scene perfectly, and afterwards I dropped the two Tonys off at their billets long after dark, and took John home to Kamen.

Such a memorable and romantic day must have made a powerful impression on John. Eight years later when he published his first novel, a day spent down the Rhine by four of his characters figured in it strongly, and its description takes up thirty pages. They swam in the Rhine while a tug towing a train of immense barges made its way laboriously upstream—would they ever make it to Switzerland? In John's fictional car were two German civilians, including one girl—not something we would have risked so openly in our day. One of the others was Oliver Childers, a Bayley-esque figure (Oliver was John's second Christian name), a young and childlike officer. The driver was Duncan Holt, a somewhat unattractive figure. Writing to tell me about the book in 1955, John said, '...the other central figure [is] a sort of dreary *alter ego*, a tough persona, quite an ugly customer in fact.' I smelled a rat at once, but he denied everything. Much later, referring to his wife the novelist and philosopher Iris Murdoch, he wrote, 'Iris used to deny emphatically that real people appeared in her novels, but of course they inevitably did, however transformed. You were an *inspiration* to me in those very early days… hence, etc. But transformation is all, and imagination, one hopes.' And at another time, recently, 'Memory of course does not suffer in old age as the body does—my recollections of you and T-Force are crystal clear. I found our set-up so congenial and delightful, but you are the one I *really* remember. Dicky Muir even, Robin Smyth of course too, but less vividly. I thought you older as well as more experienced and knowing than I was, and your wonderfully sardonic humour (esp. on car trips, etc.), so sophisticated as well as amiable and reassuring.' After he remarried, we went to visit him and his new wife, Audi. With them was a lady in her middle years who had been one of John's pupils. 'Ah,' he said to her, 'I would like you to meet Michael Howard.' 'Ah,' she replied, 'Duncan Holt!' and shook my hand. They had been talking.

Kamen

23rd August 1947

Darling Mama,

You must think that I have 'gone bad', as Robin's mama suspected of his brother when he disappeared in Bombay without writing for nine months. Anything I can say about my lapse must of necessity sound pretty flabby and gutless.

One day is beastly much like another, except the few little items which occur in the course of my own work that entertain me, but are of little interest to others. Our ranks slowly get thinner—John Bayley, a delightful Guards-man, was demobbed three weeks ago—that only leaves Robin in the Mess to attempt to make intelligent conversation with. Roy Smith the Adjutant goes out today, and Robin takes over from him. In my office now I have a civilian officer to whom I am teaching Robin's old job, and who will eventually take over from me—at a salary of £800.

The Colonel, who is really only stupid, and not vicious, is going on leave for three weeks today. A bit of a relief—we get on quite well without him. In the course of a long and not particularly distinguished soldiering career, he has learnt to dispense entirely with a moral sense of any sort, and judges everything on the basis of expediency. Trying to explain to him why something is 'right', or 'wrong' instead of 'a good thing' or 'a bad thing' is like trying to explain the colour of a sunset to a man who has been blind for fifteen years, and isn't interested in sunsets.

I am at the moment recovering from a 'booster' TAB inoculation. I had cause the other day to go into the German hospital to find a British corporal who had been wrecked in a car smash—and stayed 20 minutes there, only to find that they have 40 cases of paratyphoid there. So I hied me straight off to the Dortmund hospital for a shot. My arm isn't stiff, but for two days I had a wee bit of a temperature, and the gland under my arm and on my neck swelled up.

While I still don't get as much chance of speaking German as I should like, I find myself as capable in that direction as all but one of the interpreters employed by the unit: and although I am perhaps not as confident or fluent as I would have been with more constant practice, I am assured that I do speak it like a native.

We have had a real summer this year—all the last four weeks have been really lovely. And I have been taking photographs like a mad thing—anything from local characters to the Rhine vineyards—including a snap or two of the Dortmund races, where most of the animals appear to have six legs.

I shall not be taking another leave in England, seeing as 'ow I get demobbed before Christmas, but will come over on duty in October sometime and spend a few days. The rest of my leave allocation I shall spend at the Austrian Ski-Centre at Ehrwald.

I see as much of Margret in a slightly sort of furtive way as the various restrictions on both sides demand. My 'guilty secret' is no longer one to my brother officers who fortunately do not consider it a matter for ribald jests or

undue publicity—anyway most of them have some peculiar set-up to conceal,
so they can't afford to be too patronising.

The German press has been 'shooting' at T-Force recently—a slip-up on
somebody's part, as it should never be allowed to get into print. So I cut it all
out and sent it all up to H.Q., asking for the protection of press silence. The
question has already gone up before the D.M.G.[32]*—with my translation of*
the cuttings!

No word from the university yet as to whether I shall be given a place in
January—I shall ginger them up with a personal visit in October.

Darling—this doesn't make up for a long silence or a series of painful short-
comings—and it doesn't anything like answer all your queries—but it is a
start. More to follow.
All my love,
Michael

John Bayley was gone, and would be missed particularly by Robin and myself; his calm temperament and subtle mind added a special dimension to the life of the Mess. At least he would be able to go up to New College Oxford in time for the beginning of the new academic year, an advantage denied to us. And, of course, he would go on to earn great academic and literary distinction as a critic and author. Roy Smith, who had been filling the post as Adjutant, was also gone—a nice, modest little man, he had at least spared Robin from having to do the job for quite a while, and Robin now felt that with only four months to go he could grudgingly face it for that length of time.

With Robin's disappearance from the intelligence function, and myself like-wise having only four months to run, we had to find someone to replace me and oversee the running down of what might remain of the evacuation programme. We were lucky to get hold of Rufus Harris, the civilian officer of the CCG who

---

32 Deputy Military Governor.

had taken over as Evacuation Officer at A Detachment. His marriage had not survived the war, and he needed pastures new. Robin described Rufus's make-up as fifty per cent intellect and fifty per cent sensuality—about right, I think. One morning at breakfast he told us that the night before, returning from a show at Iserlohn, he had spotted three young women in the headlight beam of his Humber 4x4. They were attempting to thumb a lift to Kamen whither he brought them, offering to deliver them each to their door. He had instinctively noticed that one of them was perceptibly more attractive than the other two, and carefully took her home last of the three. She invited him in, and he spent the night there. Rufus was about forty, short (no more than five feet five inches but with an unusually large head), and physically and otherwise resilient. He was an enterprising, highly intelligent, educated, and cultivated man with an enquiring and retentive mind, and most amusing. I felt quite happy about my leaving my job to him in due course. And I didn't mind where he slept, so long as he didn't frighten the horses. He later got to know an English lady working for the Control Commission whom he discovered to have 'a line in eroticism all her own'. He married her.

Grant's three weeks' leave was a good start to Robin's time as Adjutant; Ronnie Coe was laid-back and undemanding in his absence. It was a respite from the malady from which Grant suffered—trying to move us around merely to suit his interest—which was complicated by what seemed to me to be his other malady—a deficiency in moral sense, and an apparent unfamiliarity with the concepts of right and wrong. Could it have been several years as a prisoner of war that had imbued him instead with an instinctive bias towards the prior calls of expediency? He never revealed anything of his history before he fetched up on our doorstep, so our diagnosis that he was suffering from the effects of time spent as prisoner was no more than a charitable assumption. After all, how do you go from colonel in the Scots Guards, to commanding No 1 T-Force? Only on the way out after a hard time, I fear. We tried to make allowances for him—we could see he was not consciously wicked or vicious, and we were by no means confident that we would have reacted to the same experiences any differently.

As time had gone by I had allocated to myself fewer individual cases on the ground, and with that came fewer chances of using my German, but I was sufficiently well exposed to it for my imitative faculty to produce a good superficial effect. Best of the English interpreters posted from the CCG was one Jarvis, who now took over as married quarters the Schulze-Westen house between the Mess and the doctor's house. Bill Adams had moved from there down to Düsseldorf, while I moved my room to the Schmitt house, the last of the block of four. Jarvis' status did not entitle him to membership of our Mess. Employed as a maid-of-all-work in the Jarvis household was Johanna Kenzian, a.k.a. 'Hanni the Honeyblonde', our Shakespeare-spouting waitress in the Mess, who was also dubbed 'Sourpuss' by Ronnie Coe because that was the face she invariably showed to him. It ill concealed her disdain. She had reserved the same face for Tony Chance, who tended to bark orders at her. But treated nicely, she would smile.

I was reckoning on a trip home on escort duty in October, and a spot of skiing at Ehrwald in Austria before the turn of the year, but neither came

Johanna Kenzian - the two faces of Eve. 'Hanni the Honeyblonde' and 'Sourpuss'.

about; there were too many loose ends to tie up before we left. We did get some time at Winterberg which was not such a major expedition.

Time spent with Margret was becoming scarce. She had won a place to read medicine at the University of Bonn, and would be gone in early October. With all the offices and now also the clerks having a view out over the garden, our meetings lacked privacy and had either to be very formal in appearance, or late in the day, or to take place elsewhere. I ran the risk of the latter. The pleasant wooded farmland in the vicinity of Unna round the Bimbergerhof, reached by crossing only one main road and a stream, afforded a trysting-place where we could be alone together during those hot late summer afternoons. Or there was the dark. One night at half past ten, when I was lying on my bed listening to broadcast music in my room at the end of a baking day, the phone rang. *'Ich muss unbedingt dich sehen.'* ('I absolutely have to see you.') I told her I would meet her at the garden gate, where she arrived, breathless, on her bike. The urgency? She suddenly had a 'certain feeling'. We were neither of us wearing much. Would our status as *demi-vierges* survive? By the skin of our teeth only.

The task of evacuating the diminishing number of serials was becoming harder and more liable to obstruction or objection. A degree of press censorship still prevailed on sensitive subjects, of which T-Force was one. We could well do without censure or even publicity in the press, so when a critical and prejudicial article in the German press was brought to my notice, I cut it out, translated it, and sent it up to HQ for the Brigadier to draw to the attention of the Deputy Military Governor, who was T-Force's point of contact with the Military Government. It had been an oversight to allow the article to slip through; we were promised protection in future.

A sense of 'eat, drink and be merry, for tomorrow we shall be demobilised' had already set in, and it was generally agreed that, before too many of us had gone, we should hold a party on a Saturday evening at the Essener Hof Hotel in Essen. This time, to avoid an inebriated voyage home, we booked accommodation in the hotel. There was a dance band, and a sizeable dance floor. Ronnie Coe was there (his friendship with the Town Major had proved useful), but Roddy Bennett was absent doing Duty Officer. A number of ladies had been invited: Tony Scolding had invited Patsy Cross who worked for the Control Commission, and whose marriage had failed and so was always open to any kind of entertainment; Tony Lucas was friendly with Joey Ekins, the daughter of a colonel in the Military Government, but I do not remember whether she was there. Robin and I were there, both unattached. And a number of our growing tally of civilian officers was there, some with wives and some without. All in all, a very mixed bag. No-one remained entirely sober, and somehow the event was ripe for disaster.

The two Tonys and I found ourselves in the men's toilet, using a bank of three adjacent urinals hung on a wall which was about five feet high, with open space above it. Tony Scolding's sense of humour sometimes tended toward the childish. As we adjusted our dress, he suddenly announced, 'Last man over the wall's a sissy!' As one, we responded immediately, and no less childishly, to the challenge by simultaneously putting a foot on the urinal in front of us to lever ourselves over the wall. All three fixtures promptly crashed to the ground and shattered. Worse was to follow. The flow of water was regulated with such Teutonic efficiency that it flushed each of the three urinals every two minutes, with no apparent way of turning it off. Very soon not only the floor of the toilet was flooded, but the levels were such that water seeped out unrelentingly into the corridor and thence onto the dance floor. Understandably, this new circumstance brought that particular aspect of the party to an abrupt conclusion. Hotel staff who knew where the stop-cock was concealed were nowhere to be found for quite some time, and when the water had reached a certain level, the party was abandoned. Ronnie Coe, draped for some reason in an unidentified lady's fox fur, waded across the floor, seized a trumpet from a member of the band and blew the 'Retreat', the mournful notes echoing over the rising waters. We needed no second bidding. Pausing only to save the life of a gentleman ex-Guards driver who had passed out and slipped to the floor face down, we went upstairs to prospect for our accommodation for the night. Robin and I found a double to share, Tony Scolding disappeared with Patsy, and how the rest arranged themselves we didn't bother to enquire.

At breakfast Tony Lucas did not appear, so naturally we all agreed that, being the man in the chair in Essen, he should be the one to go and see the manager of the hotel to apologise for our quite disgraceful behaviour, and to offer to make good the damage. He was treated with courtesy, and with the observation that the manager had never before in a long career in hotel management suffered the *démontage* of his *pissatoria*. *Démontage*—dismantling—was after all a T-Force speciality, but we really had gone a little far. The hotel's facilities were quickly restored. A bit of bad luck, we thought, that the urinals were not better secured to the wall.

After breakfast, I was taken aside by a puzzled Patsy Cross. 'Michael,' she said, 'I am so worried. Do you think there is something wrong with me? Tony just won't. When it comes to the point, he just won't.' 'Patsy, I'm sure there's nothing wrong with you, you're gorgeous, but I just can't speak for Tony.' Who was I to disparage Tony's resistance to the promptings of this attractive and willing young woman? Just like me, he was carrying the matter of playing, nay carrying the role of *demi-vierge* to lengths which were unusual for that time and place. His time in Germany was coming soon to an end, and he was playing the part *à l'outrance*, exhibiting the stamina of the long-distance runner. He was a very attractive chap, and Patsy was not the only one. At Leichlingen, working for the detachment, there was a beautiful young German woman of his own age, whom I knew only as Erika, possessor of the most startling 'bedroom eyes' which had an unmistakeable come-hither quality about them. The look was natural, and come-hither was certainly her message to Tony. One late summer evening he took her out on the lake, the Blauer See, in a rowing boat. They drifted out into the middle of the lake, whereupon she stripped off and offered herself to him. When he turned away, she jumped overboard and made as if to drown herself. Plunging in after her, he eventually managed to coax her back into the boat. It was a scene belonging in the front rank of the ludicrous, and serve him right. Another time she was with him in his billet, and he was presented with the same scenario. So was she, but having no convenient lake to jump into she rushed naked from the house down the road toward the railway. No doubt she intended him to prevent her, but he did not. Fortunately, she came to no serious harm and somehow an open scandal was avoided. He was very single-minded. Poor Erika. I only met her once at Leichlingen, and from the way she looked at Tony I didn't reckon the eyes, although I received the full benefit of them, were for me; some other bedroom.

One evening, Tony was given a lift by Roddy in his Volkswagen up to a party at the Investigators' Mess in the Schloss. After a couple of hours, feeling that he had had more than enough to drink, yet not wanting to take Roddy away from the party too early, Tony clambered into the back of the Volkswagen where he curled up on the back seat and went to sleep. His trust in Roddy to get him home in due course was no doubt well-placed; the problem was that he had got into the wrong Volkswagen. It actually belonged to one of his own sergeants. Roddy eventually emerged from the party and, seeing no sign of Tony, made his way home alone. Meanwhile, once the party was over, the possessor of the wrong Volkswagen followed his customary route, like a homing pigeon, to join his girlfriend who lived in a cellar underground in one of the most terribly bombed suburbs of Cologne on the east bank. He parked as usual on the vestiges of a street among the ruins of that wilderness, with almost nothing standing above shoulder height for hundreds of yards around except a few common buddleias. Tony slumbered on, his sergeant noticed nothing. At first light Tony came to, alone in the car and utterly disoriented. He hadn't the slightest idea where he was or how he got there; he may as well have been on the moon, so desolate was the landscape. After he had spent about twenty minutes wondering what to do next, the sergeant came up the cellar stairs and out of a hole in the ground. The two men were dumbfounded to see each other; neither of them should have been there. After a quick orientation exercise, the sergeant drove Tony home and returned to the Sergeants' Mess for breakfast. They both avoided referring to the occasion again.

Kamen

26th October 1947

Darling Mama,

Not a word more from Stewart and Ardern. I am writing to find out the nature and cause of the hitch.

I had said that I hope to be doing a Vienna trip—a chance came up a fortnight ago, and Robin, the prior claimant, got the job. As I did Adjutant for 12 days while he was away I have been promised a trip in the near future, by way of recompense. Just now, when the leaves are falling, is the time to go. There is a scheme on foot to send some three thousand students to universities out here for short terms. If Peterhouse can't let me up until October they might at least sponsor my coming out here under that scheme. If you think it a not bad idea, I shall broach the matter with Peterhouse. It would be just the chance to polish up my German.

We gave a dance at our hotel in Altena last night. I was with the Colonel's party—escorting his daughter, a perilous position—when the thing started. By midnight it had dwindled down to about 24 bodies and merged into one mass. Those who had come expressly to enjoy themselves did so, and we didn't pack up until five in the morning. I find that I can really dance as competently as the average bloke on the floor, but I refuse to rumba or tango—I find it too artificial and don't enjoy it at all. I need more confidence really— it takes about six gins to get me on the floor at all.

Some ten of us who had spent the night at the pub collected together during the course of the morning, and drove down through lovely autumn country

for lunch at the Belgian N.A.A.F.I. Officers' Club at Lüdenscheid—and
sipped tomato juice, Worcester sauce, and sherry until our strength returned.
The night before last Sgt. Wigg and I caught a youth trying to get into our
house—Wigg's married quarters are in a flat on the ground floor of our
billet. By following up such clues as there were, we recovered a great deal of
kit stolen from Wigg about three weeks previously, including his radio, and
his wife's gold wrist watch. But it took us until 3 in the morning before we
could get into bed!

If my watch could be put in the safe custody of the Bank, they could give it
to any of my officers whom I send over on duty, to bring back to me.

Not much news else.

All my love,

Michael

In *Die Welt* of Hamburg on 17th October all of page three and most of page four had been devoted to a Decree by the Joint Commanders-in-Chief of the Bizone, General Lucius D Clay and Air Chief Marshal Sir Sholto Douglas, listing 358 plants due for dismantling in our area, Land Nordrhein/Westfalen. This caused a good deal of fluttering in the dovecotes which was audible in T-Force. The numbers had been very much reduced from the original figure (which had been several hundred higher), and in the event only a fraction of those plants was eventually dismantled—first and foremost those listed as armaments factories contributing an absolutely direct input into the jaws of the German war machine. The others also contributed in one way or another, in greater or lesser degree, to German war-waging capacity. Forty-two were chemicals factories, ninety-two were iron and steel mills, and 224 were classed as being involved in mechanical engineering and the production of machine tools. The measures were intended to be penal. Under the terms of the Allied 'Level of Industry' plan of 29th March 1946, the destruction of these plants was intended to strike at the heart of the capacity of Germany ever to wage aggressive war again. But there was a worm in this particular rose: the language of the Decree paid some lip-service to the idea that the programme should not create local unemployment. Since the terms of the Decree openly threatened the jobs of the workers of 358 factories, these two objectives were clearly mutually exclusive. Neither the Germans nor the officers of the British Control Commission responsible for the functioning of the different sectors of industry fully understood that the dismantling prescribed in the Decree had nothing directly to do with reparations, nor with the Inter-Allied Reparations Agency in Brussels (among whose members the UK and USA figured, but the USSR and Poland did not). Dismantling in order to disable is not the same as dismantling to evacuate for use elsewhere. The IARA was only just getting round to identifying its targets, and had nothing to do with T-Force, which was now moving towards the conclusion of its evacuation programme. So the arguments following on the publication of *Die Welt*'s list didn't touch us, but they were genuine enough. For instance, there was great disillusionment that after certain factories in Siegen to our south were dismantled (not by T-Force), the equipment was left out in the open to rust, within sight of the homes of the workers who had thus been put out of their jobs. The conduct in this respect of the British, and of their allies, was eventually counter-productive, not unusual in the aftermath of conflict. For the Germans, it was the price of losing; for us, the price of winning. Lieutenant-Colonel A Vaughan Jones, GSO1 and successor in title to David Edwardes, telephoned me with an admonition not to panic. We had not met, he did not know me. There was very little chance that I would panic.

Stewart and Ardern in Berkeley Square were MG distributors from whom I had ordered my TC Series MG, and the convenience of taking delivery of it within, say, forty-eight hours of being demobbed was manifest. They very nearly managed it.

Robin got the first trip to Vienna, and as usual I filled the Adjutant's slot while he was away, on the understanding of a firm commitment of a Vienna

297

trip before I left. It still seemed possible that I might not go up to Cambridge until October 1948, and thus I might have some ten months to fill, almost a 'gap year'. I toyed with the idea of going to the university of Bonn (where, by chance, Margret was) courtesy of a Foreign Office scheme to send up to a thousand students to German universities for the short term. I had heard from her that any young woman going up to Bonn had to spend the first term cleaning bricks amid the bombed ruins. Each day, a '*Trümmerfrau*' ('rubble-woman') had to clean her quota of bricks before there was any chance of attending lectures and getting on with the business of becoming a doctor. I hoped I would be excused the brick-cleaning.

Our Altena hotel was more precisely on the road to Altena from Iserlohn, at Nachrodt. It was the modern and comfortable hotel Haus Helbecke, named for an ancient property in those parts, and it lay in a beautiful situation on the river Lenne. The river was about fifteen metres wide at that point, and on the other side there was a steel rolling mill which passed and re-passed red-hot lengths of steel tens of metres long at great speed through the rollers. The activity was visible from our side, and it certainly made an absorbing sight at night. My duties as escort to the Colonel's daughter, whose appearance and name have entirely escaped me, did not last until very late in the night. Lack of confidence made the dance-floor a place of torture for me without the benefit of alcohol as an agent in dispelling inhibition, so the early bedtime call for the Colonel's daughter brought welcome release. Patsy Cross was of the party, and she had brought with her a protégée, a young woman not yet twenty, the daughter of a professor of English at a provincial university. When the lady appeared with me at breakfast, I reassured Patsy that I had not harmed a hair of her head. I think Patsy was a bit disappointed. The end of the party and the commencement of breakfast were separated by only about four hours; we returned to normality in a quiet and civilised manner, with a restorative 'hair-of-the-dog' tonic that the Belgians found a bit puzzling.

The ground floor of the Schmitt house at Sesekedamm number 10 had been turned into a flat for Sergeant Wigg and his wife Margarete, and they had already been robbed about a week after moving in—rather unsettling for a new bride. As was the habit in these cases, we did not bother the local police since they could not provide the disincentive for the culprit ever to attempt such a thing again. The Provost Sergeant and a couple of his men could, and they did.

Kamen

17th November 1947

Darling Mama,

[I look like getting my car now—I might as well.]

Another lapse! I have had an unsettling week. Last Monday I reported to H.Q. to start my duty trip to Vienna, but was put off for 72 hours. Then on Thursday I was put off until Friday, and then until Sunday. Now I don't start until tomorrow night, and can see no reason why I shouldn't be put off again.

I think I am well on the way toward being accepted for a 'Semester' at Bonn University. And while I am sure that it is in no way a bad thing at this juncture to get in touch with Courtaulds, I can hardly expect them to find me a job even in the most junior capacity for ten months, especially if I am going to ask for six weeks off in the middle of it, and to disappear for two or three years at the end of it.

Most of me pals are civvies again, and most of them seem happy enough. Michael Corbett is out, and I have written to him. I hope to renew contact with him when I get out. There will be an appalling number of my T-Force and R.B. contacts up at Cambridge with me, a lot of really nice blokes among them. One has a greater sympathy with those with whom one has 'soldiered' under trying circumstances at any time, much rather than with one's school companions in balmier days. One can't help noticing that those who have done their turn have got just something which the others lack and which one has cause to be grateful for.

The routine part of my work has for all practical purposes ceased. I still have one or two violent rearguard actions to fight: T-Force has been my hobby as much as my job, and there are several battles going on which I should be very sorry to see lost. We have been forced by the change of policy to come out with our hands up in a lot of cases, and I don't like it. About every third day I put up a very strong protest, and one of these days I am going to be jumped on. It is proving an excellent exercise in expressing myself tactfully. It is all rather fun because we are under heavy cross-fire in the press and parliament, as well as most branches of the Control Commission.

My journey to Vienna should prove interesting. I go via Frankfurt, Stuttgart, Ulm, Augsburg, Munich, Berchtesgaden, Salzburg, Linz, Vienna, and back I hope through Bruck, Innsbruck, Ulm, and so forth. As long as the weather is not too inclement it should be great fun. Cold it is certain to be, but most of the roads are Autobahn and that relieves the strain a certain amount.

Papa's crème de cacao I have obtained. Other goodies I hope to get from PX stores in the Yank Zone—I am well-provided with dollars.

My group starts getting demobbed on 17th December, and I shall be there. I see no reason for further extending my service. Robin and I will be interested to see who else is with us at the demob centre at York, where we kicked off!

All my love,
Michael

One of the battles I was hoping not to lose was over documents which I had demanded for T-Force from IG Farben in August, copies of which had already been taken by us for our allies (*anglice*—industrial competitors). Our demand was made under the Additional Terms of Surrender, which was still the law of the land, but was resisted not so much by the Germans as by the British Controller at IG Farben and the Chief of the Industries Division at the CCG. I had written at length and in detail on 5th November to Lieutenant-Colonel Vaughan-Jones, my GSO1 at HQ T-Force. His rather broken-backed and somewhat irrelevant reply arrived on 8th November:

While my whole sympathy is with you over documents, I am afraid there can be no question of raising the whole matter again, since we have no support from B.o.T. & M.o.S.

I am left, as no doubt you are, with a feeling of frustration & a mild sense of irritation by our failure to secure our just demands.

The Commander is quite adamant on this point & looks with disfavour on any action of ours which might prejudice the position of T-Force.

I should explain that T-Force is under fire from influential quarters at home & in Germany, & we have necessarily to tread very carefully.

You can see the trend of high policy in Germany & it is, clearly, at any cost to put Germany back to work so that we can be repaid some of our current expenses—the future can apparently look after itself. In this light T-Force activities in the document & equipment field are obviously a hindrance & they must be terminated willy-nilly at the earliest opportunity.

Believe me I have fought against the inevitable for many months & I feel very bitter that we should have been deprived at the last of obtaining our full demands by the accidental personal intervention of the Deputy Military Governor. However, there is nothing for it but to stifle one's personal feelings & to get on with the attenuated task in hand.

You are clear, I believe, on what we may or may not have?

He was not the man that David Edwardes had been.

Three weeks since writing my last letter, my trip to Vienna was still subject to a series of frustrating delays. Apart from unsettling me, they made planning almost impossible—I had been ready to go since the 10th, and had been put off a number of times in the week that followed. I did not take well to idleness. Although the trip was meant to be a bit of a jolly for me, the mission was nevertheless a real one. I was to escort an Austrian member of Wernher von Braun's rocket team, who had been under interrogation in London, back to his home in Vienna. Once there, I was to tell him how to get in touch with Daphne Park[33] at our office there in case at any time he had something he wished to communicate on a personal or technical level. The hiatus did at least allow me the opportunity to let Rufus Harris have a dummy run at managing the intelligence office by himself, which was no bad thing. But it left me in a vacuum, which I abhorred, and after the second postponement, my morale began to deteriorate along with the weather. I began to take an extra drink at lunchtime, and several extra at night.

What I did not tell my parents was that on the Friday night, returning late from the Mess building to my room, as I made my rather hesitant way in the dark outside the Schulze-Westen house at number 6, I felt an arm placed around my waist. The owner of the arm (indeed of an admirable and full set of body parts, decoratively arranged, as it turned out) guided me firmly, and with soft words of encouragement, the remaining short way to my door, and up the stairs to my room. It was guidance which I did nothing to resist. I knew at once it was Johanna Kenzian—'Hanni the Honeyblonde'. Supposing me perhaps to be more drunk than I was, she began to undress me, a function which I was well able to resume for myself without discovering within me the will to indicate by so much as batting an eyelid that she should leave me. That preliminary out of the way, she lay down beside me, naked except for her little frilly panties. I was somehow unsurprised by the occurrence. We had been in almost everyday contact, albeit in formal circumstances, for eighteen months or more. Since the first exchanged smile there had existed between us a natural sympathy of which I was aware, but never on either side

---

33 Later principal of Somerville College Oxford and Baroness Park of Monmouth.

by so much as a gesture did either of us betray that such a thing was possible or might be desirable. I cannot think that for her part it was not premeditated; she had judged it, and me, to a nicety. We talked and talked, we kissed, we lay in close embrace in silence, from time to time we slept. At dawn she dressed and crept back to her house two doors away; the Jarvis family was away, and she held the key. We made no assignation, but nonetheless the next night we came together thus again, and the next night, and the next. Except for that first night, I was always sober; we did not need to be fuelled by drink. My colleagues noticed my relative silence during those days. Was it a case of *'post coitum triste'*? Was it, in Hanni's word, just a *'poussage'*—a flirtation, a dalliance? Sergeant Wigg and his wife, in their flat downstairs, were a model of discretion. They must have suspected something, for we were hardly silent. Were they complicit?[34] On the Tuesday I left for Vienna, exhausted. It didn't matter—I was to be driven, I could sleep.

What did all this have to do with Margret and me? Nothing, apparently. If I could not go up to Peterhouse until the following autumn, my plans to spend a semester at the university in Bonn, drawn there by feelings for her which were ever stronger, were near to fruition. My earlier intentions not to let an entanglement complicate my plans for my future were fading. If I was honest with myself, I could not really envisage a semester passing at Bonn without a relationship developing which would inevitably be given full sexual expression, and nor could she. But Margret soon became immersed in her medical studies, and she for her part cannot have contemplated with equanimity the disturbance which a love affair with someone who was soon to disappear yet again would create in her life. Later she wrote, 'I did not want you to come.'

A spell at Bonn was still only one of the options, nothing was yet certain. Otherwise perhaps a bit of what is now called 'work experience'

---

34 In the New Year, my letters to Hanni were sent care of the Wiggs. We corresponded for more than a year. The last words she ever wrote to me were, *'Michael, ich liebe Dich wohl auf immer.'* ('Michael, I love you for ever.') Was that possible?

would be useful, perhaps with Courtaulds. A number of their senior people visited the Ruhr factories of Vereinigte Glanzstoff at Wuppertal and IG Farben at Dormagen, and no less than three of them had at sundry times kindly suggested that when I left the army I should go at once to work for them at Courtaulds instead of going to university. But in truth, I was far from appalled by the thought of the number of brother officers from the Regiment or T-Force who would be with me at Cambridge. In the event, there would be fewer than half a dozen. Those with intellectual pretensions tended to go to Oxford, and my correspondence with Robin Smyth and John Bayley there was to continue throughout our student years, and beyond. The same distinction was true of those with whom I had been at school; at Cambridge there were three from Rugby for every one at Oxford, and eight of them at Peterhouse in my time. Historians and classicists, philosophers and theologians went to the other place, engineers and architects, linguists and lawyers went to Cambridge—a seemingly sweeping generalisation, but broadly true. Sharing three years and more in the service with young men of my own age created a stronger bond even than the rigours of a public school education.

Crème de cacao for a while became an essential ingredient. My father tended to dislike cocktails of the sweeter sort, but he had come across one called an 'Alexander', which could be made on a gin or a brandy base, with milk (or cream) and *crème de cacao*, finished with a dusting of chocolate powder and nutmeg. The recipe was revived at a party for my twenty-fourth birthday at Peterhouse in 1950. The gathering was held at noon on a Sunday at the end of May, and we were due to play Girton at croquet in the afternoon. Almost all of our team came to the party, and most of us went onto the field of battle without first having had lunch. The Alexanders wreaked considerable damage. The poor girls were not sure what had hit them, but they can't have thought we were taking it very seriously. There is no record of who won; it was not a consideration.

Altena

2nd December 1947

Dear Papa,

Little that I can say could be of much comfort for the loss to you of a sister. I cannot remember my Auntie Gee so very well. I know that she was the same sweet sort as all your sisters, and do feel keenly a sense of loss. You do, darling, have all my love and sympathy in what must be a moment of bitter sorrow for you all. I am sorry I cannot be at home to help even a little at a difficult time like this.

I cannot at this moment say whether I shall manage to secure a leave vacancy before New Year even. We are of course released according to a strict rota, and I have a 50–50 chance of a vacancy for 21st December. If I miss that I probably won't be out until just in the New Year. I shall of course let you know as soon as I can fix anything definite. There is little for me to stay for now—my job is done.

I had a good look at the various Wogs who line the route to Vienna, the Yanks, the French and the Russians. The first-named were friendly, the others treated me as one would hardly treat a dog: I hate their guts too. It took four days in fine weather to get to Vienna, staging nights at Frankfurt, Munich and Wels, arriving in Vienna Saturday pm. I hit one of the night-spots that evening, saw the sights on Sunday morning, and that afternoon took to my bed with flu, which I sweated out in eighteen hours.

I was fit for travel on Tuesday morning, and spent that night in Salzburg, then past Hitler's hideout at Berchtesgaden to Innsbruck the next night, then over the Arlberg Pass (6,000 ft) to Bregenz on Lake Constance, on to Ulm (Yanks) for Thanksgiving night. Then Frankfurt again, and home. The unit had in the meanwhile moved down to Iserlohn, and now Robin and a few others and I have established ourselves in one of our hotels a few miles out of the town—very pleasant and quiet.

Next Sunday we go to the skiing centre—Winterberg—for five days. Quite a party, Robin, the Orderly Room Staff-Sergeant and his wife, Sergeant Wigg and his wife, and I. The snow is falling here tonight, and lying, and should be fairly deep up there.

The idea of going to Bonn is part of a regular but little-patronised interchange scheme. I would under normal arrangements be billeted on a British family here in the neighbourhood, but I would try to live with a German family. Further details I know little about—the scheme is in its infancy, and one could make more or less what one liked of it. I await an answer from the Foreign Office.

Little other news for the moment.

All my love,

Michael

On Tuesday 18th November I went up to HQ T-Force at Bad Oeynhausen to receive my brief, collect my man, and put together my small convoy—two Austin 16s complete with drivers. My rocket scientist and I were to share one vehicle, the other was dedicated to the carriage of about four hundredweight of canned goods and other food which I was to deliver on the return journey to the wife of another scientist. Her husband was being detained at Spedan Towers in Hampstead for longer than expected for the purpose of further interviews, and the food was intended to keep her going until his return. Having been embroiled with Hanni over previous nights, I was unlikely to offer sparkling company for my charge, at least for a couple of days. I intended to let sleep take over for as long as it felt inclined. Our first night was in Frankfurt where FIAT, our opposite number in the US Zone, had booked accommodation for me and my scientist, and for the two drivers, plus secure space for the vehicles with their cargo. It was autobahn all the way, and we drove down the Rhine without my giving the Lorelei even a glance. I excused myself to my companion on the grounds of lack of sleep. Was I seeking forgetfulness in slumber? I don't think so—recent memories were quite sweet.

The next day took us past Pforzheim where, in February 1945, the RAF had attacked the town in force on the grounds that it was a centre for precision instrument manufacture for weapons, and also that it was a communications centre for troop movements. Apart from the damage to the road network, eighty-three per cent of the built environment within the limits of Pforzheim was destroyed and seventeen thousand inhabitants killed, more than one in four of the population—the highest proportion in any German city attacked from the air. The bomb-damaged autobahn had been pretty well reconstructed and I'm afraid the shattered landscape rated little more than a glance from me as we sped past. The British have done penance there since; it was a slaughter on a scale hardly justified by the importance of the targets. And even if it had been, it was none the less appalling.

By nightfall I was beginning to sit up and take more notice. We arrived in Munich and I even managed to have a look round the damaged fifteenth century *Frauenkirche*, with its hundred-metre-high twin towers still standing. From there on I started to share the wheel with the driver. When I was not sleeping, being a passenger was something of a trial for me; my driver wouldn't change down early enough and tended to labour up the hills. I was glad to do more than my share at the wheel. The next day was especially memorable because it was the first time I ever approached really high mountains from a low-lying plain. I didn't really notice the Austrian Alps until they already occupied quite a slice of the horizon, and for me it was spine-tingling. I had to stop the car and photograph the scene.

Our drive on Friday 21st took us past Salzburg, where the autobahn ran out, and on to Linz on the Danube, which formed the border between the US and Russian Zones. Most of the city, including the railway station, lies south of the river, and it was to the railway station we went, or near to it. It was important that I should not be seen with the scientist. There was a strong chance, only a mile from the Russian Zone, that a Russian agent would be watching the trains to Vienna; anyone escorted by a British officer would be suspect. The scientist—how can I have forgotten his name?—thanked me for the good treatment he had received in England, and at our hands in particular. He complimented my Scottish driver and myself on our splendid driving skills—he did not drive himself, and it was the first time that he had ever been in a car without being positively sick with apprehension! I told him how and when to find me in Vienna, and left him to it. He caught a late afternoon ordinary stopping train to Vienna, while we retraced our tracks fifteen miles west to Wels for the night.

British and other Allied vehicles travelling to Vienna passed of necessity through the Russian Zone which surrounded it, and were obliged by the Russians to enter the city from the south via the Semmering Pass and Wiener Neustadt. So we had to go the long way round through Klagenfurt and Graz in the British Zone to the south. The drivers had been told where to hole up in Vienna for the two days and three nights, and they were looking forward to it. Leaving me at the officers' transit hotel, they disappeared until early Tuesday morning. It was a jolly for them too, and the journey had not been too testing.

The transit hotel was comfortable, the food was excellent, and over dinner a pianist was playing Viennese light music, Lehár and the like, on the grand in the corner. It seemed to me he might have had a classical training but felt unable to indulge his preference, given what he presumed to be the taste of the audience with which he was faced in order to earn a crust. (Crusts were still hard to come by in Vienna in 1947.) I thought I would take a chance, so I asked the waiter to take over a little note from me, which simply read, 'Would you like to oblige me by playing the Opus 90, No 4?' He read it, and when the waiter pointed me out to him, he waved and then played quite beautifully the Schubert Impromptu in A Flat Major—that same opus whose number I had only so recently discovered. I hoped I had done us both a favour.

The concierge recommended a nightclub. My heart wasn't in it, but I felt it incumbent upon me to visit one. At least it qualified me a couple of years later to maintain that Carol Reed had captured perfectly the essence of Vienna at that time in his film *The Third Man*. The mists of autumn and the gas lamps at night certainly helped, and the sense that there was something going on under the surface. I toured the city on foot the next morning, before feeling rotten and retiring to bed with aspirin and whisky after lunch. On Monday I considered trying to get to see the soprano Irmgard Seefried who had joined the Vienna State Opera in 1946, but I still did not feel well enough. On Tuesday we drove to Salzburg, quite a hard day's drive although there was as yet no snow lying on the lowlands, and sampled the rather offhand American hospitality there. They had at least got the musical life of the city moving again, including the summer Mozart Festival. After dark, the streets and alleys were at least as atmospheric as Vienna had been, despite the presence of drunken US soldiery.

The next day our destination was Innsbruck, which was in the French Zone, evidenced in part by the Rugby football goal posts in the few flat stretches of the valley of the River Inn—not a normal feature of the Austrian countryside. Our overnight accommodation was in a French barracks in the middle of town. The soldiers were slovenly and surly, the barracks were dirty, broken windows were left unrepaired letting snow drift in, and rats ran in the corridors. The food was basic, the service *negligé*. We couldn't wait to get out of there, so we left early, having heard that there was snow four feet deep in the Arlberg Pass which was on our route. On the steady climb up from Landeck a snowplough had cleared the deeper snow, but we were without chains and still driving on snow and ice.

I made it in my car to the pass six thousand feet up, but the other Austin lost traction and failed. The driver managed to turn and go back to a level stretch to take another run at it which succeeded, and he rejoined us.

We had come sixty-five miles, and had another sixty to go. Our target was Fussach in the little Austrian enclave of

Snow in the Arlberg Pass, 24th November 1947.

Rheineck on the Swiss side of the Rhine, where it flows into the south-eastern end of the Bodensee, otherwise known as Lake Constance. The lake is at 1,300 feet above sea level, so we must have dropped some 4,700 feet to a level where there was just a scattering of snow. The lady and her daughter to whom we delivered our cargo had never seen so much food. They were so delighted that they wanted to give us some, but we declined and explained that its purpose was to keep them alive, not us. We went on to a late lunch at Bregenz, still just in Austria, and discovered that when we re-entered Germany we would still be in the French Zone as far north almost as Ulm, about another ninety miles. We couldn't face the prospect of another night at the mercy of the French, so there was nothing for it but to drive like hell for the US Zone.

The two Austins, down from the pass, to deliver food to the family of a scientist detained at Spedan Towers.

At the frontier post of the French Zone I had an altercation with the French lance-corporal to whom it fell to examine my papers. He told me that I had made a mistake, it was not possible that I had been born in 1926 as stated on the form I had filled in. I had stated my rank as captain, and in the French army such young men were never given the rank of captain. I grasped him by the lapels of his tunic and shook him, shouting, '*Impudent!*' Fortunately at that moment the sergeant in charge of the post arrived, and we were able to laugh the matter off. I did not care to reveal the nature of the mission which had brought me to that part of Austria. My over-reaction to the argumentative lance-corporal was hardly designed to avoid drawing attention to our little party.

We reached Ulm just as darkness was falling. The first unit we came to was a US Constabulary Mess, a company of military police, and it was not until I entered and was shown into the dining room that it dawned upon me that it was Thursday 27th November: Thanksgiving Day. The company was commanded by a lieutenant, senior grade, and he was sitting at the head of the dining table among the ruins of the lunch, with his three other officers around him. Even had they thought it appropriate, they were quite incapable of getting to their feet. They addressed me as 'lootenant' and it would have been churlish to correct them, not least because they were rather older than me. They could not have been more hospitable, and insisted that they would gladly find us, as refugees from the French, sleeping quarters—which they did, and they also fed us at about seven o'clock on the plentiful remains of their Thanksgiving feast. There was still turkey in abundance, and squash. Given the nature of the occasion, conversation was full of maudlin reminiscence of the family scene back home (mostly Texas), and repeated fulsome reassurance of goodwill toward their British brothers-in-arms, with particular reference to myself. With too much bourbon pressed on me, hardly to be refused in the circumstances, I was glad that none of them could really keep awake beyond half-past-nine. We promised to meet at breakfast. There we learned that they operated the speed-trap on the autobahn. They pointed it out for us on the map, and we later steamed through at full speed without being challenged. The Austins, despite a two and a quarter litre capacity, had a distinctly unsporting performance. A sustained sixty miles per hour was probably all they could manage anyway.

Only one more night at Frankfurt stood between me and my return to No 1 T-Force, which had in my eleven days' absence moved the HQ office to a house in Iserlohn, and the Mess to Haus Helbecke on the road to Altena, where we had so recently had our party. A Detachment were left where they were. All my personal effects had been moved for me. I had been given no prior warning, probably in case I dredged up some sound operational reason why we should not move. Clearly I was not to be given the chance. Anyway, on my return I had just eighteen days to go, and part of that was to be spent skiing.

My semester at the university in Bonn now looked as if it could well become reality, and the absurdity of following the proposed practice of having digs with a family where no German was spoken was manifest. Of course, there were difficulties, principally to do with food rations. But surely those could be overcome by, for instance, having a main meal at midday under the aegis of the British Council. More to the point, would discharged officers, used to an expansive and privileged way of life, make good lodgers and good ambassadors?

Winterberg

9th December 1947

Darling Mama,

I got your letter telling about Auntie Gee on Saturday afternoon, and immediately wrote to Daddy. I left the letter addressed on my desk on Sunday morning for the post Cpl. to call for on Monday—I then came here for five days skiing. Ringing through to confirm with Rufus Harris my deputy and successor that it had been safely dispatched, I found that he knew nothing of it. So I am writing another note to Daddy in case: if two arrive please make my explanation for me: if not, no word need be said.

Robin and I have scrounged vacancies for release on the first day of our group. We leave our unit a week tomorrow—17th. I get to York on the afternoon of the 19th, and should be home with you some time on the evening of the 20th. We shall have dinner at the Station Hotel, York, with Barry Smith, who is now A.D.C. to Monty Stopford there—stay the night, and travel down the next day.

I feel rather cold and naked at the idea of it all, but can see no point in deferring it all for so much as an hour. My job here is finished, I don't want another. My first 'duty to myself' will be once more to belabour Peterhouse in an attempt to make them let me go up at once. Failing that, I can make them prescribe a course of reading for me to carry on with. If that proves fruitless, I then go on to persuade the Foreign Office German Division to let me go to Bonn. If that flops, I shall trade on my now pretty wide and specialised knowledge of the subject to get the Technical Intelligence Branch of the B.o.T. German Division to give me a temporary job. Then I would turn to Courtaulds. Further than that I cannot at the moment look—at the worst, I can always drive a tractor!

You can imagine perhaps how difficult it has been from where we are for Anne and me to think up a silver wedding present for Daddy. We felt that if we could get him a couple of seats for the whole sitting of the Olympic Athletics, although it is an insubstantial sort of gift, it might well be an occasion not easily forgotten. Could you sound Alfred Hayes for us? Or suggest anything you think he might like better.

Before shuffling off this Khaki coil, I find it reassuring that not a few people out here have admiration for the efficiency of the organisation, the running of which has been my particular affair—and within of course a fairly limited sphere automatically associate my name with that efficiency. And yet all the good it will do me is to allow me to look back with pleasure in days to come—and to assure myself that any time spent out here has not been entirely wasted.

Robin is with me here. Over the road we have Robin's Orderly Room Staff Sergeant with wife, and my Sgt. Wigg with wife. We have already had two days pleasant if strenuous skiing, and may have more if tonight's north-east wind brings snow. We were able to pick up where we left off last January and have gained a degree of confidence not really commensurate with our competence. Nevertheless our instructors are enthusiastic about our progress. The pub is comfortable and the price of the drink is too appalling to permit of excess.

My trip to Vienna I won't put on paper but will describe direct shortly

*(20th) with photos. For the moment let it suffice that I covered 21 hundred
miles in ten days—spending three in Vienna, and managing to go to most
of the eight places en route.*

*I did as you suggested, and have got myself a nice pair of fur-lined flying
boots, more than welcome they are up here in the snow.*

*Unfortunately we have had a mist up here the whole time so far, and so I
haven't been able to take any views of the scenery. I did however forego my
morning's skiing and went out taking snaps of the Wiggs and Duffners,
and managed to get most of them just before or just after coming to grief.
Unfortunately it froze and hailed a bit last night, and the surface is like
glass, and the going very heavy—likewise the falls.*

*Jack Griffiths collected my watch for me a fortnight ago—it is a gem and
goes beautifully. As for the car, I have heard nothing since I wrote just before
the budget. I can pepper them up as soon as I get home.*

No more news for the moment.

All my love,

Michael

Our release date was fixed as early as it could have been for both of us, so
Robin and I could go through the process together. Still no word from Peterhouse. Even though it was getting towards the end of term, it was still too
early for the college to be sure of any vacancy created by those who had come
up for the first time in October but had decided to quit. And still no decision from the Foreign Office as to whether they would let me go to Bonn
for a semester. I had just learned that the German Division of the Board of
Trade had something called a Technical Intelligence Branch—the fruits of
our labours had probably been coming their way. *Prima facie,* I was qualified
by the last two years' experience to work for them, if they could use me as a
temp. Or, lastly, I could try to exploit my contacts with Courtaulds for a spot
for ten months. Early in the New Year would be time enough for all that.

New Year's Day was my parents' silver wedding anniversary, and presents were always a problem in those days of shortages. Tickets to the Wembley Olympics were a thought; my father had been a bit of an athlete, and he had generated an interest in athletics in the family which persisted into the next two generations, to the point where my wife and all our children went with me to the Olympics at Munich in 1972.

I was writing from Winterberg in the middle of our five-day stint. Unusually, Robin and I were allowed away at the same time, and even to take our sergeants and their wives with us. It was rather in the nature of a honeymoon for the Wiggs—the first time they had been away together. The Orderly Room Staff-Sergeant was Eric Duffner whom we had inherited from one of the Pioneer Companies. Duffner's Belgian wife he had acquired on the way through Brussels. She was younger, ambitious for him, demanding and hard to please. Neither of them had the figure for skiing, nor any other vertical sport. The only advice I gave him was that if he came to a tree, he should ensure that

Sergeant Duffner meeting an obstacle and 'getting it wrong'.

both legs passed on the same side. He failed spectacularly. Quarters for officers and NCOs were segregated, but we were able to ski together. I regarded it as my job to provide them with a photographic record of their successes and failures, mostly the latter.

I felt entitled, in my last letter from Germany, to look back with some satisfaction. I flatter myself that I had created and earned my opportunity, and taken full advantage of it. I was probably wrong in assuming that to look back on it with pleasure would be the only good it would do me. I am quite sure that when I secured my first job in 1950, my record in T-Force was a determining factor in the face of competition from thirty-six other Oxbridge graduates. For twenty-one months I had done my best to carry a substantial load of responsibility, during which period the service at HQ T-Force was being performed by a sequence of staff officers: two lieutenant-colonels, three majors and six captains, counting Jean Hughes-Gibb: they operated, in North Rhine/Westphalia, through me. I hope I provided an element of continuity and consistency. It was a record of continuous service exceeded only by the invaluable Sergeant Wigg, with his amazing memory, and the handful of NCO and riflemen clerks who made up the section. I had been sounded out more than once as to whether I might agree to sign on for a further period, which would have to be at HQ. It would have meant another pip at the age of 21, a Majority, which would have had its attractions. But I was not going to be deflected. I suspected that there would be difficulty enough in settling to academic work again after a break such as I had already had, without compounding it.

Within ten days of my having written from Winterberg, I was released from active service. Things happened very fast. One evening, Robin and I fitted in a concert in the theatre in Iserlohn, which was now on our doorstep. The Berlin Philharmonic Orchestra performed under the baton of the Romanian Sergiu Celibidache, who had the benefit of being seen as politically 'clean' while other notable conductors such as Furtwängler and von Karajan still had a question-mark of sorts hanging over them. We were given a Brahms symphony preceded by a Berlioz overture, the *Carnaval Romain*. The theatre had been slightly bomb-damaged, so part of the roof had been temporarily covered with corrugated steel sheeting. A violent rainstorm commenced precisely as the orchestra struck up the Berlioz overture which was, as several of his overtures are, loud and sometimes strident. In order to compete with the elements—the high wind and the rain beating deafeningly on the tin roof—Celibidache had them playing *fortissimo* all the time to hold their own. The contest was much applauded. The storm subsided, and in the Brahms we experienced calmer waters, none of them on the roof. At the end of the concert Celibidache was presented first with a bunch of imitation flowers, then a bouquet of real flowers, and then with a large bag of coffee beans—two kilos, I should think, and worth much more on the black market than his Reichsmark concert fee. This last was wildly applauded.

Hanni, who had remained in Kamen, working for the Jarvises, came down one evening to say goodbye. It had to be in public. We shook hands, and she accused me of being so '*Englisch kühl*'—cool in the English fashion. It was nevertheless a bit of a wrench; my feelings for her were, unsurprisingly, warm. To Corporal Fox's girlfriend, who had become my secretary, I bequeathed the contents of my zinc-lined trunk filled with cigarettes. These she used, I later heard, to purchase an appendectomy and three weeks' stay at the best hotel in Baden-Baden for her mother and herself by way of recuperation. Apart from 200 for Christa who loved a cigarette, I could not give the entire cache to the Kunsemüller girls. Two hundred was a smoke, twenty thousand would have been a monetary gift, and might have seemed to create an obligation. I would not have wished thus to cloud my relations with Margret and Christa.

It was unthinkable that I should leave Germany without saying goodbye to Margret in person, now in Bonn. At this stage I needed no pretext, fictitious or otherwise, to make the trip. In any case, it was only thirty miles the other side of Leichlingen, where I could stage and pick up a meal. Christa gave me Margret's address, we made a date, and one morning in hard frost and pale sunshine down I went. She had a bedsit on the second floor, where we could at least be private. There was much sighing, some tears, many promises—promises to write, promises to meet again. We knew that neither of us would be deflected from our immediate aims, she to qualify as a doctor and I to get my degree and find financial independence. But there was still the prospect that I might spend a semester at the university in Bonn in the New Year, which we both knew would pose a serious threat to our standing as *demi-vierges*. In the event, we were to correspond, often and passionately. Soon she was to write '*So ausgesprochene Liebesbriefe kann ich nicht schreiben, nur kannst*

Du, wohl einer poetischen Ader wegen.' ('I cannot write such open and frank love letters, only you can, perhaps because of your poetic vein.') In fact, her love letters became no less open, poetic vein or no. We continued writing for most of two years, by which time, starved of actual face-to-face contact, our correspondence had assumed a calmer character. It has continued, as between friends, for over sixty years.

Robin and I kissed T-Force goodbye on Wednesday 17th December, and crossed from the Hook of Holland to Harwich that night. Strolling round the boat after an evening meal, we came across two young officers of the 1st Battalion The Rifle Brigade going on their first home leave. They must have been still nineteen—goodness, how young they looked, and how pleasant they were. We sat with them and bought them brandy. While we sat talking, we were approached by a young Grenadier Guards lieutenant whose face was vaguely familiar. We had seen him somewhere before, probably in the 21 Club at Bad Oeynhausen. He introduced himself as James Taylor, and explained that he, too, was on his way to York to be demobilised.

'The trouble with you Riflemen,' he declared provocatively, 'is that you can't hold your liquor.' It was intended as a challenge, and accepted as such.

'Is that so?' I replied. 'Would you care to join us in a brandy?'

He would, and there were half a dozen more rounds, before the two younger men said it was their bedtime. Giving an impeccable impression of sobriety, they excused themselves and the party broke up. Half an hour later Robin and I were taking a turn round the deck to get a breath of fresh air before turning in, and as we came to the stern rail, there bent double over it, his weight nicely balanced on either side, was James Taylor, insensible. We carried him inside, brought him round with a douche of cold water, and put him in his bunk. Game, set and match.

We found ourselves once more at Fulford Barracks, York, where we had both spent our first day in the army, bringing our military careers nicely full circle. Thirty-two months, plus demobilisation leave, would make it three and a half years. Those of our contemporaries who had elected to join the Navy or the Air Force got out and up to university much earlier—their services did not have Germany to occupy. Robin and I went through the formalities of demobilisation in the very same barrack room as we had spent our first night in the army in September 1944. By now we had more or less adopted James (he clearly needed looking after), and we all picked the same pattern for our civvy suit. James wore his, we stayed in uniform. We didn't fancy a night-train south, so we had got our mate Barry Smith to book us in at the Royal Station Hotel in York[35] for the night of the 19th December. Barry had been in the 2nd Battalion in Germany but was now ADC to General Montagu Stopford—a Rifleman, of course. When one of our Greenjacket generals needed an ADC he would ask the regiment for a name, and appoint one of our own. Barry, who had likewise joined with us at York, had signed on for a further term in order to do the job.

After a taxi ride from Fulford Barracks, we claimed our huge room at the Royal Station Hotel. There was a spare day-bed in the room, so we let James join us. We each had in turn a symbolic hot bath. James' horrid civvy suit was an appalling fit, so he first got into the bath in it and then abandoned it, getting back into uniform. We had a late, lengthy but quiet and civilised dinner on English soil, to wrap up three and a quarter years of time passed, during the greater part of which we had been 'otherwise occupied'.

On the Monday when I reached home, there was a phone message waiting for me. There would, after all, be a place for me at Peterhouse the next term, starting on Tuesday 6th of January. Robin got a similar message from Trinity. In January I discovered that James, who was destined for Pembroke College just across Trumpington Street from Peterhouse, had been equally fortunate.

---

35 The Royal Station Hotel was a good class, four-star hotel belonging to the London North Eastern Railway. As recruit Riflemen in September to November 1944, we used sometimes to go and have dinner there on a Saturday night courtesy of our fellow recruit Michael Holland of the KRRC, whose father was a director of the railway. It made a nice change from getting tanked up on beer in the pubs of York though, of course, we were derided by those who did.

We got into the habit of taking coffee or tea with our respective friends at Tulliver's (on the same side as Peterhouse but opposite Pembroke). We passed the time of day, but he never presumed upon our acquaintance in an earlier incarnation, and certainly never risked denigrating my capacity to hold my liquor. Nor did I ever remind him that he had been within an ace of making food for the fishes. At Cambridge Dicky Muir was already up at King's, and Tony Lucas at Trinity. Arriving at Trinity College Oxford, Robin was to find Johnny Pepys Cockerell already there before him, John Bayley at New College, and Tony Chance at Corpus Christi. Had Sir Peter Macdonald only asked the question in the House now, '*Where* are all these bright young men?'—I could have given him a precise reply and some decent addresses.

POSTSCRIPT

Throughout my time at Cambridge I saw quite a lot of Tony Lucas. Visiting him at Trinity, in the gatehouse at Whewell's Court, I found his rooms on the third floor opposite a set retained by Prince Ludwig Wittgenstein until his death in 1951 (though the great philosopher had resigned his chair at Cambridge in 1947). Our conversations were,

The author, Salzburg, August 1949.

unsurprisingly, often far from philosophical. Sharing a similar taste in music, we decided in the spring of 1949 to go to the Mozart Festival at Salzburg that summer in my MG convertible. For ten days we covered many miles to swim in the lakes of the Salzkammergut in the mornings, share a bottle of wine over lunch in a lakeside village, and then return to rest, shower and snooze before attending a concert. Evening performances focussed on *The Magic Flute* and *Fidelio*, both featuring the divine Irmgard Seefried under the baton of Furtwängler. On the Sunday at noon there was the performance of von

At the summit of the Grossglockner Pass on the way back to Germany.

321

Hofmannsthal's *Jedermann* in the Cathedral Square, still using Max Reinhardt's production six years after his death. We went on to Venice for three days, and then back to Germany to revisit old haunts: Düsseldorf to look up Bill Adams; Mülheim to search for Tony's Airedale, Alastair, whom he had left behind (alas, no trace); on up to Minden where Rufus Harris and Bob Wigg and a handful of others, the rump of T-Force, had now been subsumed into G Branch, Research Division at the Headquarters of the Control Commission, to work on a valuation of the proceeds of our evacuation programme which had come to an end in early 1948.

On our way to Salzburg three weeks earlier, aiming to get there from Flushing inside twenty-four hours, we had slept in Bill's house briefly between two and six in the morning, then breakfasted and hurried on. Now we would have time for a chat. Our warning message had gone astray so, upon our unexpected arrival at his office, he bade us stay the night. We went minutely over old ground into the small hours. More than twice my age, Bill was a wise old bird. We were glad to be assured that our heyday had been the best of times, and that we had done well to go when we did (not that we wavered). He would soldier on to the end—as he had done one war ago. Like the BBC in 1943, the CCG were by now taking very seriously the satirical lyrics of Noel Coward's *Don't let's be beastly to the Germans*. They had paid their debt in due time, and we had certainly helped them to do it.

It was the same story at Minden where the admirable Rufus was at the heart of a small, comfortable and typically well-catered Mess. A mere half dozen represented the last remnants of T-Force, together with a small handful in the Finance Division—chartered accountants all—who had been put to the common task of putting a price upon the depredations of T-Force from April Fools' Day in 1945 to the bitter end. One of the latter was Janet, the lady who, Rufus had confided, had 'a line in eroticism all her own'. We spent a day and a half with them, and were royally wined and dined, with caviar and vodka as a late late supper. Rufus and Janet were not to stay there much longer. They had

had enough, and in six months they were gone. Wigg stayed on, immutable, charming, funny, omnicompetent. A lovely man, I missed him.

And then there was Kamen. It was of course impossible to drive past the Kunsemüllers' house where I had first lived and then had my office over a period of some twenty months. When I had gone to say goodbye eighteen months before, it had been Christa who bade Robin and me farewell from the front door, and I had been moved to see the tears in her eyes as she shook our hands without speaking. Now it was Christa again at the door. At first she looked at my feet which were sandaled, then at my slacks, not as clean as they had been, then to my red and white sweatshirt and shabby green sweater. Still no sign of recognition. Then she looked me in the face for perhaps three seconds before her beautiful eyes lit up as she spoke my name—spoke it not as it would be pronounced in German, but as in English. Then without another word she threw the door wide open and rushed back into the house, calling to the rest of the family that Michael had come back. Soon Margret appeared too. I was glad to be spared the ironic formality of a hand-shake. 'For heaven's sake,' she said, 'come on in.' I explained that Tony was in the car, and they called to him to come in as well. They were evidently amazed by our arrival, and I wondered what had become of the warning letter I had sent.

It was in the middle of the doctor's consulting hours, but when he heard we were there he made Christa—who was by now fully qualified—take over from him while he came in and chatted for a few minutes before returning to his patients, a most friendly gesture. Then forward came the Frau Doktor followed by Hans-Gerhard. She was most friendly and civil, and brought us through into the sunny morning-room which had once been my office, and bade her children serve us with schnapps. Christa came back into the room, and I asked her after her husband, Eberhard. He was doing a refresher course at a hospital in Stuttgart and, from the look of sudden seriousness that came over their faces, I could tell that he was in rather worse shape even than they had expected. He had recovered from the spotted typhus which he had caught on the way back home to Germany, but his chief problem was read-justing to everyday life—as it was with all the others. If only his letters had not been so optimistic, they might have been better prepared.

I asked after her child, Ina-Maria. I had spent hours photographing the child, helping her to walk and to talk, and playing with her. At a very early age she had called me '*Onkel Michael*', when she knew but few other words, and had always seemed to trust me. She was a lovely infant, sturdy and fair, blue-eyed and good-humoured. They brought her in and presented her to Tony, to whom she curtsied sweetly. Her astonishingly blond hair had all but faded to brown, except for a few strands in the front which gave it a silver-gold sheen, but her eyes were still bright blue, and her expression was lively and intelligent. She was led before me. Her mother asked her, '*Kennst Du den Onkel Michael?*' ('Do you know Uncle Michael?')

'*Ja, der Onkel ist lieb, ich brachte ihm Walderdbeeren.*' ('Yes, I am fond of him. I used to bring him wild strawberries.')

It was almost too much for me.

While Tony was complimenting Christa on her child, I asked Margret what Eberhard had thought of all the many snaps I had taken. With a swift glance to see whether Christa had heard my question, she said in a low voice, 'No, not yet.'

Then Margret was sent off by her mother to cook us a plate of ham and eggs, for we had shown signs that we would soon have to be on the road again, and she would not let us leave the house until we had eaten there. Over the eggs, we sat and chatted with the three children, each of us speaking in our own lan-guage, as I had almost always done with them. Margret remembered that she had once promised me a book, *Der Trompeter von Säkkingen,* a collection of verse by Viktor von Scheffel, and that it still lay in her bedroom upstairs, the room which had for a while been mine. She ran and fetched it, wrote her name in it, and gave it to me. Then we had to go. The doctor and his wife came in again to say goodbye, and Margret and Christa saw us to the door.

I felt strangely light-hearted as I drove away. Often one struggles with the fear of being forgotten by those by those whose remembrance one seeks, and it is balm to the soul to find that you are remembered after all, and with affection. Margret wrote to me later that, after Tony and I left, her mother admitted that she had intercepted and concealed the letter in which I said that I would be coming to Germany. How many more of my letters had never reached Margret? The Frau Doktor may have been less impressed by my poetic vein, but in the end it was of no moment. I found the von Scheffel marked, at a point in the poem of Hiddigeigei, the old tom-cat, at Stanza IX:

> *Hiddigeigei spricht, der Alte:*
> *Pflück die Früchte, eh' sie platzen;*
> *Wenn die magern Jahre kommen,*
> *Saug' an der Erinn'rung Tatzen!*

> Hiddigeigei speaks, the Ancient:
> Pluck the fruit, before it rots;
> If lean years come,
> Lick the paws of memory!

APPENDIX A

The legitimacy and evolution of T-Force

The modern reader may find it difficult to appreciate the frame of mind of the victors in the aftermath of a second long and bitter world war. Perhaps it would be useful to note the position in which T-Force began to carry out its operations, which might otherwise appear to have lacked legitimacy.

In the first ten days of February 1945, the three participating powers at the Yalta Conference, Britain, the Soviet Union and the USA, confirmed the policy of unconditional surrender which had been adopted at the earlier Casablanca Conference. This was a concept without precedent in international affairs, and it was predicated upon the supposition that when the time came for hostilities to be terminated, there would be in existence a German government capable of delivering the German nation into the Allies' hands.

However, as the machinery of government began to disintegrate in Germany by the end of March, no government competent to sign a general surrender of the nation seemed likely to survive in order to effect the necessary transfer of supreme authority. No documents had been drafted to meet this situation; there was no precedent. An entirely new basis for occupation and control had to be devised. It was to take the form of a Declaration that Germany had been completely defeated, her unconditional surrender had been effected, and the Allied governments had assumed supreme authority in Germany. This declaration of the assumption of power and the consequent formation of the Allied Control Council was signed and promulgated by the Allied Commanders-in-Chief in Berlin on 5th June 1945, as Proclamation No 1 ('The Terms of Surrender') of which Article 13B provided for further terms to be promulgated. They were, subsequently, as Proclamation No 2, of 20th September 1945 ('The Additional Terms of Surrender') in which six Articles, listed below, made provision for the activities carried out by T-Force. This was the law of the land, and its legality has never been challenged, not even by a confident post-war German government. No limit was placed upon the penalties for disobedience under the Terms and Additional Terms of Surrender. They were to be obeyed. The operations of T-Force were legal.

THE PROVISIONS
SECTION V
Article 13 (b)
The German authorities will immediately place at the disposal of the Allied Representatives all research, experiment, development and design directly or indirectly relating to war or the production of war material, whether in government or private establishments, factories, technological institutions or elsewhere.
Article 17 (b)
There shall be no destruction, removal, concealment, suppression or alteration of any documents, records, patents, drawings, specifications, plans or information, of any nature, affected by the provisions of this document. They shall be kept intact in their present locations until further directions are given. The German authorities will afford all information and facilities as required by the Allied Representatives in connection therewith.
SECTION VI
Article 19 (a)
The German authorities will carry out, for the benefit of the United Nations, such measures of restitution, reinstatement, restoration, repara-

tion, reconstruction, relief and rehabilitation as the Allied Representatives may prescribe. For these purposes the German authorities will effect or procure the surrender or transfer of such property, assets, rights, titles and interests, effect such deliveries and carry out such repair, building and construction work, whether in Germany or elsewhere, and will provide such transport plant equipment and materials and equipment of all kinds, labour, personnel and specialist and other services, for use in Germany or elsewhere, as the Allied Representatives may direct.

SECTION XII

Article 45

Without prejudice to any specific obligations contained in the provisions of the Declaration or any proclamations, orders, ordinances or instructions issued thereunder, the German authorities and any other person in a position to do so will furnish or cause to be furnished all such information and documents of every kind, public and private, as the Allied Representatives may require.

Article 46

The German authorities will likewise produce for interrogation and employment by the Allied Representatives upon demand any and all persons whose knowledge and experience would be useful to the Allied Representatives.

Article 47

The Allied Representatives will have access at all times to any building, installation, establishment, property or area, and any of the contents thereof, for the purposes of the Declaration or any proclamations, orders, ordinances or instructions issued thereunder, and in particular for the purposes of safeguarding, inspecting, copying or obtaining any of the desired documents and information. The German authorities will give all necessary facilities and assistance for this purpose, including the service of all specialist staff, including archivists.

The unit had been formed on 1st April 1945 in Brussels, and the targets which gave their initial 'T' to T-Force were to be, at first, any weapon or weapon system, or 'warlike stores', or information or intellectual property which could be of value to the Allies in the further prosecution of the war, firstly against Germany and then against Japan. This remained the priority until the war with Japan ended in mid-August 1945, by which time T-Force came under the control of the British Intelligence Objectives Subcommittee (BIOS), which was a subcommittee of the Chief of Staff's Committee. Most of the targets would already have been identified by battlefield and air reconnaissance, or industrial and other intelligence during the course of the war; others would be discovered as targets of opportunity as the army advanced.

The wartime establishment of T-Force was not dissimilar to that of an infantry brigade, consisting primarily of two infantry battalions.[36] They were selected because they were not directly engaged in combat operations and were now available promptly for a new role. Operating in small independent groups, often down to the level of a platoon, they would deploy closely on the heels of the leading army formations, and sometimes even in advance of them. Their great early prizes were the ports and naval bases on the Baltic, upon which the Russians were known to have their acquisitive eyes: an early exercise in T-Force interdiction.

Once targets had been identified, seized and guarded, T-Force would bring up the assessors and investigators, specialists who had been called upon by BIOS. They would evaluate what had been found, and T-Force would evacuate anything of interest into the hands of the Services' and other research establishments in the UK for further examination of its usefulness as a weapon or engine of war. T-Force was also responsible for providing communications, accommodation, rations and transport for these people and, when things had settled down, opened Messes and later even hotels throughout the Zone for this purpose.

---

36 5th Battalion the King's Regiment, 1st Bucks Battalion of the Oxfordshire & Buckinghamshire Light Infantry, with a third added briefly: 30th Royal Berks.

After VJ Day and by the end of the year, 1st Bucks and 5th Kings had settled into locations in which they would remain for the next couple of years, the latter in an area defined by the borders of Lower Saxony and Schleswig-Holstein, and 1st Bucks in the provinces of North Rhine and Westphalia which incorporated the Ruhr.

As this second phase of their operations developed, the unit was able to concentrate less on weapons and weapon systems, and more on the entire German military-industrial complex, including anything which caught the attention of the investigators sponsored by BIOS as representatives of British industry—a single machine or a section of a plant, a blueprint or patent, or even an idea existing only in the mind and memory of a German scientist or technician. Interest therefore focussed heavily upon the huge industrial concentration of the Ruhr, in which eighty-six percent of German heavy industry in the British Zone was located. It lay in the territory of No 1 T-Force Unit which took over from 1st Bucks in early April 1946.

On 29th March 1946, the four Allied Powers had signed the 'Level of Industry Plan' stating that German heavy industry was to be reduced to fifty per cent of its 1938 levels by the destruction (i.e. dismantling) of 1,500 listed manufacturing plants. This represented an intent which was already becoming frayed at the edges even as it was expressed, but it was nonetheless indicative of the Allied view up to that time of the way forward for a Europe which, industrially, Germany had hitherto dominated. This was the background against which BIOS's more selective approach, intended to concentrate on British needs and given effect through the activities of T-Force, may be viewed.

APPENDIX B

The emergence of T-Force into the public domain

Nearly twenty years had elapsed by the time I approached the Ministry of Defence in 1966 announcing my intention to write, or cause to be written, a history of T-Force and requesting a degree of cooperation, perhaps in the disclosure of documents still under embargo. I got the usual po-faced *nihil obstat* with regard to the project, but the manuscript would have to be submitted for their scrutiny. There would be no cooperation; I put the file away.

In the early eighties Tom Bower was researching his second book, *Klaus Barbie, Butcher of Lyons* (1984), when he felt the need to consult on points of international law with the distinguished academic and jurist Professor Colonel Gerald Draper at Sussex University. While doing so he met Julia Draper and learned from her of the existence of T-Force, where she had held the 'personalities' portfolio at HQ T-Force. Bower was sufficiently intrigued to adopt the subject for his next book. At the time, I had only just written to Julia (formerly Jean Hughes-Gibb) and told her of my own intentions, so she sensibly brought me together with Tom Bower. He was at that time deputy editor of the BBC's investigative flag-ship *Panorama*, and therefore enjoyed access to good research facilities. As I was still in full-time employment in the City, we agreed that it would be sensible for him to write the book and for me to help him in any way I could.

In the event, as he undertook his researches in the Public Records Office, Bower found that the record was in many important respects defective; documents were either missing or under long-term embargo. So he turned his attention instead to the corralling and employment of Wernher von Braun and many of his rocket scientist colleagues in the United States. The project came to fruition as *The Paperclip Conspiracy: The Battle for the Spoils and Secrets of Nazi Germany* (1987). Three or four of its fourteen chapters include substantial reference to T-Force activities, and the author was kind enough to name me first among the acknowledgements in his book.

The records and documents of the Control Commission for Germany, including those of T-Force, came ultimately under the aegis of the Foreign & Commonwealth Office, and in 1983 I corresponded with Ellie Blaney, head of the FCO Library and Records. From her I learned that a large quantity of CCG files, including those of T-Force, were destroyed in Germany between 1948 and 1956. The remainder, some 240 tons, were brought to the UK where the destruction continued unabated to the point where by 1986 less than two tons remained. Much of this material remained secret, even after forty years, and some remains so even today (in particular, I suspect, any that quantify the monetary value of the depredations of T-Force). It is still a sensitive and controversial subject.

In 1996 I thought I might dip my toe in the waters again, so I wrote a brief, six-page memoir for my brother Riflemen which, with the blessing of the Army Historical Branch, was published in the 1999 issue of the *Royal Green Jackets Chronicle.*

By 2007 most of the reserved T-Force documents had been disembargoed and released for inspection in the National Archive. Among the parties carrying out their 'due diligence' on the released documents was the *Guardian* in the person of senior reporter Ian Cobain. He chose one in particular to set the tone for a two-page article published on 29th August 2007 under the headline: 'How T-Force abducted Germany's best brains for Britain'. The reader is given the impression that T-Force carried out the 'enforced evacuation' of German scientists in a disgraceful and inhuman way. Everything we did was, of course, 'enforced'. Cobain focuses upon a memorandum written by a so-called senior civil servant, since identified to me as Mr E A Bearder, who was employed by the CCG as head of the Chemical Industries Section of the Trade and Industry Division—the body to whom he addressed his memo. Describing how T-Force operated, Bearder wrote:

'Usually an NCO arrives without notice at the house or office of the German and warns that he will be required. He does not give him any details of the reasons, nor does he present his credentials. Some time later the German is seized (often in the middle of the night) and removed under guard. This procedure savours very much of the Gestapo methods and, quite apart from causing great and unnecessary inconvenience to the individual and to the industry employing him, it is bound to create feelings of alarm and insecurity. I have not been able to get to the bottom of the matter, but there appear to be two bodies which carry out these kidnappings.'

One of these bodies, said Cobain, was the British Intelligence Objectives Secretariat, 'answerable to the Cabinet', on whose instruction T-Force carried out the so-called abductions and kidnappings. The other was the Field Information Agency (Technical), or FIAT, an Anglo-American military intelligence unit that earmarked scientists for evacuation. Bearder was right in just one particular: that he had been unable to get to the bottom of the matter (nor indeed anywhere near it).

The *Guardian* did not have the nerve to name any of those to whom it fell to carry out these duties, of whom I am, with Roddy Bennett, the youngest of the four left alive. None of us was approached, even though (because?) we could have told them that it was not like that. There was no need to carry out such operations by night, and we did not. Nor did we need the threat of arms to coerce or seize compliant individuals, many of whom were only too eager to travel to England in the hope of being offered a job in industry there, and to avoid any possible detention by the Russians. We treated them with all the consideration due to any human, nor was it in my nature or that of any of my officers or their men to do otherwise.

Cobain had the courtesy to come and see me at my request, but he was not about to publish any correction. Letters of protest from survivors of No 2 T-Force to the *Guardian* remained unacknowledged, and readers of this book must judge for themselves whether there is any likelihood of his allegations being true.

Most recently, in September 2009, has come Sean Longden's book *T-Force: the Race for Nazi War Secrets, 1945*. It is the culmination of two years of painstaking research, including many personal interviews with survivors—particularly those from 5th King's/No 2 T-Force Unit who doggedly maintain an Old Comrade's Association. Longden has been more than kind about the help I was able to give him. I was pleased to comply with a request from the *Journal of the Royal United Services Institute* to write a review of Longden's book for inclusion in their issue dated December 2009.

ACKNOWLEDGEMENTS

Without my mother's decision—of which I was long unaware—to preserve the letters which I wrote to her and to my father, this memoir could never have come into being. Though I wrote them often without taking enough time or care over them, she may have sensed that I was embarking upon some interesting adventure. Discovering them among her effects when she died twenty years later, I left them in a file which lay unread for four decades.

I first skimmed through them while looking for material which might be a help to Sean Longden when he began his research for his history of T-Force in 2007; the dialogue between us that this established has been both agreeable and helpful to me. It was from a realisation that they could provide a chronological framework for a story which I had felt needed telling, that I decided to have the manuscript letters transcribed and lodged on my hard disk. In February 2009 I consulted Sarah Aldridge about this, and amazingly she asked that she might be allowed to do it herself, and for that, and her first kind correction of my commentary on the letters which followed, I am much indebted to her.

Repeated admonitions from John Bayley in his letters to me over a period of some years prior to this, that I "really should write" —without saying quite what—sustained me in this early phase, and I am grateful for his encouragement.

In May 2009 my friend Yves Bonavero, who was privy to what I was doing, gave my efforts a crucial impetus by introducing me to David Reynolds, commissioning editor at Old Street, and they both persuaded me that I should by all means continue further on the course on which I was embarked, and

David asked that he might have first read of the MS when it was ready, which by Christmas it was: he was, it seemed to me, keen to give me my very first rejection slip. However he, and the publisher, Ben Yarde-Buller at Old Street, both took a sympathetic view of what I had done, and wished me to take it further. My dealings with them have given me the greatest pleasure. Ben put me in the hands of my editor Henry Howard, who has treated me with much tolerance and great good humour, and with real sympathy for material harking back two whole generations: there again I have been most fortunate.

Val Hoskins gave me good advice at several points when I suspected that I was out of my depth.

For much of this period, from August last, I have enjoyed the unstinting support and help of a friend who has wished for her own reasons not to be named. Restrained by her seat-belt in the front passenger seat of my car, she had already been unable to escape hearing a certain amount of my tale. She has drawn freely upon her contacts, her considerable experience in a cognate field, and assorted professional and technical skills to make it possible for this to be a more readable book than it might have been without her help. My friends whom I have told of my venture are all aware of her identity, of the depth of her support and the quality of her work, and of my gratitude for it.

Michael Howard, August 2010